RACE, GENDER, & COMPARATIVE BLACK MODERNISM

RACE, GENDER, & COMPARATIVE BLACK MODERNISM

SUZANNE LACASCADE
MARITA BONNER
SUZANNE CÉSAIRE
DOROTHY WEST

Jennifer M. Wilks

 LOUISIANA STATE UNIVERSITY PRESS   Baton Rouge

Published by Louisiana State University Press
Copyright © 2008 by Louisiana State University Press
All rights reserved
Manufactured in the United States of America
First printing

DESIGNER: Amanda McDonald Scallan
TYPEFACES: Minion, Trebuchet MS, and Eccentric Std
TYPESETTER: J. Jarrett Engineering
PRINTER AND BINDER: Thomson-Shore, Inc.

Portions of the Introduction first appeared in "Writing Home: Comparative Black Modernism and Form in Jean Toomer and Aimé Césaire," *Modern Fiction Studies* 51.4 (2005): 801–23. Portions of Chapter 1 first appeared in "La mulâtresse nègre: Exoticism and the Gaze in Suzanne Lacascade's *Claire-Solange, âme africaine*," *MaComère* 6 (2004): 57–62. Portions of Chapter 4 first appeared in "New Women and New Negroes: Archetypal Womanhood in Dorothy West's *The Living Is Easy*," *African American Review* 39.4 (2005): 569–79.

Library of Congress Cataloging-in-Publication Data

Wilks, Jennifer M., 1973–
    Race, gender, and comparative Black modernism : Suzanne Lacascade, Marita Bonner, Suzanne Césaire, Dorothy West / Jennifer M. Wilks.
        p.   cm.
    Includes bibliographical references and index.
    ISBN 978-0-8071-3364-4 (cloth : alk. paper) 1. American literature—African American authors—History and criticism. 2. American literature—Women authors—History and criticism. 3. Caribbean literature (French)—Black authors—History and criticism. 4. Caribbean literature (French)—Women authors—History and criticism. 5. Race in literature. 6. Women, Black, in literature. 7. Modernism (Literature)—United States. 8. Modernism (Literature)—Caribbean Area. 9. Literature, Comparative—American and Caribbean (French) 10. Literature, Comparative—Caribbean (French) and American. I. Title.
    PS153.N5W495 2008
    810.9′896073—dc22

                                                                              2008014734

The paper in this book meets the guidelines for permanence and durability of the Committee on Production Guidelines for Book Longevity of the Council on Library Resources. ♾

For
Catherine O'Neal
Susie Wray
Elaine Sanders
and
Jacqueline Wilks

Contents

Acknowledgments

However much its pages evoke the solitude experienced by many a modernist, I am well aware that this book would not exist had I truly been working on my own. My heartfelt thanks to those friends and mentors who offered criticism that was both challenging and stimulating from the project's earliest stages: Natalie Melas, Anne Adams, Biodun Jeyifo, Angel David Nieves, and Michelle Scott. As the manuscript evolved, so my circle of readers grew; I am particularly grateful for the astute commentary and moral support offered by Joanna Brooks, Lisa Moore, John McKiernan-Gonzalez, Frank Guridy, Juliet Hooker, Meta Jones, Nhi Lieu, Julia Mickenberg, Deborah Paredez, Jemima Pierre, Cherise Smith, and Shirley Thompson. The final step in the journey from manuscript to book would not have been possible without the careful guidance of my editor, John Easterly, and the readers and staff at the Louisiana State University Press.

I have been fortunate to receive the generous encouragement of colleagues in Austin and beyond. The University of Texas at Austin Department of English and Center for African and African American Studies have provided the fertile intellectual ground needed to develop such a project. Ann Cvetkovich, Edmund T. Gordon, Joni Jones, and Helena Woodard have been instrumental in transforming my professional base into an academic home, as have Jafari Allen, James Cox, John Gonzalez, Neville Hoad, Domino Perez, James Lee, and Phillip Alexander. Whether they've realized it or not, the students in my graduate and undergraduate courses have also been an invaluable resource. Thank you for allowing our literature classrooms to become a test site for new texts and ideas. From their respective corners of the world David Agruss, Cherene Sherrard-Johnson, Guy Bellance, Viviane Sévérin, Michèle Yung-Hing, and Jonathan Eburne continually prove that collegiality and friendship can trump geography. Je vous remercie tous. I am also indebted to the editors of the *African American Review, MaComère,* and *Modern Fiction Studies,* in whose pages portions of this manuscript first appeared.

My scholarship has been equally enriched by research conducted at the Bibliothèque Nationale de France in Paris, the Centre des Archives d'Outre-Mer in Aix-en-Provence, the Beinecke Rare Book and Manuscript Library at Yale University, the Schlesinger Library at the Radcliffe Institute for Advanced Study, the Bibliothèque Schoelcher in Fort-de-France, and the Bibliothèque Universitaire of the Université des Antilles et de la Guyane in Schoelcher. In addition, Ina Césaire was kind enough to grant me an interview during my time in Martinique. These trips were facilitated by generous financial support from Cornell University, the Andrew W. Mellon Foundation, the Social Science Research Council, the Woodrow Wilson National Fellowship Foundation, and the University of Texas at Austin.

If I first encountered examples of remarkable womanhood within my family, I have had the pleasure of meeting more among the inimitable women of Bryn Mawr College. A special "Anassa Kata" to Angie Emery Henderson, Erika Merschrod, Ingrid Nelson, and Tamara Rozental as well as to Mary Blockley, Ellen Cartsonis, Hillary Hart, Madeline Maxwell, Sue Sheppard, and Tam Voynick.

Finally, I would like to express my profound gratitude to the Wilks and Sanders families for the love and warmth with which you sustain me. Thank you to my parents, Jacqueline and Carl Wilks, for introducing me to the life of the mind; to my brothers, Carl and Eric, for being my friends as well as my siblings; and to my sister-in-law Cheryl and my nieces, Jasmine and Erica, for replenishing me with your wit and wonder. My world is because all of you are.

RACE, GENDER, & COMPARATIVE BLACK MODERNISM

Introduction

Model Modernity

In a Bambara myth of origin, after the creation of the earth, and the organization of
everything on its surface, disorder was introduced by a woman. Disorder meant the
power to create new objects and to modify the existing ones. In a word, disorder meant
creativity.
—MARYSE CONDÉ, "Order, Disorder, Freedom, and the West Indian Writer" (1993)

If the narrative of comparative American modernity begins with wandering
Italian men in the form of Christopher Columbus, it also begins with the character of Miranda, the Italian woman who propels Shakespeare's dramatic encounter with the New World and haunts the racialized gender norms confronted by American women of color. If the narrative continues with Haitian
revolutionary heroes such as Toussaint L'Ouverture, who articulated Caribbean nationalism through Enlightenment principles, it also develops through
the experiences of outsiders such as Défilée, who symbolically reassembled

1

the first black republic through her collection of Jean-Jacques Dessalines's remains. And, if at the dawn of the twentieth century this story erupts in the masterful speech of Booker T. Washington, who insisted on the centrality of African Americans in the South to the realization of U.S. democratic ideals, it also materializes in the compelling declarations of Anna Julia Cooper, who insisted on the integrity of women to questions of race and nation. It is, in sum, a story that includes not only European-descended subjects but also African diasporic ones; not only fiery rhetoric but also subtle critique; not only archetypal men but also atypical women.

Race, Gender, and Comparative Black Modernism recuperates and critiques four early-twentieth-century African American and Francophone Caribbean women writers—Guadeloupean Suzanne Lacascade (dates unknown), African American Marita Bonner (1899–1971), Martinican Suzanne Césaire (1913–66), and African American Dorothy West (1907–98)—whose works defy the gendered and periodized boundaries of literary categorization. To trouble such boundaries further, the book concludes with an examination of the late-twentieth-century writings of Guadeloupean Maryse Condé (b. 1937) and African American Toni Morrison (b. 1931) and the ways in which their respective texts continue to confront the conflation of gender roles with social and literary conventions. If the multiple moves suggested by this sketch—from modernity to modernism, modernism to postmodernism, protofeminism to feminism—seem disorderly, they are intentionally so. Inspired by Condé's equation of disorder with creative freedom, I am interested in how a critical construction that may at first seem counterintuitive can in fact produce new ways of reading African diasporic women's writing.[1] There is no physical ground, no literal soil, on which the earlier quartet of writers met, and the relationships between their respective engagements with race and class, genre and gender, cannot be seamlessly equated. Yet, when read collectively and alongside the later works of Condé and Morrison, the writings of Lacascade, Bonner, Césaire, and West "traverse all of the.... boundaries instituted to keep [their critical] dislocations in place."[2] They are artistically provocative, politically complex, unquestionably modernist.

I have chosen the title *Race, Gender, and Comparative Black Modernism* over the perhaps more obvious "Race and Gender in the Harlem Renaissance and Negritude" in keeping with the themes of provocation and disorder. In an immediate sense comparison forms the book's methodological core because, as Rey Chow observes, "more often than not, it is assumed that comparison occurs as a matter of course whenever we juxtapose two (or more) national languages and literatures, geographical regions, authors or themes."[3] This study juxtaposes the work of Caribbean women writing in French with that of African American women writing in English, and, although it does not address modernist women writers from the Anglophone and Hispanophone Caribbean or from continental Latin America, my hope is that the project will nonetheless provoke questions and observations that exceed its limited scope. In a more far-reaching sense, however, comparison is also pivotal to my endeavor because, as much as its theoretical underpinnings promote the possibility of parity, stability, and universality, its practical applications often entail disciplinary instability. In his lead essay in the American Comparative Literature Association's 2004 State of the Discipline report, Haun Saussy argues that, because of its development outside of the rubric of national literature (i.e., British, American, French, etc.), "comparative literature contests the definition of *literature* (as well as aesthetic norms, genre definitions, literary-historical patterns, and the rest) by throwing examples and counterexamples at it."[4] This tradition is, admittedly, not without its own variants of the exclusion and oversight often attributed to monolingual or national literary studies. "Languages and cultures rarely enter the world stage and encounter one another on an equal footing," Chow notes, and nineteenth- and early-twentieth-century incarnations of comparative literature were dominated by what she calls the "Europe and Its Others" model of comparison, with Europe as the analytical control and other sites as its experimental counterparts.[5] My work dovetails with that of Chow and Saussy, as well as postcolonial comparatist Natalie Melas and feminist scholar Susan Sniader Lanser, in its efforts to recoup the contestatory, redefining possibilities of comparative literature, to disrupt the balance of Europe and Its Others by pursuing comparison through specificity rather than a universality that ultimately becomes a stand-in for hegemony. Such an approach allows, to borrow from Melas, for the consideration of texts in terms of their "standing *in* the world" rather than their "exemplary representativity" or capacity to "[stand] for the world."[6] For comparison is most insightful and most engaging not when it ignores or "dissolve[s]" difference but when it connects works from different literary traditions in order to "transform them, then send them out [into the world] again."[7]

It is in this spirit of contestation and transformation that my title uses comparison to invoke the category of race. In her essay on tensions between Francophone African and Caribbean officials in interwar Paris, historian Alice Conklin's titular inquiry recalls Condé's interrogation of West Indian literary order:

3

"who speaks for Africa?"[8] In other words, who has the right or authority to represent the continent and its inhabitants? The contenders at play in the incident discussed by Conklin were two men, West African deputy Blaise Diagne and Martinican novelist and former colonial administrator René Maran, and, as Hazel Carby forcefully argues in her 1998 work *Race Men*, the question of African American representation has been similarly gendered. Carby calls on scholars "to expose and learn from the gendered, ideological assumptions which underlie the founding texts [written by the *founding fathers* of black American history and culture] and determine that their authors become the *representative* figures of the American intellectual."[9] My endeavor here is to ask what happens to "blackness," both as a lived identity and a social construction, when articulated by women who have not been considered representative because of their gender and their emphases on individual rather than collective expression. Similarly, what happens to understandings of race when the terms used to discuss the inherently thorny category are not directly translatable from one language to another? The most striking example of Brent Hayes Edwards's theory of *décalage*—the difference or disjunction that underscores relations across the African diaspora—comes in his discussion of the linguistic intricacies that hampered French translations of Alain Locke's anthology *The New Negro* (1925).[10] On a final note, how is the term *black* destabilized when modern black identities are negotiated from and through positions of relative cultural and/or economic privilege? Regardless of geographic or linguistic context, neither "authentic blackness" nor resistance is the exclusive province of men or of intellectuals explicitly identified with the "black working and lower classes," and for this reason I want to continue the important work of disproving the limited literary and political expectations that contemporaries and critics alike have held of middle-class black women writers.[11] The practice of comparison not only encourages such questions but in many ways requires them if one is indeed to benefit from the critical possibilities that Chow, Lanser, and Melas ascribe to specificity.

"Modernism," the final link in my conceptual chain, returns us to the issue with which I began to negotiate my title. If specificity is indeed key, why stake this project's claims in the larger, unfamiliar terrain of comparative black modernism instead of in the more immediate, and in many ways more clearly defined, terrain of Harlem Renaissance and Negritude studies? With the exception of Maryse Condé and Toni Morrison, the "atypical women" in question wrote during the historical periods traditionally associated with the aforementioned literary movements; my disruption of the "exemplary representativity" that Melas examines, however, depends in part upon reading women writers against and outside of the gendered archetypes and genealogies of African diasporic literary production. The inventive, paradigm shifting output of early-twentieth-century African American and Francophone Caribbean authors neither begins nor ends with the "representative colored men" of the Harlem Renaissance and Negritude: Langston Hughes, Claude McKay, and Alain Locke, for example, within the former, and Aimé Césaire, Léon-Gontran Damas, and Léopold Sédar Senghor within the latter.[12] I am no less concerned, however, with rethinking the parameters of the contemporaneous and, I argue, inextricably related emergence of modernism. For, if one considers modernism nothing less, or nothing more, than "the loosely affiliated movements and individuals in the arts and literature that reflect and contribute to the conditions and consciousness of modernity," its study should not be limited to the works of white writers.[13]

Early-twentieth-century African diasporic literary expression is not exclusively indebted to Anglo-American T. S. Eliot, author of the sweeping text *The Waste Land* (1922), nor to French poet Charles Baudelaire, creator of the groundbreaking verses of *Les fleurs du mal* (*The Flowers of Evil*, 1857). Neither is Spaniard Pablo Picasso, whose Cubist and primitivist art introduced "Africa" to twentieth-century European and American cultural centers, an apt point of departure. Such framing genealogies yield, in the English and U.S. literary canons, bibliographies dominated by the work of Eliot and the likes of James Joyce, Ezra Pound, Gertrude Stein, and Virginia Woolf and, in the French canon, a roster that stretches from Baudelaire to Breton but is no less Eurocentric.[14] As these litanies provide a sense of what modernism was, to transpose the title of Harry Levin's 1960 essay, they also indicate what, in the eyes of many critics, modernism was not: studies of "high" modernism often omit the Harlem Renaissance and Negritude, just as surveys of these movements have often neglected the substantive and groundbreaking contributions of women writers.[15]

A comprehensive reconsideration of modernism must also include the interrogation and expansion of concepts and categories of modernity. My reach back to notions of modernity, or "the radical *rupture* from rather than the supreme embodiment of post-Renaissance Enlightenment humanism and accompanying formations in the West," may suggest a critical framework that is largely chronological, but I am also interested in the conceptual blocks that have excluded African American and Francophone Caribbean women from narratives of literary modernism.[16] The word *period* suggests an alluring intellectual neatness, a logically ordered group of texts that are both exceptional and representative. But the term also implies foreclosure, containment, and elimination, and for all the innovation and experimentation of the age it chronicles, criticism that discusses modernism as a unitary rather than plural entity is no exception.[17] I propose these hermeneutic shifts not to produce a new but no less problematic gynocentric or Afrocentric canon but to stage a critical conversation that reflects the early-twentieth-century circulation of artists and ideas rather than the late-twentieth-century balkanization of them. When one resists the collapse of text and writer, of typescript and type of artist, more complex, more interesting pictures of modernism, the Harlem Renaissance, and Negritude, as well as of their various interrelationships, emerge. It is scholarly output, not historical circumstance, that has disconnected authors who exchanged ideas in the same intellectual circles, responded to each other's work, and published in the same venues. Because of the critical prominence of figures such as Gertrude Stein and Alain Locke, the voices of women of color have been ostensibly represented but ultimately elided by works such as Stein's *Melanctha* (1909), which features a mulatta heroine, and Locke's "The New Negro" (1925), who is introduced as a composite of all African Americans, women as well as men.[18] Using questions of modernity to pluralize modernism reverses the positing of the African diasporic individual in general and the African diasporic woman in particular "merely as an object or subject of art, not as an artist."[19] Similarly, loosening the Harlem Renaissance and Negritude from critical moorings constructed around 1920s New York City and 1930s Paris, respectively, facilitates the discussion of how black women writers from outside of these temporal and geographic boundaries negotiated early-twentieth-century concerns about social upheaval, industrialization, and war. Through such critical moves *Race, Gender, and Comparative Black Modernism* rejects the orderliness of periodization for the creativity of disorder.

Definitional Complications

To declare modernity the province of African American and Caribbean peoples is to assert the role of formerly captive, enslaved, and silenced voices and bodies in the formation of the brave New World. From European perspectives modernity may signal the march of "progress" and the attendant emergence of new economic, national, and cultural identities (a prime example of this march being Christopher Columbus's 1492 voyage), but such models seem less constructive when considered from African American and Caribbean perspectives. According to Simon Gikandi, the designation of 1492 as inaugural modern moment posits modernity as that which happens to, rather than that which is effected by, indigenous American populations and the enslaved and indentured transplants who succeeded them: "If Columbus's 'discovery' of the Americas and his initial encounter with the peoples of the New World have paradigmatic value in the European episteme because they usher in a brave new world, a world of modernity and modernist forms, . . . these events also trigger a contrary effect on the people who are 'discovered' and conquered."[20] Paul Gilroy extends the critique of Eurocentric narratives of modernity by faulting them for discounting slavery, which is either deemed the "special property [of blacks] rather than a part of the ethical and intellectual heritage of the West as a whole" or declared "a premodern residue that disappears once it is revealed to be fundamentally incompatible with enlightened rationality and capitalist industrial production."[21] As a result, to question modernity, to move beyond the limited options of ahistorical concern and "premodern residue," is to interrogate not only historical timelines but also the soundness of the historical enterprise itself. One must trade cohesive stories of European expansion for the disruptive complications of conquest.

This exchange, however, should not entail the eventual assertion of a new, Americas-centered vision of modernity that seeks to install its own historical and conceptual order. Édouard Glissant deems totalizing historical narratives "un fantasme fortement opératoire de l'Occident, contemporain précisément du temps où il était seul à 'faire' l'histoire du monde" ("a highly functional fantasy of the West, originating at precisely the time when it alone 'made' the history of the world").[22] Rather than posit a Caribbean-centered seamlessness, Glissant embraces complication as constitutive of and even necessary for American (in the broad hemispheric sense rather than exclusively national one) literary production: "Il leur [les littératures nationales] faut tout assumer tout d'un coup, le combat, le militantisme, l'enracinement, la lucidité, la méfiance envers soi, l'absolu d'amour, la forme du paysage, le nu des villes, les dépassements et les entêtements. C'est ce que j'appelle notre irruption dans la modernité" ("They [national literatures] must include all at once struggle, aggressiveness, belonging, lucidity, distrust of self, absolute love, contours of the landscape, emptiness of the cities, victories, and confrontations. That is what I call our irruption into modernity").[23] With its insistence on simultaneity and plurality

("all at once," "our"), Glissant's formulation challenges alternative modernities not to replicate the exclusion of Eurocentric models. He calls for the revision of "History" through collectivity, not singularity: "'Là où se joignent les
histoires des peuples, hier réputés sans histoire, finit l'Histoire.' (Avec un grand
H.)" ("'History [with a capital *H*] ends where the histories of those people
once reputed to be without history come together'").[24] While Glissant's explicit
discussion is limited to the broad categories of the West and the Americas, his
theory is equally applicable to the question of gender. Just as Western narratives
of modernity that exclude American perspectives are functional but fantastic,
so, too, are African diasporic narratives of modernity that omit the experiences
of women serviceable but, ultimately, incomplete.

Is Columbus, then, the only Italian specter in need of an American exor-
cism? How does Miranda, the woman at the center of Shakespeare's *The Tempest* (1611), haunt the New World women who preceded and succeeded her?
Long read as a dramatic interpretation of the colonial encounter in the Americas, *The Tempest* features a veritable host of traveling Italians, but Miranda is
the lone woman on the tropical island cohabited by her father, Prospero, the de-
posed duke of Milan, and his slaves, the spritely Ariel and the monstrous Caliban.[25] Through this isolation Miranda becomes the "'idealized' object of desire for all classes . . . and all population-groups."[26] Where Sycorax, Caliban's
deceased mother and the absent woman of color, is a "foul witch" (1.2.258),
Miranda is a wondrous "goddess," the epitome of womanhood (1.2.423). Despite uttering the oft-quoted "O brave new world / That has such people in't!"
(5.1.183), however, Miranda serves mostly as a figure through which the male
characters mediate their respective power struggles. Her romance with survi-
vor Ferdinand, the son of the king of Naples, is orchestrated by Prospero to facilitate his triumphant return to Europe. Caliban, meanwhile, laments his failed
sexual assault of Miranda as a missed opportunity to "people . . . else / This isle
with Calibans" (1.2.350). His struggle may be one of liberation, but it, like the
elision of Sycorax, is one contingent upon misogynist violence. Thus, while
Miranda escapes—because she embodies—the racialized limitations of the
Eurocentric feminine ideal, she does so only to meet the gendered limitations
of masculinist interpretations of modern agency.

A range of female agents, from historical figures to mythico-religious ones,
populate Haitian revolutionary history, yet their stories, like Miranda's, have
been presented more as complementary rather than central to the emergence
of the first black republic. For this reason Joan Dayan couches her explora-

tion of figures such as Dédée Bazile as a means of redressing the presentation of women's "stories [as] something of an interlude in the business of *making history*."[27] It was Bazile, a meat vendor traveling with Jean-Jacques Dessalines's army, who gathered his scattered remains for burial when dissidents murdered Haiti's first president and emperor in 1806. Remembered by history and legend as Défilée, Bazile is alternately described as Dessalines's unrequited lover or his adopted daughter; one factor linking all accounts is Défilée's reputed madness, thought to have been induced by the barbarity of French colonial rule. Dayan reconstructs Défilée's story to look past the allegations of insanity and read the figure as instrumental to Haiti's national development: "If Défilée summons the tale of a republic, fallen and then resurrected through transformative love, she also remains an image that goes beyond this blessed conversion. . . . More like the oungan [priest] or manbo [priestess] who prevents the dead from re-turning to life to harm the living, Défilée assembles Dessalines's remnants in order to make sure they are suitably buried, thus thwarting their resurrection by a sorcerer."[28] By restoring one of Haiti's early national symbols, Défilée en-ables the country to move beyond the mortal existence of its seminal liberator, ruler, and, after Dessalines's elevation to "*lwa* (god, image, or spirit) by the Hai-tian people," deity.[29] She facilitates, to return to Glissant, the republic's "irrup-tion into modernity."

Less than one hundred years later, African American educator Anna Julia Cooper initiated a different type of modern emergence, that of an "African-American intelligentsia [that was] male *and* female."[30] She published *A Voice from the South*, a collection of essays and speeches, in 1892, and her analysis of "the Negro problem" differs markedly from that offered by the more readily cited "Atlanta Exposition Address" (1895) by Booker T. Washington and *The Souls of Black Folk* (1903) by W. E. B. Du Bois.[31] In the chapter "Womanhood: A Vital Element in the Regeneration and Progress of a Race" Cooper ties the fate of African America not only to geography, not only to the interplay of the sacred and the secular, but also to the relationship between the aforementioned categories and gender. She posits the plight of black women as the barometer for the fortunes of the race, and she does not consider her male peers able to grasp or represent this unique position: "At any rate, as our Caucasian bar-risters are not to blame if they cannot *quite* put themselves in the dark man's place, neither should the dark man be wholly expected fully and adequately to reproduce the exact Voice of the Black Woman."[32] In other words, however educated and however talented, the Race Man (to recall Carby) should not presume to speak for African American women. Equally astute in her reading of the interracial politics impeding gender solidarity, Cooper also "critiques the burgeoning white women's movement for its racist exclusions."[33] Indeed, I imagine that, just as Cooper might have praised Haiti's Défilée for taking the birth of the nation into her own hands, she might also have challenged Shakespeare's Miranda for not linking Sycorax's fate to her own. For Anna Julia Cooper the conscientious representation of both modern African American-ness and modern womanhood demands the inclusion of African American women's perspectives: "Only the BLACK WOMAN can say 'when and where I enter, in the quiet, undisputed dignity of my womanhood, without violence and without suing or special patronage, then and there the whole *Negro race enters with me.*'"[34]

What Cooper's call offers twenty-first-century readers is a charge to question the predominance, not the presence, of heroic men in the articulation of African diasporic modernities, just as scholars have interrogated the predominance of white Europeans and Anglo Americans in the defining moments used to map American modernity. J. Michael Dash dates Caribbean modernity from the 1804 Haitian Revolution "because it was in Haiti that Caribbean thought first emerged as a contestation of the reductive mystification of colonialism"; neither African nor European yet both, Haiti asserted its independence by creating itself through a "new composite culture."[35] As befits the political context of the late-nineteenth-century United States, where the emergence of an independent African America was not imminent, Houston A. Baker Jr. traces the advent of African American modernity to the rise of Booker T. Washington as a national leader. The richness of Dash's and Baker's respective studies stems in part from their considerations of the human fallibility behind L'Ouverture the General and Washington the Race Man. The former sought to craft Haiti by combining Enlightenment principles with local resistance, and the latter mastered the racist rhetoric of accommodation to "[set] forth strategies of address . . . designed for Afro-American empowerment."[36] Yet the very same political investments—L'Ouverture's in French Revolutionary philosophy and Washington's in accommodationism—that generated these accomplishments also led the two figures to significantly, if not excessively, trust white interlocutors and allies, hence the capture of L'Ouverture by Napoleon's forces and the critique of Washington as the (instrument) of white southern racists.[37] These men clearly asserted black agency through radical social change, but they did so through methods that were neither unanimously popular nor wholly unproblematic.

In *Silencing the Past: Power and the Production of History,* Michel-Rolph Trouillot writes that "history, as social process, involves [peoples] in three distinct capacities: 1) as *agents,* or occupants of structural positions; 2) as *actors* in constant interface with a context; and 3) as *subjects,* that is, as voices aware of their vocality."[38] If Miranda, Défilée, and Anna Julia Cooper complicate definitions of New World modernity, it is because their stories enable the consideration of women as agents, actors, and subjects rather than as supporting characters to their heroic male counterparts. Miranda's positioning reveals the gender dynamics of (early) modern agency, Défilée's collection of Dessalines's limbs symbolizes the unification of Haiti, and Cooper's mastery of uplift ideology "challenge[s] the terms of contemporary debate about gender and about race."[39] All three examples demonstrate the possibility of seismic discursive and conceptual shifts even in the absence of political earthquakes or national prominence. Perhaps when an individual's gender, race, or class identity does not fit prevailing notions of the modern subject, the limits of modernity rest not with the concept itself but with the models used to describe it.

BLACK MODERNIST TYPE(S)

The relationships between reason and terror, modernism and imperialism, that one might be tempted to dismiss as the abstractions of latter-day literary theorists are the same relationships that defined the sociohistoric dynamics in which African diasporic modernists lived and worked. In the 1945 essay "Poésie et connaissance" ("Poetry and Knowledge") Aimé Césaire traces the emergence of French modernism to the "depersonalized," "deindividualized" ("dépersonnalisé," "déindividualisé") self produced by the increasing dominance of science and technology; his semantic play, however, suggests a much longer lineage, one that explicitly stretches back to the Judeo-Christian creation story ("Au commencement était le verbe"/"In the beginning was the word") and implicitly recognizes the historical phenomenon of chattel slavery, which dehumanized enslaved Africans and their descendants.[40] To many African American and Caribbean modernists history was not simply "a nightmare from which the aesthetic imperative was going to rescue the artist" but a narrative to be engaged and critiqued in order to "affirm the power of historicity" of those for whom Columbus's New World "discoveries" were more tragedy than triumph.[41] To do otherwise would be to accept, tacitly or overtly, portrayals of African diasporic Americans "as either an ahistorical figure of European desire or simply a victim of the history of conquest and enslavement."[42]

On the contrary, to many Anglo American and European modernists the constitutive break of modernity was one from "occidental rationality," not from the "racial terror" that was its historical sibling.[43] Racial and ethnic differences were often decontextualized and depoliticized as they were celebrated artistically as the fount of an invigorating primitivism. Simon Gikandi attributes this disconnect to a particular brand of modernist anxiety: canonical modernists "needed the primitive in order to carry out their representational revolution, but . . . once this task had been accomplished, the Other needed to be evacuated from the scene of the modern."[44] There are, of course, other ways of reading canonical modernism's limited engagements with difference. Fredric Jameson attributes the absence of imperial sites and bodies in English modernist narratives to geography. He argues that metropolitan writers physically divorced from "a significant structural element of the economic system . . . located elsewhere" were unable to know or imagine life in Europe's colonial holdings.[45] Texts such as E. M. Forster's 1910 novel *Howards End,* Jameson continues, emerged to reflect the conflicts of a metropole irrevocably changed by, but ever separated from, its colonial doubles. However convincing with regards to Forster's novel and its subsequent analysis of Joyce's *Ulysses* (1922), Jameson's reading does not, or cannot, account for the resonances between primitivism, the modernist school fascinated with ahistorical, non-Western objects or Others, and its predecessor, exoticism. In exoticist discourse Europe's colonial "elsewhere" did not have to be known or seen; it only needed to serve as a "site for that liberating, guilt-free naturalness that had been stifled within European cultures."[46] Thus, while imperial expansion produced the anxiety and absence discussed by Jameson, it also produced the attendant escapism and objectification through which exoticist thinkers, as well as modernist successors like Picasso, managed the shifting dynamics of life in eighteenth-, nineteenth-, and early-twentieth-century Europe.

However obscured or ignored, such racialized politics extended from the production and reception of mainstream modernist works to that of African American and Francophone Caribbean texts. The formal experimentation that renders Gertrude Stein's *Autobiography of Alice B. Toklas* (1933) innovative and, at times, inaccessible, for example, was not attractive to African American poet James Weldon Johnson because he sought artistic liberation in standard-ized language free of the distorted dialect of minstrelsy and other misrepresen-tations of African American culture.[47] Although Harlem Renaissance impre-sario Alain Locke interpreted choices such as Johnson's as artistic license and thus a sign of the flowering of African American modernism, other critics—during and after the Renaissance—read the usage of standard literary forms as evidence of the movement's "'failure' to produce *vital, original, effective,* or 'modern' art."[48] Conversely, those African diasporic (identified) writers who did choose to experiment with language and form were credited not with artis-tic virtuosity but with tapping into some fundamental aspect of their Negro-hood, new or otherwise. Much to Jean Toomer's dismay, Sherwood Anderson praised the former's genre-bending *Cane* (1923) for capturing its author's Af-rican American "essence"; twenty-five years later Jean-Paul Sartre celebrated Negritude poetry in similar language, praising its depiction of "ces multiples aspects de l'âme noire" ("the multiple aspects of the black soul").[49] Black women modernists whose innovation turned on nuanced subversions of stan-dard forms often found themselves in the cross-hairs of both critiques: Claude McKay described novelist Jessie Redmon Fauset as "too prim school-marmish and stilted" for his taste, and white reviewers and publishing insiders openly wondered whether the African American elite depicted in her novels "really ex-isted."[50]

Idiosyncratic and ignorant at best, masculinist and racist at worst, the as-persions cast upon Fauset's artistry and authenticity nonetheless reveal a key conceptual difference between African diasporic modernisms and Anglo and European variants. Whereas the latter became (in)famous for their practitioners' refusal "to represent any *thing* other than [their] refusal to represent," the persistent historical and cultural reduction of African diasporic subjectivities to stereotypes yielded a body of early-twentieth-century African American and Francophone Caribbean literature fascinated, if not obsessed, with representation.[51] If black modernists negotiated questions of art, race, and self-representation textually through form and language, they negotiated these issues metatextually through the projection of representative African diasporic—and predominantly male—figures. In seeking to construct black modernism in their respective, and some-times overlapping, contexts, African American and Francophone Caribbean writers as a whole faced the challenges of proving their artistry (as writers who created rather than merely recorded "natural" black expression), their subjec-tivity (as writers whose work demanded to be read alongside that of their Anglo and French counterparts), and their mastery (as writers who could both use and reinvent prevailing discursive forms). For a subset of this larger group the figures that propelled this re-presentation, this movement from stereotype to subject, proved to be no less than the defining archetypes of comparative black modernism: the New Negro and the Negritude hero.

To "make it new" in modernist-era African American and Caribbean cultural production meant to negotiate both occidental rationality, from which Anglo and European writers declared their artistic independence, as well as the racial terror it produced, rationalized, and institutionalized.[52] Such negotiations entailed not merely assertions of individual, self-fashioned identities that recall the figure of "the solitary modernist" but also articulations of archetypal blackness that borrowed from earlier eras and embodied an enterprise usually considered anathema to modernist art: the consolidation of group identities.[53] In other words, newness for many of the gatekeepers of the Harlem Renaissance and Negritude involved situating African diasporic peoples with regard to histories and conventions that had long denied or denigrated their collective existence. As a result, over the course of repeated creative and critical deployments the African American New Negro and the Caribbean Negritude hero grew from literary examples of emergent blackness into symbols charged with embodying model African diasporic modernity.

The New Negro owes its prominence as the Harlem Renaissance archetype par excellence to the high-profile vehicles through which it was launched. In March 1924 sociologist and *Opportunity* editor Charles S. Johnson hosted a dinner at the New York Civic Club. Foreshadowing the eventual elision of women intellectuals from Harlem Renaissance narratives, the event held in Jessie Fauset's honor is more commonly remembered as the catalyst behind *Survey Graphic* magazine's special "Harlem: Mecca of the New Negro" number. Howard University philosopher Locke wrote the issue's lead essay, "The New Negro" (1925), and shepherded its transformation into the expanded and re-titled anthology *The New Negro*.[54] Locke posited the eponymous figure as a national symbol, one who would solve America's race problem through the intellectual, social, and, presumably, economic strides that distanced him—the modern African American subject—from the "Old Negro." The New Negro promised change not only within African American communities but across the American sociopolitical landscape as well: "the choice is not between one way for the Negro and another way for the rest, but between American institutions frustrated on the one hand and American ideals progressively filled and realized on the other."[55] On the international stage Locke envisioned an African American community led by the New Negro as no less than "the advance-guard of the African peoples in their contact with Twentieth Century civilization."[56]

Despite the eloquence and sweep of Locke's prose, his vision falls short of acknowledging the social intricacies that complicated New Negrohood. He does not address the manner in which the intersection of gender, race, and class impeded the advancement of modernist-era African Americans, and his arche-type is representative not "in the sense of mode, or mean, or median" but in the sense of being "the most presentable."[57] As Cheryl Wall notes, "With its imagery drawn from industry, technology, and war, and the extended citation of poems by Langston Hughes, Claude McKay, and James Weldon Johnson, [Locke's] es-say takes on a masculinist cast."[58] And yet to discuss women's relationships to New Negrohood would not have been inconceivable; in July 1923 the *Messen-ger,* the journal of the Brotherhood of Sleeping Car Porters, published a "New Negro Woman" number. Two years later, within the pages of Locke's own an-thology, Elise Johnson McDougald queried and critiqued "The Task of Negro Womanhood."[59] The gender exclusivity of Locke's New Negro is compounded by his advocacy of class-based racial vanguardism; "the only safeguard for mass [interracial] relations in the future," he argues, "must be provided in the care-fully maintained contacts of the enlightened minorities of both race groups."[60] The southern-to-northern, rural-to-urban migration of working-class African Americans may have been the catalyst behind the young century's social trans-formation, but it is the "Young Negro, [with] his poetry, his art, his education, and his new outlook" that Locke imagines directing this change for the collec-tive benefit of the race.[61]

Henry Louis Gates Jr. ascribes such literary rehabilitations of the Negro to a Reconstruction-era desire to counter the negative discursive legacy of slavery, to reassemble "blackness" in the American imagination as the country itself had been rebuilt.[62] Indeed, aspects of Locke's vision can be found in earlier and contemporaneous formulations of New Negrohood. Both J. W. E. Bowen's *An Appeal to the King* (1895) and Booker T. Washington, Fannie Barrier Wil-liams, and N. B. Wood's *A New Negro for a New Century* (1900) presented the New Negro as a figure that would " 'turn' the new century's image of the black away from the stereotypes scattered throughout plantation fictions, blackface minstrelsy, vaudeville, racist pseudo-science, and vulgar Social Darwinism."[63] W. E. B. Du Bois espoused similar sentiments—although without using the phrase *New Negro*—in his essay "The Talented Tenth" (1903), a group whose members he posited "as models of Negro gentility for the dominant white society and subordinated blacks."[64] Taking a more recognizably radical stance, socialist and *Messenger* coeditor A. Philip Randolph championed the perspectives of a group largely underrepresented by those engagements with New Negrohood: working-class African Americans. Unlike Locke, who describes his archetype as a reluctant radical, Randolph introduces his New Negro as one ready to confront early-twentieth-century racial violence directly and without regard for the concerns of Anglo American patrons or African American elites.[65] What joins these portrayals, from the genteel revolution of Du Bois's Talented Tenth to the open revolt of Randolph's working class, is the connection between the achievement of an individual or select group of individuals and the advancement of African Americans as a whole.

Early articulations of Negritude devoted more attention to connections between race and diaspora than to those between race and nation. Although the social climate in France and the Francophone world prompted Negritude poets Aimé Césaire, Léon-Gontran Damas, and Léopold Sédar Senghor to claim their blackness, the idiosyncrasies of the French political system rendered the interrogation of citizenship perhaps less urgent for them than it was for their African American peers. As residents of Martinique and French Guyana, respectively, two of France's *vieilles colonies* (old colonies), Césaire and Damas were French citizens by birth, and the government policy of *assimilation* encouraged colonial subjects—particularly those whose educational achievements seemingly confirmed the ideal of France as a colorblind, meritocratic republic—to consider themselves French first and foremost.[66] Senghor was not born with French citizenship, but the prominence and wealth of his family made him a similarly favorable candidate for assimilation, and he became a naturalized French citizen in 1933.[67] Although assimilation allowed for the incorporation of African diasporic subjects into the French body politic, however, it was less accommodating to the open acknowledgment of the ways in which race impacted such incorporations. Universal humanism, the Enlightenment philosophy that became a founding principle of French republicanism and, by extension, assimilation, in fact promoted a very particular ideal of Frenchness, one that was white and bourgeois.[68] Because of this conceptual impasse, the more well-known early forays into Negritude negotiated the cultural, social, and political ramifications of blackness through "Africa" as much as, if not more than, through France.

In *Pigments* (1937), the first volume published by a member of the Negritude triumvirate of Césaire, Damas, and Senghor, Damas introduces a nascent hero who yearns for the ancestral sources that European colonialism has denied him. Damas's persona is unlike the wistful figure of African American Countee Cullen's 1925 poem "Heritage":

> *One three centuries removed*
> *From the scenes his father loved,*
> *Spicy grove, cinnamon tree,*
> *What is Africa to me?* [69]

On the contrary, the speaker of "Blanchi" ("Whitewashed") is angry and rebellious:

> Se peut-il donc qu'ils osent
> me traiter de blanchi
> alors que tout en moi
> aspire à n'être que nègre
> autant que mon Afrique
> qu'ils ont cambriolée

> It may be [thus] that they dare
> treat me as whitewashed
> while everything within me
> wants only to be black
> as negro as the Africa
> they robbed me of.[70]

The struggle becomes more personal in "Hoquet," in which Damas explores the internalized racism that further proscribes the desire to reconnect with Africa and, in turn, with blackness. In a confrontation between a black-identifying mulatto son and his mother, the repressive matriarch chastises her child for crossing the line between mulatto respectability and black coarseness: "les *mulâtres* ne font pas ça / laissez donc ça aux *nègres*" ("*Mulattoes* don't do that / leave that to the *Blacks*"; 36).[71] The offense that sparks this closing rebuke is the son's desire to study the banjo; instead of embracing the more "refined" violin, he would rather play the instrument immortalized by Claude McKay as the symbol of diasporic primitivism.[72] Damas further transgresses the boundaries enforced by the disgruntled mother by italicizing both "mulâtres" and "nègres," thus rendering the terms graphically equal.

The link between blackness, heroism, and Africa emerges more explicitly in Aimé Césaire's 1939 epic *Cahier d'un retour au pays natal (Notebook of a Return to My Native Land)*. Césaire's male persona rejects the wandering of the diasporic subject for the permanence of an African-centered identity and, over the course of three movements, progresses from despising his island home to accepting it and its complex, often tragic history: "J'accepte, j'accepte tout cela" ("I accept, I accept it all").[73] Ultimately, the cultural roots that the hero rediscovers are reflected in physical roots plunged into African soil:

> A force de regarder les arbres je suis
> devenu un arbre et mes longs pieds
> d'arbre ont creusé dans le sol de larges
> sacs à venin de hautes villes d'ossements

> From staring too long at trees I have
> become a tree and my long tree
> feet have dug in the ground large
> venom sacs high cities of bone.
>
> (50/51)

Africa is an integral part of the persona and, through this poetic *enracinement* (putting down of roots), he of it. This journey of self-discovery—from the Caribbean to Africa and back—culminates in the articulation and embrace of *négritude* (blackness), a category that Antilleans of Césaire's generation customarily associated not with themselves but with Africans.[74] In reclaiming and representing the history of the slave trade and its aftermath, Césaire transforms what had been a source of shame into a source of pride.

The Negritude interrelation of a virile male persona and "Africa" comes full circle with Senghor, the poet who knew the continent as a "living, profuse" entity rather than a lost ancient site.[75] In his first collection, *Chants d'ombre (Shadow Songs;* 1945), Senghor's depiction of this intimacy repeatedly turns on the association of companion and continent. His imagery ranges from the subtle in "Nuit de Sine" ("Night in Sine"), in which the speaker posits the simply named "Femme" ("Woman") as a medium through whom he can access his ancestors, to the overt in "Femme noire" ("Black Woman"), in which the title figure becomes indistinguishable from the landscape:

> Femme nue, femme obscure!
> Fruit mûr à la chair ferme, sombres extases du vin noir, bouche qui fais
>   lyrique ma bouche
> Savane aux horizons purs, savane qui frémis aux caresses ferventes du
>   Vent d'est
> Tam-tam sculpté, tam-tam tendu qui grondes sous les doigts du
>   Vainqueur

> Naked woman, dark woman
> Ripe fruit with firm flesh, dark raptures of black wine,
> Mouth that gives music to my mouth
> Savanna of clear horizons, savanna quivering to the fervent caress
> Of the East Wind, sculptured tom-tom, stretched drumskin
> Moaning under the hands of the conqueror.[76]

This image of woman as landscape simultaneously praised and pleasured by the male speaker recurs in the poem "Congo," in which the phallic roots of Césaire's *Cahier* reappear in the mountains overlooking the Congo River: "Oho! Congo couchée dans ton lit de forêts, reine sur l'Afrique domptée / Que les phallus des monts portent haut ton pavillon" ("Oho! Congo, lying on your bed of forests, queen of subdued Africa / May the mountain phalluses hold high your pavilion").[77] These portrayals of women are more complimentary in that, in the move from Damas to Senghor, women have gone from rejecting to representing Africanness; they facilitate rather than foil the poet's celebration of his negritude. But the transition from antagonistic mulatta to African ideal also suggests a decline in the agency exercised by women of color in canonical Negritude. However noble, the task of embodying Africa is not the same as articulating one's own relationship to the continent and its cultures.

The predominance of male interpretations of Negritude continues in the poetic, Francophone analogue of Alain Locke's *New Negro*, the Senghor-edited *Anthologie de la nouvelle poésie nègre et malgache de langue française* (*Anthology of New Black and Malagasy Poetry in French*; 1948). Its exclusively male list of contributors includes Césaire, Damas, and editor Senghor, along with Malagasy writers Jean-Joseph Rabéarivelo and Jacques Rabémananjara; more important, the volume prefaces these poems with Sartre's "Orphée noir," which alternately presents Negritude as androgynous, "à tour la femelle de la Nature et son mâle" ("both Nature's female and its male"), and masculine, driven by a spirituality that is "phallic" ("phallique") and "spermatic" ("spermatique").[78] As practiced, Negritude may have been a literary movement that spanned the Francophone world (with the exception of the former Indochina), but, as collected and theorized, it seemed to be coalescing in a decidedly masculinist fashion: Damas went so far as to deem Senghor, Aimé Césaire, and himself "the Holy Trinity of Negritude—with philosopher-poet Senghor as the Father; the poetic son, Césaire, . . . and the Holy Spirit, Damas."[79] While Damas's metaphor would seem to leave the role of divine mother (Mary) open, this option seems no less restricting than that of the race traitor of "Blanchi" or the cultural icon of Senghor's poems.

As limiting the conception of African American modernism to New Negro-hood glosses over the perspectives of early-twentieth-century African Americans who either could or would not conform to Locke's masculinist bourgeois ideal, so limiting one's understanding of Francophone modernism to the Negritude poets elides the contemporaneous experiences of Francophone individuals whose lives did not exemplify "radical" masculinism. While some members of the Francophone bourgeoisie unquestionably produced literature encouraging cultural assimilation and social complacency, others, including Guadeloupeans Oruno Lara and Suzanne Lacascade, rehabilitated the formerly pejorative term *nègre* in popular fiction published before the advent of Césaire, Damas, and Senghor. In Lara's 1923 novel *Question de couleurs (Blanches et noirs)* a Guadeloupean gentleman of color instructs his equally refined countrywoman in the ways of racial pride, and the *mulâtresse* title character proudly proclaims her African ancestry throughout Lacascade's 1924 novel *Claire-Solange, âme africaine.*[80] Similarly, before German ethnologist Leo Frobenius's influential rehabilitation of African culture was translated into French, the Martinican Nardal sisters orchestrated diasporic cultural exchange in person through salons hosted in their Paris home and in print through the publication of the bilingual journal *La Revue du Monde Noir/Review of the Black World* (1931–32).[81] Despite the review's promotion of racial pride and consciousness, the journal and its editorial team, much like Jessie Fauset in the African American context, have been famously dismissed as insufficiently engaged.[82] As illustrative and inspiring as archetypes such as the New Negro and the Negritude hero are, then, their centrality to studies of the Harlem Renaissance and Negritude has obscured the ways in which black women modernists, in spite and because of their respective class positions, produced progressive literary negotiations of race, gender, and nation by using, subverting, and, ultimately, rejecting discourses of model black modernity.

THINKING OUTSIDE THE ARCHETYPE: COMPARATIVE BLACK MODERNISMS

Seeking to disrupt canonical narratives of early-twentieth-century African American and Francophone Caribbean literary production, *Race, Gender, and Comparative Black Modernism* links questions of race, gender, and modernism to think outside the archetype. Womanhood in model black modernism is not unlike blackness in Zita Nunes's discussion of racial democracy in Brazil: "Blackness, in terms of racial democracy, [becomes] the name given to that which exceeds it and makes it visible—it is the remainder that makes the notion of racial democracy possible and sustainable, yet always destined to fail."[83] Within the Harlem Renaissance and Negritude canons, the figures of the heroic male and the nurturing female facilitate black modernist representation while others, particularly the black woman who falls outside of the category of mother/lover/partner, threaten the ideals reinforcing that representation. Gender at large and womanhood in particular are to be controlled; they are to be "complementary" rather than challenging, subordinate rather than subversive, remaindered rather than incorporated.[84]

In order to move from "representative colored men" (or representative Europeans and Anglo-Americans) to atypical black women, scholarly expectations of modernist type must be distinguished from preconceived notions of modernist types. Hortense Spillers argues that the exclusion of African American subjects from mainstream American discursive communities produces the impulse "to break apart, to rupture violently the laws of American behavior that make such syntax possible [and] to introduce a new *semantic* field/fold more appropriate to his/her own historic movement."[85] How have the semantic fields and intellectual folds of the Harlem Renaissance and Negritude been shaped by perceptions of archetypal blackness? How have criteria for "intellectual citizenship" and belonging within the respective movements been determined: through the production of literature whose social relevance is evaluated by the presence or absence of sanctioned racial archetypes, through the form and content of works, or through some combination of the two?[86] How does the examination of understudied women's voices from the early twentieth century disturb the Eurocentric and masculinist canons—or laws—of modernism, the Harlem Renaissance, and Negritude? Intellectuals Jessie Fauset and Paulette Nardal were much more than literary midwives and godmothers, the titles often used to describe their participation in black modernist circles, just as the social impact of their respective writings exceeds their middle-class backgrounds.[87] As such, they and other women writers belong in the same critical discussions as their African diasporic male, European, and Anglo American peers.

Such is the conversation that I launch, but by no means conclude, with this study. I am interested in the new understandings of comparative black modernism that emerge with the discussion of a nonuniform group of women writers across historical moments, genres, and languages. How do differences between *francité* (Frenchness) and "Americanness," between *la francophonie* and African America, factor into these writers' respective engagements with race, nation, and diaspora? How does removing the convergence of African diasporic writers in New York and Paris as a ground of comparison alter the critical landscape of modernist studies? In addressing these questions, I wish to demonstrate that, when read through the work of noncanonical writers, womanhood within black modernist discourse operates not only as a site of representation but also as one of contestation.

Chapter 1, "A Dying Exoticism: The Enigmatic Fiction of Suzanne Lacascade," reads Lacascade's *Claire-Solange, âme africaine* as a protofeminist, proto-Negritude articulation of Caribbean identity. Central to Lacascade's narrative are the discourse of post-exoticism, which I introduce as the simultaneous deployment and destabilization of exoticist images and tropes, and the representation of the *mulâtresse* protagonist as a living tableau that invites and controls the male metropolitan gaze. Reading Claire-Solange's evolving racial consciousness through the lens of post-exoticism demonstrates the interdependence of exoticism and Negritude: in *Claire-Solange* the former functions not as an entity from which the latter signals a distinct literary and ideological break but, rather, as a movement that is inextricably bound to Negritude articulations of place and identity. In addition, I examine the novel's interracial marriage subplot as one that challenges the Fanonian narrative of *lactification*, or whitening, by reversing the traditional balance of power in the woman of color–white man relationship and presenting this romance as an allegory of

France's relationship to its overseas colonies. Throughout the novel Lacascade's multifaceted protagonist counters not only the romanticized *doudou* of exoticism but also the objectified primitive of European modernism à la Josephine Baker and the soon-to-emerge idealized hero of Negritude.

Chapter 2, "The Limits of Exemplarity: Marita Bonner's Alternative Modernist Landscapes," examines the fissures left unexplored in New Negro visions of African American community. Whereas Lacascade forgoes a discussion of class in order to foster diasporic unity, Bonner's essays, plays, and short stories foreground the issue as she contends that any viable conception of community must grow out of an initial acknowledgment of internal divisions. In Bonner's writing the center of New Negrohood does not hold because the unifying facades promoted in the project of achieving social advancement through artistic production were also instruments by which segments of African American communities, particularly the upper middle class, preserved boundaries of intraracial difference. Bonner's work further transforms traditional conceptions of Harlem Renaissance landscapes in a literal, geographic sense. Challenging the primacy of the U.S. eastern seaboard as the nexus of early-twentieth-century African American intellectual production, Bonner locates modernist struggles for individual and communal self-determination in a variety of sites ranging from the sleepy southern hamlet of the 1938 short story "Hate Is Nothing" to the abstract wilderness of her 1928 expressionist drama *The Purple Flower*. I identify Bonner's Frye Street stories, which imagine the problems and possibilities of community in a multiethnic, working-class Chicago neighborhood, as the culmination of her project of constructing alternative modernist landscapes.

Chapter 3, "Surrealist Dreams, Martinican Realities: The Negritude of Suzanne Césaire," interrogates the obscurity of Martinican essayist and playwright Césaire, who challenged the hegemony of French culture through surrealist practice much in the same way Bonner confronted American racial and gender stereotypes through abstract and expressionist forms. Césaire is more often remembered in Negritude criticism as an enigmatic icon rather than as an instrumental theorist, yet her writings from *Tropiques* (1941–45), the journal she cofounded with husband Aimé Césaire and fellow Martinican René Ménil, directly and insightfully engage the intellectual influences that informed the work of canonical Negritude. The "other" Césaire's essays deftly outline the impact of surrealism and Frobenian theory on Caribbean reclamations of the region's African and American roots. Furthermore, in a departure from the work of her peers, Césaire deploys notions of a primeval African past in order to examine key social problems facing interwar Martinique, not to reify a distant, idealized "mother" continent. The chapter concludes with an examination of the links between Césaire's nuanced interrogations of Caribbean social relations and the work of postcolonial theorist Édouard Glissant and Créolité proponents Jean Bernabé, Patrick Chamoiseau, and Raphaël Confiant.

Chapter 4, "Black Modernism in Retrospect: Dorothy West's New (Negro) Women," returns to the genre of fiction with an examination of West's 1948 novel *The Living Is Easy*. I read the text as a retrospective critique of the forces that continued to circumscribe women's lives in the midst of the social and cultural awakening presumably embodied in the New Negro. Like Lacascade, West builds her narrative around an unexpectedly recalcitrant protagonist, and, like Bonner, she examines how social and moral stratification compounded the problem of race in the lives of early-twentieth-century African American women. My critique turns in large part on the tension that West builds between her protagonist's stance as anti–New Negro woman (and perhaps nascent New Woman) and a competing character's status as what I call True Negro Woman; the novel's conclusion finds all of the principal women characters in some way trapped between the traditional past and the modern(ist) present. I conclude that this uneasy condition casts more doubt upon the viability of the cultural paradigms that polarize the women than upon the integrity of West's characters. Indeed, their respective predicaments reveal the inherent paradox of the presumably representative, but ultimately exclusive, New Negro and New Negro Woman.

In the conclusion, "Atypical Women Revisited," I turn to two late-twentieth-century novels, Maryse Condé's *Heremakhonon* (1976) and Toni Morrison's *Tar Baby* (1981). One question often posed about African diasporic modernisms is that of whether any of its manifestations "succeeded" in fostering significant artistic or social change. While Dorothy West, writing in 1934, concluded that she and her fellow New Negroes failed to realize their "fine promise," I arrive at a very different conclusion when revisiting black women modernists through fiction produced out of the emergent black feminisms of the late twentieth century.[88] For, if the protofeminist, atypically political work of Lacascade, Bonner, Césaire, and West has been underappreciated, their writings have nonetheless paved the way for women writers who have continued their predecessors' interrogation of masculinist notions of modernity, identity, and community. In *Heremakhonon* and *Tar Baby*, respectively, Condé and Morrison introduce protagonists who are unabashedly *contestataire* (antiauthority). Whereas the diasporic travels of Lacascade's Claire-Solange are implicitly sanctioned by the presence of chaperoning family members, Condé's Veronica travels between Guadeloupe, France, and Africa largely at her own discretion. Whereas West's Cleo manipulates the gender dictates she so despises in order to achieve self-fulfillment, Morrison's Jadine rejects traditional womanhood outright. In short, in keeping with Condé's critical call for literary disorder, the protagonists of *Heremakhonon* and *Tar Baby* are neither male nor messianic, their respective returns "home" reveal that concept to be a construct built across multiple locales instead of associated with a single ancestral site, and women's sexuality does not serve the exclusive purpose of regenerating a male protagonist or, through procreation, the native land.[89] Neither novel ends with a definitive resolution, but I argue that it is precisely this lack of narrative restriction that signals the sustained and successful contestation of model modernity and its attendant demands of communal, racial, and diasporic solidarity.

Ultimately, what interests me about these and other atypical women is not so much the answers that their lives and writings provide as it is the questions they provoke. In Shakespeare, Miranda does not challenge her father's Eurocentric, patriarchal usurpation of Sycorax's power, but imagining such a rebellion pushes readers to rethink the depth and breadth of the racialized constructions of gender confronted by black modernist women writers; in Haiti, Défilée is not cured of her madness by the gathering of Dessalines's remains, but appreciating the national import of her individual act opens the door to revising notions of social engagement; and in the United States, Anna Julia Cooper does not end the predominance of race men in early-twentieth-century African American intellectual life, but using her work to revisit this era can correct gender imbalances in studies of the period. For it is the unexpected qualities of these figures, as well as of the writers and characters featured in *Race, Gender, and Comparative Black Modernism,* that are constitutive of, rather than inconsistent with, their respective explorations of modernity.

1 A Dying Exoticism

The Enigmatic Fiction of Suzanne Lacascade

Qu'est-ce après tout que l'engagement sinon la restitution de quelque aspect de la vérité que l'on a choisi d'illustrer?

What is engagement, after all, if not the restoration of some aspect of the truth that one has chosen to illustrate?

—MARYSE CONDÉ, "La littérature féminine de la Guadeloupe" (1976)

When *Claire-Solange, âme africaine* was published in 1924, the novel allegedly created such a stir that its author, Guadeloupean writer Suzanne Lacascade, was forced to leave her island home.[1] Yet Lacascade is perhaps best known for being unknown; that is, it is her inscrutability that often precedes and intersects with critical examinations of *Claire-Solange,* her sole publication.[2] What little biographical information is available verges on the nonexistent, as in writer-critic Maryse Condé's admission that "nous ne savons rien de Suzanne LACAS-

CADE, de sa vie, de ses expériences" ("we know nothing about Suzanne LACAS-
CADE, about her life, [or] about her experiences").[3] As a result, *Claire-Solange* is
not only a literary text but also a historical document, the record of an otherwise unknowable black modernist woman writer. While such a claim rightly
raises concerns about collapsing authorial and fictional identities, my aim here
is to read the intersection between Lacascade's life and her novel as evidence
of the enigmatic nature of much early Francophone Caribbean fiction. Written between the death of exoticism and the birth of Negritude, *Claire-Solange*
conjures and contradicts the work of predecessors, successors, and peers alike.
It is fluent in the rhetoric of exoticism yet nevertheless advances a project of racial valorization that foreshadows Caribbean Negritude's reclamation of the region's African heritage. It coincides with the literature of regionalism yet embraces a diasporic perspective whose reach extends far beyond the Caribbean
archipelago. And, finally, *Claire-Solange* recalls the models of exemplarity prof-
fered by Negritude and regionalism yet does so through a protagonist who is
too feminist for the former movement and too acerbic for the latter.

As a result, I am interested in how Lacascade's novel, rather than conform-
ing to fixed literary models, instead slips between them, revealing their per-
meability, points of contention, and, ultimately, interdependence. If the narrative of *Claire-Solange, âme africaine* is at times melodramatic, an assessment to
which I will return later, it is a narrative whose flaws reveal the shortcomings
of both exoticist escapism and Negritude "engagement." When the protagonist's unmitigated praises about her native (Caribbean) and ancestral (African)
homes seem to reach a fever pitch, it is then, and perhaps only then, that one realizes the extent to which much of Claire-Solange's persona is deliberate, strategic performance. The character not only boldly asserts a self-determined identity but, being conscious of others' desire to define her, also positions herself
as a living tableau to be read critically, indeed, to be regarded carefully, rather
than through the rose-colored lenses of exoticist or Negritude stereotypes. It is
in this unexpected and original narrative turn that I locate Lacascade's modernism.

Set principally in World War I–era Paris, *Claire-Solange* opens with a cable
announcing the imminent arrival of the title character, the twenty-year-old
daughter of Aurore Duflôt Hucquart, a deceased Martinican *mulâtresse* (mulatta), and Étienne Hucquart, a white Frenchman.[4] A devoted daughter, Claire-
Solange reluctantly leaves Martinique to accompany an ailing Étienne to France.
There father, daughter, and various members of the Duflôt family settle into

the home of Étienne's widowed sister-in-law. This generous but strained hospitality soon proves more mercenary than altruistic: convinced that she married the wrong brother, Jeanne Hucquart, the consummate Parisian *bourgeoise*, plans to woo Étienne by welcoming his Caribbean extended family into her home. To ensure success Jeanne enlists Jacques Danzel, her godson, to court Claire-Solange, thus persuading her to remain in Paris with Étienne. Yet neither Jeanne nor Jacques is prepared for the vehemence with which Claire-Solange rebuffs their advances. She dismisses the former as her "tante blanche" ("white aunt"; 63), the latter as her "pseudo-cousin" (62). Claire-Solange further distances herself from French society by proudly declaring her difference, alternately identifying herself as *nègre, africaine,* and *mulâtresse française.* This resistance extends to the physical environment: Claire-Solange prefers the French capital's Caribbean enclave to the smart neighborhood where Jeanne lives. In brief Claire-Solange considers her visit to France more an occasion to assert her ties to Martinique than to appreciate or participate in life in Paris.

Ultimately, however, Claire-Solange finds herself more and more drawn to Jacques Danzel and, by extension, France. The woman who once responded to her cousins' teasing prediction that she would marry Danzel with the denial "Jamais je n'épouserai un blanc, *jamais pas, jamais pas*" ("I'll never marry a white man, *never, never*"; 28) begins to reconsider her formerly staunch opposition to all things, her father presumably excluded, white and French. After a series of monumental defining events—the departure of her maternal family (save her aunt and chaperone Émilienne), the experience of meeting her paternal family, and the outbreak of World War I—Claire-Solange acknowledges her change of heart. The novel casts her eventual union with Jacques Danzel as a triumph of love over pride, as Lacascade's heroine at last recognizes the European heritage intermingled with her "African blood" and her suitor, wounded during the war, trusts that it is love, not pity, that has won Claire-Solange's heart. While the fate of Jeanne's pursuit remains unknown, the return of the prodigal Étienne is completed through his daughter: as he once exiled himself from France for his wife, so Claire-Solange exiles herself from Martinique to remain with Jacques Danzel.

It is perhaps because of the incongruity between *Claire-Solange*'s politicized narrative of race and identity and its apparent rehearsal of the more conventional marriage plot that reception of the novel has been uneven. At the time of its publication the novel was reviewed by the mainstream *Le Petit Parisien,* in which it was declared "de réelle promesses" ("of real promise"), and in the

Francophone organ *La Dépêche Coloniale et Maritime,* in which Lacascade was praised as a writer "de réel talent" ("of real talent").[5] These positive statements aside, the manner in which the latter assessment was qualified speaks to the social discomfort and critical silence that the novel went on to produce:

> Mais pourquoi l'auteur insiste-t-il autant sur l'intimité des races? C'est trop fort exagéré, Mademoiselle, je vous l'assure, et il y a beau temps que le préjugé de couleur n'existe plus en France, et que nous en avons laissé toute la cruelle sottise aux chrétiens anglo-saxons!

> But why does the author insist so much on racial intimacy? It's overexaggerated, Miss, I assure you, and it's been a good while since color prejudice has existed in France and we've left its cruel foolishness to Anglo-Saxon Christians![6]

Whatever the critic's own political position, his words spoke to prevailing trends in both radical and conservative streams of Francophone Caribbean thought: interracial romance was not a progressive topic in the eyes of militant intellectuals advocating for sociocultural independence from France, nor was French racism a favorite subject among moderates or conservatives in the Guadeloupean and Martinican middle and upper classes. As part of its *mission civilisatrice* (civilizing mission), French colonialism initially strove to transform colonial others into French subjects through language, instruction, and—in the case of *les vieilles colonies* of Martinique, Guadeloupe, French Guyana, and Réunion—citizenship.[7] The assumption of this new, French identity by the colonized was called "assimilation," of which an important component was the belief that the France of the 1789 Revolution was incapable of fostering racism.

Paulette Nardal (1896–1985) and Étienne Léro (1910–39) are two key interwar Francophone intellectuals who were publicly vocal about questions of race and assimilation yet curiously silent about *Claire-Solange.* Although both Martinican, middle-class, and, during much of their writing careers, Paris-based, Nardal and Léro illustrate the aforementioned complexities of French colonial policies and politics. With her sisters Jane and Andrée, Nardal hosted a weekly salon where guests from throughout the African diaspora gathered to "[discuss] interracial and colonial problems, racist injustices, and current events."[8] These conversations continued in the pages of *La Revue du Monde Noir/Review of the Black World,* the bilingual journal the Nardals cofounded with cousin Louis-Thomas Achille in 1931. Paulette Nardal specifically addresses the intersection of gender and racial consciousness in the essay "Éveil de la conscience de race" ("Awakening of Race Consciousness"), her contribution to the *Revue*'s final issue:

> Les femmes de couleur vivant seules dans la métropole moins favorisées jusqu'à l'Exposition coloniale que leurs congénères masculins aux faciles succès, ont ressenti bien avant eux le besoin d'une solidarité raciale qui ne serait pas seulement d'ordre matériel: c'est ainsi qu'elles se sont éveillées à la conscience de race.

> The coloured women living alone in the metropolis, until the Colonial Exhibition, have certainly been less favored than coloured men who are content with a certain easy success. Long before the latter, they have felt the need of a racial solidarity which would not to [*sic*] be merely material. They were thus aroused to race consciousness.[9]

Nardal concludes "Eveil de la conscience de race" by cautioning that embracing blackness does not necessitate rejecting whiteness; in Nardal's eyes the latter move could precipitate an unfortunate "retour à l'obscurantisme" ("return to ignorance"; 31). Yet there is no mention of Lacascade either in conjunction with these comments or in the chronological review of Caribbean literature that precedes them (27–29). Instead, the author who would seem to have been an ideal subject for Nardal's analysis is nowhere to be found.

Lacascade is similarly absent from the writings of Nardal's compatriot Léro, who was part of the Marxist-surrealist collective that published the single-issue journal *Légitime Défense* in 1932. While Nardal and her editorial team largely envisioned racial vindication through cultural awakening, Léro and his collaborators primarily advocated social revolution. Accordingly, in his signature essay, "Misère d'une poésie," he uses a survey of Caribbean literary history to denounce early-twentieth-century Martinican and Guadeloupean writers for producing unimaginative work from within "une société mulâtre, intellectuellement et physiquement abâtardie" ("a mulatto society, intellectually and physically corrupt").[10] He continues by accusing this same society—his own, it should be noted—of being beholden to and manipulated by the French bourgeoisie (10).[11] That Lacascade does not appear in the litany of authors critiqued by Léro is especially noteworthy because the novel was the literary form that Surrealists found the most restrictive of expressive freedom and the use of such an unimaginative, bourgeois form to depict a *mulâtresse* protagonist falling in love with a white Frenchman would seem all the more cause for Léro's critical attention.[12] If, as critic Valérie Orlando states, only thirty copies of *Claire-Solange* were printed, one might attribute these otherwise perplexing omissions to scarcity: perhaps Nardal and Léro were simply unable to access a copy of the novel.[13] Yet, in light of the publicity Lacascade's text received and the relative intimacy of Francophone intellectual circles in Paris (despite their markedly different social politics, for example, Léro contributed to *La Revue du Monde Noir* before going on to cofound *Légitime Défense*), it is surprising that neither Nardal nor Léro would not at least have heard of and been moved to mention *Claire-Solange*. These circumstances suggest another scenario, one in which Lacascade's anomalous politics—too Afrocentric for the *Revue,* too bourgeois for *Légitime Défense*—may have posed too much of a critical conundrum for her peers to tackle. However much Nardal and Léro may have wished to challenge existing gender and class politics, respectively, they may not have been ready for a text as slippery as *Claire-Solange*.

One critic who would have been poised to tackle Lacascade's novel is Frantz Fanon, whose landmark 1952 work *Peau noire, masques blancs (Black Skin, White Masks)* incorporates gender in its analysis of Caribbean racial consciousness. His work, however, like much of the pre-1950 Francophone Caribbean literature critiqued by scholar Nicole Aas Rouxparis, is largely male-dominated and devoid of representations of women as complex, nuanced subjects.[14] In the collection's now (in)famous chapter "La femme de couleur et le blanc" ("The Woman of Color and the White Man"), Fanon reads Martinican novelist Mayotte Capécia's 1948 *Je suis martiniquaise (I Am a Martinican Woman)* as a narrative of *lactification,* or the desire to whiten the race.[15] He contends that for Capécia, whom he uncritically conflates with her character and reads as representative of all Antillean women of color, the way to achieve this whitening is "choisir le moins noir" ("to select the least black of the men") and, if possible, a white man, as a lover.[16] Fanon complicates his reading in at least two ways: (1) he acknowledges the problematic nature of reading *the* woman of color— whomever this representative, all-encompassing figure might be—through *a* literary character; and (2) he follows the Capécia discussion with the chapter entitled "L'homme de couleur et la blanche" ("The Man of Color and the White Woman"), in which he discusses Martinican writer René Maran's 1947 interracial romance *Un homme pareil aux autres*. Nonetheless, it is Fanon's castigation of Capécia, not his admission of analytical irresponsibility, that has indelibly marked the critique of Francophone Caribbean women's literature, and his critique of Maran is filtered through the following explanation:

> Le Blanc étant le maître, et plus simplement le mâle, peut se payer le luxe de coucher avec beaucoup de femmes. Cela est vrai dans tous les pays et davantage aux colonies. Mais une Blanche qui accepte un Noir, cela prend automatiquement un aspect romantique. Il y a un don et non pas viol.

> Since he is master and more simply the male, the white man can allow himself the luxury of sleeping with many women. This is true in every country and especially in colonies. But when a white woman accepts a black man there is automatically a romantic aspect. It is a giving, not a seizing.[17]

The statement astutely recognizes the social dynamic and power imbalance that formed the subtext of many colonial-era interracial relationships but does so in a one-sided fashion; Fanon denies not only the agency of the woman of color, who, in his reading, can only be victimized by the white man, but also that of the white woman, who, in turn, can only love the black man. The resulting framework reduces all women-authored novels about women of color in relationships with white men to narratives of *lactification* and elevates all male-authored texts about inverse relationships to narratives of true love. In any case both models render a novel like *Claire-Solange,* whose *mulâtresse* protagonist embraces her blackness even as she falls for a white suitor, a literary impossibility.

The late twentieth and early twenty-first centuries have brought a variety of studies reconsidering the place of *Claire-Solange, âme africaine* within Francophone Caribbean literary history. Early analyses by Maryse Condé and Jack Corzani offer qualified praise, albeit with different terms of qualification than the novel's initial reviewers: it is Lacascade's style, not her subject, that Condé and Corzani find deficient.[18] In particular Condé argues that, although Lacascade appropriates stereotypes for the purpose of racial valorization, the author eventually drowns her protagonist and narrative in a sea of exoticist images. Similarly noting the interplay between Lacascade's form and content,

Roger Toumson describes *Claire-Solange* as "une lecture plaisante et instructive" ("pleasant and instructive reading") whose primary significance rests in its representation of a growing ethnic consciousness among the Antillean mulatto intelligentsia.[19] As critical attention to the novel has increased, the focus seems to have shifted from questions of form back to those of content. Thus, although Brent Edwards tempers an initial argument for recognizing Lacascade as an important pre-Negritude writer with the observation that *Claire-Solange* rehearses conventional exoticist narratives, his reading and those by Micheline Rice-Maximin, Valérie Orlando, and T. Denean Sharpley-Whiting ultimately privilege issues of gender and intertextuality over interrogations of Lacascade's style.[20] These assessments demonstrate critical balance in that they provide astute readings of *Claire-Solange* as they recover it and early Francophone Caribbean women's writing from the lingering impact of Fanon's Capécia indictment, but they also speak to a critical uncertainty about how to assess previously marginalized texts that straddle, confuse, and challenge literary boundaries.

Upon initial readings Lacascade's novel may seem to enhance more than clarify this confusion, but the questions it raises are key to rethinking how masculinist or gender-neutral articulations of Negritude operated within a larger field of comparative black modernism. Foremost among these questions is that posed by Edwards in his study of interwar black intellectual culture: "What would it mean . . . to stake out a new, or 'forgotten,' genealogy of Negritude," one in which women are not simply invoked but empowered to speak for themselves?[21] Lacascade's outspoken protagonist predates and radically differs from the female iconography of canonical Negritude. Unlike the repressive mother who, in Léon-Gontran Damas's poem "Hoquet," admonishes her son to maintain the social demarcations between "mulattoes" and "blacks," the mixed-race Claire-Solange, as the novel's title indicates, embraces her African heritage.[22] The child of a French father ensconced in the colonial bureaucracy and a Martinican mother equally well situated in that island's *bourgeoisie de couleur,* Lacascade's protagonist enjoys a life of privilege unknown to the urinating peasant woman or self-sacrificing seamstress in Aimé Césaire's *Cahier d'un retour au pays natal.*[23] Nor is Claire-Solange the idyllic, silent embodiment of an ancestral motherland found in Léopold Sédar Senghor's 1945 poem "Femme noire," which depicts the titular figure as a ripe landscape caressed by the wind.[24] And, finally, unlike essayist Suzanne Césaire, Lacascade consistently links questions of racial identity to questions of gender. In addition to these thematic differences, *Claire-Solange* predates the first "official" Negritude volume, Damas's *Pigments*, by thirteen years. It is a text that rests "on the liminal edge of the accepted [and] expected" boundaries of Negritude, but its explicitly articulated, clearly progressive racial politics suggest that perhaps these boundaries should be redrawn chronologically as well as thematically.[25]

I would be remiss if I did not also consider Lacascade's position with respect to the exoticist writers she succeeded. But, as Lacascade foreshadows Negritude's vindication of blackness without using the same strategies and symbols as its paragons, so she celebrates the Caribbean in a manner reminiscent of, but not equivalent to, the practitioners of exoticism. The result is what I call "post-exoticism," a discourse that simultaneously employs and exceeds exoticist tropes. I propose this term fully conscious of the problems raised by such literary critical postings. Having found postcolonialism inadequate in addressing the work of black women writers, Carole Boyce Davies questions the validity of declaring any literary movement, political system, or critical school "over": "the ideology of most 'postings' conveys that the older systems, as well as their after-effects, are carried over into the present or future. Bereft of their singular and prominent identifications which fuel the opposition or energy of resistance, they become empty positionalities which obscure oppression (i.e., post-feminism means one no longer has to struggle against patriarchy)."[26] Rather than obscure the problematic elements of exoticism or prematurely pronounce its death, I wish instead to challenge canonical notions of black modernism by restaging the relationship between exoticist and Negritude representations of the Caribbean. Roger Toumson argues that any insistence on an impassable breach between literary styles and periods is not only false but also dangerous; such a stance impedes the comprehensive analysis of Francophone Caribbean poetics by relegating atypical or unusual texts to the critical dustbin.[27]

I also label *Claire-Solange* post-exoticist in order to pursue the more productive interpretive possibilities of privileging the novel's relationship to the so-called decadent, imitative works of early-twentieth-century Francophone Caribbean literature over the reputedly more "authentic," "inventive" works of Negritude. My goal is to escape the reading of Lacascade as a mere precursor to her more celebrated successors and highlight her engagement of issues of racial identity through exoticism rather than in spite of it. Moving beyond the archetype of the exotic—or tragic—woman of color and the representation of the Caribbean as paradise on Earth, Lacascade troubles the idealization of "tropical" people and places to facilitate the racial valorization once thought to be the sole province of Negritude. Central to this valorization is a strategy identified by Édouard Glissant as essential to articulating the "lived modernity" of the Caribbean: "Nous devons développer une poétique du 'sujet,' pour cela même qu'on nous a trop longtemps 'objectivés' ou plutôt 'objectés'" ("We need to develop a poetics of the 'subject,' if only because we have been too long 'objectified' or rather 'objected to'").[28] What Lacascade begins to develop in *Claire-Solange*, through its inversion of exoticist dynamics, is a poetics of the black woman subject.

L'Exotisme Est Mort! Vive l'Exotisme?

Lilyan Kesteloot's conclusion that "il n'y avait effectivement aucune littérature originale aux Antilles" ("there was no originality in West Indian literature in French") prior to the 1932 publication of *Légitime Défense* is to black Francophone literary history in general what Frantz Fanon's commentary about Mayotte Capécia is to Francophone Caribbean women's literature in particular: a defining moment, a line of demarcation between imitation and innovation, self-hatred and self-acceptance.[29] In a sense Kesteloot is restating, albeit more diplomatically, the Étienne Léro declaration noted earlier: that most pre-1930s Guadeloupean and Martinican literature was the amateurish output of a bastardized mulatto intelligentsia. Questions of diplomacy and polemic aside, both the Kesteloot and Léro statements effectively posit pre-Negritude writers as personae non gratae. Why would these critics—especially Kesteloot, whose comment appears in an academic study rather than a cultural manifesto— propose or effect the wholesale dismissal of a body of literature? Was exoticism so pernicious as to warrant its erasure as a precursor to Negritude? What of those texts, such as *Claire-Solange*, written between the final throes of exoticism and the early cries of Negritude? Should one follow preexisting literary historical models for reading such work? According to Corzani, *Claire-Solange* could be read as an example of "regionalism" *(le régionalisme)*, literature that was written between 1910 and 1935 and that, if somewhat picturesque, was more realistic than exoticist literature. Toumson uses roughly the same historical parameters but argues that regionalism and Negritude originated "d'une seule et même entreprise ayant pour fin un détournement culturel" ("from one and the same enterprise, having as its goal cultural change").[30] The precursor of regionalism, in turn, was none other than exoticism.

The history of literary exoticism in the Francophone Caribbean stretches from the colonization of the islands to the early twentieth century. Fueled by what Régis Antoine describes as "l'esthétique d'esprit colon" ("the aesthetics of the colonial spirit"), the work of early exoticists functioned as propaganda intended to lure European settlers to the Americas.[31] Written in the seventeenth and eighteenth centuries by missionaries and explorers, these texts tended to gloss over the often inhospitable terrain of the Caribbean, instead presenting the archipelago as "les Iles Fortunées," or "the Favored Islands."[32] As the colonization it paralleled developed, exoticism simultaneously facilitated Europe's "comprehension . . . of the new, strange cultures it had encountered" and its "consolidation [of] unified national communit[ies]": the definition of the colonial Other/elsewhere served to clarify perceptions of national space and identity.[33] Over time island residents across racial categories adopted exoticism as a means of highlighting the merits and charms of the New World relative to the Old. Les békés, or white Creoles, began writing about their tropical lives, and in the late nineteenth and early twentieth centuries mulatto and black Antillean writers steeped in metropolitan French literary culture joined les békés and their European predecessors by offering their own exoticist interpretations of the Caribbean.[34] Regardless of the identity or intention of these subsequent chroniclers, their writing as well as that of their predecessors stemmed from a mutual, problematic organizing principle: the transformation of the Caribbean from a colonized site marked by slavery and genocide into an apolitical space offering wonders and riches unavailable in Europe.

This contradiction between colonial politics and artistic perspective is evident in the work of Daniel Thaly, the Martinican poet alternately hailed as "le Prince des Poètes" ("the Prince of Poets") and a bard of exoticism.[35] The scion of a wealthy béké family, Thaly published widely in the early twentieth century, and the island home that he left to pursue medical study in France became a principal subject of his poetry.[36] Featured in Thaly's 1911 collection Le jardin des tropiques (The Garden of the Tropics), the poem "Chanson" celebrates a breathtaking, if depopulated, Caribbean landscape and warrants being cited in full:

> La lumière coule en cascades d'or
> Sur les frais vallons d'Ile charmée;
> Tes yeux sont pour moi le plus cher trésor;
> Vive le soleil, ô ma bien-aimée!

La muscade saigne au fond du verger.
Ta chair amoureuse est toute embaumée
D'une odeur de miel, d'ambre et d'oranger;
Vive le soleil, ô ma bien-aimée!

Qu'importent demain, le deuil ou la mort,
Sur mon cœur je sens ton âme pâmée,
La lumière grise et l'amour est fort;
    Vive le soleil, ô ma bien-aimée![37]

The light flows in cascades of gold
On the fresh dales of the charmed Island;
Your eyes are, for me, the dearest treasure;
Long live the sun, o my beloved!

The nutmeg seeps deep in the orchard.
Your amorous flesh is ever fragrant
With the scent of honey, amber, and orange;
Long live the sun, o my beloved!

What do tomorrow, grief, or death matter,
In my heart I feel your swooning soul,
The light is exhilarating, and love is strong;
    Long live the sun, o my beloved!

With these words Thaly immortalizes a sun-drenched, charmed island where tropical flora and fauna infuse the skin of the persona's beloved. Indeed, a cursory reading leaves one wondering whether the beloved is not a human, but "l'Ile charmée," "le soleil," or both. As Paulette Nardal comments, there is no mention here or in other poems from *Le jardin des tropiques* of race consciousness.[38] That is not to say that Thaly does not feature explicitly racialized personae in his work; when such figures do appear, however, as in the poems "Le Caraïbe" ("The Carib") and "Marchande martiniquaise" ("Martinican Market Woman"), they are generally depicted in isolation, divorced from the power dynamics that structured colonial society. "Le planteur" ("The Planter"), which implicitly acknowledges the persona's privilege through the repeated use of possessive pronouns, departs from this abstraction, but only briefly. As the planter surveys his domain, his gaze captures all: the land ("mes savanes"), its agricultural implements ("mes lourds chariots"), and the laborers ("mes travailleurs") who use the latter to tend the former.[39] This proprietary rhetoric is in no way problematized within the wistful, nostalgic poem.

If Thaly's publication record alone is not enough to trouble the aforementioned chronological boundary between exoticism and regionalism—although Thaly published his first book in 1900, the collections cited here appeared in 1911 and 1928, respectively—the manner in which Lacascade's prose resonates with Thaly's poetry might prove more convincing. From the moment Claire-Solange arrives in Paris, she begins comparing the French capital to her Martinican home: "Pourquoi conservez-vous alors ces horribles masures, près des fortifications? Chez nous la misère n'offre pas un si lamentable contraste, même dans les villages nègres par temps d'épidémie" ("Why do you keep these horrible shacks near the city walls? In our country misery doesn't offer such a lamentable contrast, even in the Negro villages during epidemics"; 21). One might argue that this comment suggests what René Ménil identifies as "natural" exoticism, the normal tendency of a traveler to find her foreign surroundings strange and remarkable, or that it offers an apt critique of French urban poverty.[40] Yet Claire-Solange's observation depends in part on the presentation of Martinique as an "île fortunée," where, the protagonist would have one believe, even disease-plagued communities are less miserable than French shacks. Celebrating the "primitive" ("villages") over the "civilized" ("city walls") and forgoing any discussion of the speaker's privilege, this France-Martinique opposition conjures the colonial exoticism of Thaly and others. Would residents of the Martinican villages in question consider their living conditions preferable to those of the Parisian poor? What of the economic capital, that is, the money necessary to finance travel, that has facilitated Claire-Solange's observation? How does that impact her perception, let alone her experience, of "misery"? These questions remain unanswered in this passage, leaving the presumably more benign indigence of the Martinican "villages nègres" to epitomize an "elsewhere," a site through which the anxieties of "the modern, industrialized state" can be negotiated or escaped.[41]

As *Claire-Solange, âme africaine* progresses, Lacascade continues to stage her protagonist's encounter with the metropole as an exercise in incommensurability. When Jacques Danzel boasts about the renowned French springtime, Claire-Solange counters with an elegiac vision of "la nuit tropicale" ("the tropical night"; 47). This "African soul" finds little in French nature, culture, or society that withstands comparison to Martinique, and, although Lacascade ably uses these utterances to articulate her protagonist's sense of regional pride, Claire-Solange's compulsion to answer every remark praising France with excessive praise for Martinique recapitulates a founding dichotomy—Old World versus New, Europe versus the Caribbean—of exoticist rhetoric. In one such instance the resemblance between Claire-Solange's vocabulary and Thaly's "Chanson" is striking:

—*Quant à ça!* Les Européens viennent-ils donc nous prendre jusqu'aux noms de nos essences? Sachez, mon pseudo-cousin, que votre pseudo-acacia n'embaume pas autant que nos arbres dont les fleurs sont de petites boules d'or chaud. Du reste votre végétation rabougrie. (62)

—*As for that!* Have the Europeans come to take even the names of our trees from us? Know, my pseudo-cousin, that your pseudo-acacia does not smell as sweet as our trees whose flowers are little balls of warm gold. Besides your scrawny vegetation.

Prompted by Claire-Solange's detection of a "peppery odor" ("odeur poivrée"), which Jacques attributes to a nearby tree, the above retort counters the fragrance of the French acacia with the vision of "[un] Paradis terrestre antillais où jamais la reproduction ne s'arrête" ("[an] Antillean heaven on earth where reproduction never stops").[42] In Claire-Solange's estimation all things French, be they family or flora, connote artifice and lack, while all things Martinican embody nature and plenitude. It is as if Lacascade has placed the words of the *béké* bard in the mouth of her *mulâtresse* character.

The similarities between Lacascade's writing and exoticist rhetoric do not end with depictions of nature. As the brief explication of Thaly's poetry indicates, exoticist rhetoric idealized and/or stereotyped not only the Caribbean's natural landscape but also the lived reality of its population of color. Early exoticist texts transformed the archipelago's "Other" residents, particularly Carib Indians and women of color, into mythical figures whose depiction facilitated the construction of colonial discourse.[43] In order to maintain a paradisiacal vision of the islands, exoticism could not accommodate sociopolitical realities such as death and displacement, enslavement and rape, for an interrogation of such matters would reveal the lie behind the ideal of the New World as a tabula rasa waiting to be inscribed by Europeans.[44] Consequently, Caribs, whose decimation preceded the repopulation of the archipelago by European settlers and enslaved Africans, were represented as "treacherous cannibals" or "noble savages" (as in Thaly's "Le Caraïbe") but not as complex beings whose maltreatment demanded attention and reparation. Women of color were also largely depicted as one of two polar opposites, either the desexualized yet maternal wet nurse known as the *da* or the hypersexualized yet submissive love interest known as the *doudou*.[45] Moreau de Saint-Méry, the eighteenth-century chronicler famous for his account of life in colonial Saint-Domingue (present-day Haiti), described the *mulâtresse* as follows: "L'être entier d'une Mulâtresse est livré à la volupté, [et] le feu de cette Déesse [Vénus] brûle dans son cœur pour ne s'y éteindre qu'avec la vie" ("The entire being of the *Mulâtresse* is given to voluptuousness, and the fire of this Goddess [Venus] burns in her heart only to be extinguished there with life").[46] As with exoticist representations of Caribbean spaces, these portrayals of the region's inhabitants provided an outlet through which Europe could articulate its relationship to racial difference in the New World and social change in the Old.

If Lacascade positions Claire-Solange as a vehicle for revisiting exoticist accounts of the Caribbean's natural and social geography, she deploys Jacques Danzel, the romantic foil, to rehearse exoticist visions of women of color. As Danzel finds himself intrigued, captivated, and charmed by Claire-Solange, his perception of her in relation to Martinique shifts from simple association, as in his description of her as "[une] femme des îles" ("[a] woman of the islands"; 45), to complete identification, as demonstrated in the following passage:

L'amour de Claire-Solange, il [Jacques Danzel] se l'imaginait merveilleux: de l'ardeur, de la spontanéité, des silences inattendus; et quelle douceur, quelle sécurité, en dépit des orages; toute la brusquerie d'une floraison enivrante, le mystère d'une forêt vierge. L'amour chez la femme, vous le savez? reproduit la nature de son pays. (92)

The love of Claire-Solange, he fancied it marvelous: filled with ardor, spontaneity, unexpected silences; and what tenderness, what security,

in spite of the storms; all of the suddenness of an intoxicating efflores-
cence, the mystery of a virgin forest. A woman's love—did you know?—
mirrors the nature of her country.

Here the key referents *amour* (love), Claire-Solange/*femme* (woman), and *pays*
(country) are sequentially correlated, interchanged, and collapsed into one,
and that which Condé explains as "le thème de la dualité de la nature antil-
laise . . . [g]énéreuse et destructrice à la fois, tendre et cruelle" ("the theme of
the duality of Antillean nature . . . at once generous and destructive, tender and
cruel") surfaces in the contrasting qualities attributed to Claire-Solange's love:
it is tender and stormy, spontaneous and secure.[47] In an apparent rehearsal of
the script of conventional exoticism it is not simply the woman's love but the
woman herself who embodies her country.

It is quite fitting, then, that Lacascade names her protagonist "Claire-Solange,"
which signifies "light" *(clair)*, "earth" *(sol)*, and "angel" *(ange)*; and that Jacques
Danzel later christens her "ma clarté sauvage" ("my wild light" or "my savage
clarity"; 101). In this play on Claire-Solange's name both the figurative and literal translations of "ma clarté sauvage" posit the character as an exotic Other:
whereas "my wild light" positions Claire-Solange as an uncontrollable, tropical
brightness within the metropolitan landscape, "my savage clarity" speaks more
specifically to the manner in which the character's rhetoric is alternately depicted as refreshingly candid or excessively brusque. Upon his return from the
war a wounded Danzel calls Claire-Solange "mon clair soleil," or "my bright
sun" (200). In all of these references the heroine ceases to be an independent
being and becomes, instead, a substitute for a stereotype or ideal larger than
herself, in the final instance that of Martinique as tropical paradise. Like her
island and her similarly situated mother before her—who is named *Aurore,*
French for the Roman goddess of the dawn—Claire-Solange seems poised to
bring warmth, tenderness, and color to the metropole. She could very well be
the unnamed beloved ("Long live the sun, o my beloved!") of Daniel Thaly's
"Chanson."

Lacascade extends this association of woman and country to *les métropoli-
taines,* or Frenchwomen from the metropole. Jacques envisions them as em-
bodiments of a Europe that, already dismissed by Claire-Solange as the land
of faintly scented flowers, is the antithesis of the Caribbean. Claire-Solange's
first Parisian ball, and first encounter (in the novel) with white women other

than Jeanne, provides the backdrop for what ultimately becomes a comparison of the relative charms of white women and women of color. Continuing his meditation on "a woman's love," Jacques Danzel imagines that, contrary to the life of passion and spontaneity promised by Claire-Solange, romance with a Russian princess "l'entraînerait dans ses neiges" ("would lead him into her snows"; 94). The narration reinforces the equation of white women with frigidity when, upon her arrival at the ball, Claire-Solange is greeted by "la froideur des jeunes filles beiges" ("the coolness of the young beige girls"; 97). These *Parisiennes* are not only as colorless as the French sky but also as inhospitable as the metropolitan climate. When considered alongside the "wonders" of the tropics, France and its residents figuratively and literally pale in comparison. Indeed, how could mere metropolitan mortals compete with tropical angels and goddesses? Whereas colonial discourse throws the weight of femininity behind white women, exoticist rhetoric throws the power of seduction behind women of color. In either case the association reduces women to the role of ciphers of their respective climates, and the potential for protofeminist solidarity between Claire-Solange and her Parisian counterparts remains unrealized, as it does between Shakespeare's Miranda and Sycorax and between Anna Julia Cooper and the Anglo American feminists she addresses. Fortunately, Lacascade rescues this precarious discursive situation by having Claire-Solange's unrelenting insistence on her right to self-definition and determination gradually destabilize the authority of Jacques's observations.

Perhaps the most intriguing and, I would argue, skillful aspect of Lacascade's deployment of exoticism comes in her turn to Baudelaire, the poet whose work, according to Aimé Césaire, signaled French literature's awakening from listless prose to dazzling poetry.[48] If vibrant and modern, Baudelaire's verse is not without its exoticist moments, and thus it is to his poetry that Lacascade turns to convey Jacques Danzel's enchantment at witnessing the mysteries of Claire-Solange's *coiffure,* or hairdressing:

Da hoche la tête pour approuver; lassé, le cou de la jeune fille ploie de côté; et Jacques songe que Baudelaire aussi avait su voir, avait aimé la nonchalance de ces attitudes exotiques:

La brune enchanteresse
A, dans le col, des airs noblement maniérés.
(49)

Da [Claire-Solange's maid] shakes her head to approve; weary, the young girl's neck bends to the side; and Jacques dreams that Baudelaire, too, knew to behold, knew to love the nonchalance of these exotic attitudes:

> This brown enchantress
> Her neck is noble, proud, her manner dignified.[49]

Drawn from "À une dame créole" ("For a Creole Lady"), the verse invites the simultaneous comparison of Claire-Solange with the poem's dedicatee, a wealthy white Creole from the island of Mauritius, and of Lacascade's prose with Baudelaire's poetry.[50] As if providing a model for Jacques Danzel's imagination of Claire-Solange via Martinique, "À une dame créole" frames the portrait of Baudelaire's Creole beauty (second quatrain) between a description of her island (first quatrain) and of the reception her beauty would elicit in France (first tercet). In both novel and poem the portrayal of the exotic Other functions as part of a larger project of depicting her native land and, as demonstrated by Jacques's direct contemplation of the relative merits of Caribbean and European women, of exploring the relationship between an elsewhere, the Other, and the metropole. The seamlessness with which these elsewheres and Others are interchanged speaks further to the exoticist conception of islands (and their inhabitants) as mythical spaces rather than as actual locales (and individuals) with distinct identities. It is through such chains of (mis)identification that Jacques can see Claire-Solange through the image of a "brune enchanteresse" who was, in fact, white as well as transpose the poem's opening image—"Au pays parfumé que le soleil caresse" ("Off in a perfumed land bathed gently by the sun"; line 1)—from Mauritius to Martinique.[51]

Prompted by the sight of Da styling Claire-Solange's hair, Danzel's intertextual reverie also evokes Baudelaire's "La chevelure" ("Head of Hair"), another poem from *Les fleurs du mal*. Inspired by the poet's *mulâtresse* mistress, Jeanne Duval, "La chevelure" is a celebration of what Robert Greer Cohn inexplicably describes as "Jeanne's dusky Caribbean hair."[52] The poem's persona marvels in his lover's dark curls, in whose depths live "la langoureuse Asie et la brûlante Afrique" ("langourous Asia, scorching Africa"; line 6). Her hair not only conjures visions of these faraway places; it itself becomes a means of travel to them. Alternately named "mer d'ébène" ("sea of ebony"; line 14), "ce noir océan" ("this black sea"; line 22), and "Cheveux bleus" ("Blue head of hair"; line 26), *la chevelure* enables the poet to enter "a world of heightened sensation," to "[rediscover] an inebriating sense of *total* existence."[53] As noted earlier, Jacques Danzel imagines Claire-Solange playing a similar role in his life. He dreams that, as mistress of his metropolitan household, "[elle] illuminerait par la clarté sauvage de ses robes un intérieur mélancolique, . . . l'égayerait par son rire de coloniale" ("[she] would, by the wild light of her dresses, illuminate a melancholy interior, . . . would enliven it with her colonial's laugh"; 91). She would, as critic Edward Ahearn observes of Jeanne Duval, "embod[y] and [open] up . . . another world—exotic, far removed from . . . urban civilization," and, as Baudelaire before him, Danzel would rediscover "this lost world . . . in the hair and the body of the black woman whom [he] loves."[54]

Whether from poetry or prose, these evocations and representations of the *mulâtresse* are relatively benign; that is, although reductive, they refrain from denigrating or attacking the figure's character. Instead, the narrator's descriptions, Jacques's daydreams, and Baudelaire's verses collectively reiterate exoticist depictions of the *mulâtresse* as the heiress to a pleasing blend of "white" and "black" traits, as the recipient "de ses géniteurs blancs et noirs une grande disposition à la tendresse aussi bien qu'à la sensualité" ("of a great predisposition to tenderness as well as sensuality from her white and black forebears").[55] Even in moments when Claire-Solange appears to be at the mercy of her black blood, as when her speech becomes a bit too colorful for Parisian society and her father attributes the gaffe to "le sang chaud de sa race" ("the hot blood of her race"; 65), this purportedly inherent passion seems emblematic of a difference that, if disorderly on occasion, is, at best, charming and, at worst, worthy of paternal indulgence. Jacques's willingness to blur the lines between reality and representation falls squarely within this tradition. In many French literary portrayals of the *mulâtresse* or her male counterpart, the *mulâtre* (mulatto), however, the figure's presumed intrinsic difference has a darker, more sinister significance, one that is lost on *Claire-Solange*'s male figures (characters and poets) but not on its other principal female character: Claire-Solange's Aunt Jeanne.

Whereas Jacques is charmed by Baudelairean visions, Jeanne is haunted by Balzacian specters. In the pseudonymously published 1824 novel *Le mulâtre*, Honoré de Balzac presents a title character who distinguishes himself by committing incest and claiming allegiance with the devil.[56] For, if excessive passion can foster love and warmth, it may also engender betrayal and deception. Although extreme, Balzac's portrayal resonated with negative perceptions of *mulâtres* among nineteenth-century white metropolitans and white Creoles. If the latter did not go so far as to consider the *mulâtre* or the *mulâtresse* evil incarnate, they did often consider mixed-race individuals shameful proof of concubinage and illegitimacy within Creole society.[57] Consequently, when Claire-Solange insists on correcting a gentleman who has mistakenly identified her as Spanish, Jeanne vehemently objects:

> Pourquoi revendiquer sans cesse ce titre de mulâtresse? Ne sait-elle donc pas? . . . Mais Claire-Solange le savait—et ceci la rendait inexcusable,— que la littérature a fait du mulâtre un être abject, perfide, n'ayant gardé que les faiblesses seules, les duplicités, les tares de sa double origine. (89–90)

> Why incessantly claim this title of *mulâtresse?* Didn't she know? . . . But Claire-Solange knew—and this made her inexcusable,—that literature has made the *mulâtre* an abject, treacherous being, having only kept the weaknesses, the deviousness, the defects of his double origin.

For Jeanne the social embarrassment that Claire-Solange's fictional precursors might generate poses a greater threat than the fact of her niece's blackness. Upon learning that Claire-Solange is mixed-race Jeanne's acquaintances might, like Jacques Danzel before them, regard her niece through the lens of literary stereotypes, albeit those that demonize rather than idealize the "double origin" of the *mulâtresse.*

The predicament that concerns Jeanne is an inversion of that detailed in *Peau noire, masques blancs.* Fanon describes "le Noir" ("the Negro") as being "sur-déterminé de l'extérieur . . . pas l'esclave de 'l'idée' que les autres ont de [lui], mais de [son] apparaître" ("overdetermined from without . . . the slave not of the 'idea' that others have of [him] but of [his] own appearance").[58] The Negro's difference is visible, and this visibility is the means through which his relations with others are filtered. For Claire-Solange in particular and *mulâtres* in general, however, it is the potential lack of visibility that poses a greater problem. Indeed, many stereotypes attribute the alleged duplicity of the *mulâtre/ mulâtresse* to the inscrutability of the figure's racial identity. I would argue, then, that, with already variable racial signifiers such as skin color made even more unreliable by miscegenation, idea takes precedence over image in early-twentieth-century French misperceptions of mixed-race individuals. Claire-Solange's difference is perceptible yet ambiguous: the gentleman who provokes the "titre de mulâtresse" comment senses that Claire-Solange is not *une métro-politaine* but incorrectly guesses that she is Spanish. Jeanne would have preferred that her niece navigate the treacherous terrain of race and stereotype by accepting this misidentification and approximating, if not claiming, whiteness. This approximation would, subsequently, control how Parisian society receives Claire-Solange and prevent her from being overdetermined by the "idea" that others have of the *mulâtresse*.

Lacascade foreshadows Jeanne's preference for continental over colonial difference in the scene depicting the character's first dinner with the Duflôt-Hucquart family. Although the meal begins with distinctions between the metropolitan hostess and her colonial guests intact, racial and discursive boundaries soon collapse along with Jeanne's composure. Jeanne fights off a fainting spell with the thought "Résisterai-je jusqu'à la fin? Trop de chocolat pour mon goût" ("Will I resist until the end? Too much chocolate for my taste"; 25). With the object of her question unidentified (what must Jeanne resist?), the signifier *chocolat* slips between the discourses of gastronomy and race. Has the taste of the food threatened to overwhelm Jeanne, or has she in fact found herself surrounded by "too much [blackness] for [her] taste"? The dinnertime context supports the former interpretation, yet Jeanne's earlier observation that there are "trop de Métèques" ("too many foreigners"; 21) in Paris implies that the comment also alludes to race. To complicate Jeanne's discomfort further, a quick glance around the dining room proves any simplistic use of the term *blackness* problematic; not only are some of the hands around Jeanne "gantées de blanc" ("gloved in white"; 25), many of them are white: "En effet, autour de sa table, les mulâtresses, jeunes et vieilles, posaient treize taches de couleur entre le masque terreux de Monsieur Duflôt, placé à sa droite, et la pâleur anémique d'Étienne, placé à sa gauche" ("In fact, around her table, the *mulâtresses,* young and old, presented thirteen shades of color between the earthy mask of Monsieur Duflôt, seated to her right, and the anemic pallor of Étienne, seated to her left"; 25). This multihued panorama challenges notions of fixed racial boundaries and grants Jeanne the visual license to reposition Claire-Solange along the European racial and ethnic spectrum. If exoticist literature can use the representation of the *mulâtresse* to negotiate national identity at home and abroad, then perhaps Jeanne can manipulate the chromatic range of racialized otherness to preserve social capital as she introduces her enigmatic niece to Parisian society.

POST-EXOTICISM AND *LA MULÂTRESSE NÈGRE*

Yet Claire-Solange refuses to whiten herself *(se lactifier)* to pass for Spanish or, for that matter, anything other than African, and it is this resistance that complicates Lacascade's appropriation of exoticism. What is more, the metropolitan characters with whom Claire-Solange interacts are as liable to be objectified as their colonial counterparts. As Jacques Danzel imagines the *mulâtresse* as an embodiment of Caribbean splendor, so the narration associates the young white women ("les jeune filles beiges") at the Parisian ball with the city's wintry climate. More important, Lacascade does not limit this objectification to other women. When Claire-Solange's cousins exhort her to speculate about Jacques's appearance, she does not swoon; she quips, "Il sera beige" ("He'll be beige"; 28). Instead of waiting to be enthralled by whiteness, Claire-Solange expects to be underwhelmed by blandness. As if on cue, Jacques appears moments later "très simple, élégant, en costume beige" ("very simple and elegant, in a beige suit"; 28). If the Frenchman can identify his *mulâtresse* love interest with her milieu, then surely she can read his sartorial correctness as representative of his Parisian bourgeois environment.

A similar astuteness informs Claire-Solange's acknowledgment and direction of the manner in which others observe her. The slippage of racial signifiers that Jeanne finds so disconcerting becomes a pedagogical tool for Claire-Solange, who discourages confusion by leading her viewer's eye away from the unstable marker of skin color to a presumably more telling indicator:

Voyez mes cheveux crépus, je ne saurais les lisser en cadenettes contre mes joues, comme les Juifs d'Aden, je ne pourrais les relever en chignon 1830 . . . Mes cheveux de nègre, il faut les séparer en bandeaux, les tordre tant bien que mal sur la nuque . . . coiffure qui exagère le prognathisme. Mesurez mon angle facial! Regardez-moi bien. (36)

See my coarse hair, I wouldn't know how to smooth it in locks against my cheeks, like the Jews of Aden, I couldn't pin it up in an 1830 chignon . . . My Negro hair, which must be parted in the center, twisted as

best one can on the neck . . . a hairstyle that exaggerates prognathism.
Measure my facial angle! Look at me carefully.

Claire-Solange does not want others to misconstrue her *mulâtresse* identity;
on the contrary, she instructs them to detect it via the texture of her hair. Having lived in the multiracial Caribbean, where it is not uncommon for the complexion of a *mulâtre* or *mulâtresse* to be as fair as, if not fairer than, that of
a white Creole, Claire-Solange turns to her hair to communicate that which
her skin does not: the presence of African ancestry.[59] The gesture bespeaks a
degree of racial literacy and self-assurance (Claire-Solange's tone is instructive, not pathetic or defensive) not shared by the character's white metropolitan
aunt. Whereas Jeanne prefers Spanishness, Claire-Solange chooses Africanness;
whereas the aunt's reaction to racial indeterminacy ranges from agitation to
nausea, the niece welcomes any opportunity to declare "what" she is.

The words that, given Claire-Solange's pronouncements about France and
Martinique, might seem more impulsive than calculated in fact mount a subtle
challenge to the pseudoscience of race. As the character defines herself, she
proves quite fluent in racial discourse. Her self-presentation includes references
to a historically specific hairstyle, the 1830 chignon, as well as to a culturally
specific and, because of European anti-Semitism, racialized hairstyle: the locks
worn by the Jews of Aden.[60] Lacascade's particular combination of verb tense
and vocabulary underscores the significance of Claire-Solange's conscious representation: the imperatives *voyez* (see), *mesurez* (measure), and *regardez* (look
at), together with the terms *prognathism* and *facial angle*, invoke the efforts
of European intellectuals to classify race. The practice of reading facial angles
was the cornerstone of the work of eighteenth-century Dutch anatomist Peter
Camper, who claimed that human and animal "types" could be distinguished
through the measurement of "the angle from the upper lip to the forehead . . .
and horizontally across the face."[61] In Camper's analysis "the European" and
"the Negro" were polar opposites, with the former most closely corresponding
to the human ideal and the latter more closely resembling monkeys. In light of
such a theory's scientifically faulty and overtly racist nature, it is important to
note the context in which Lacascade introduces it. Just prior to presenting herself as an object of study, Claire-Solange ridicules another tenet of scientific
racism, the alleged infertility of the *mulâtre:* "*Mulâtre,* vient de mulet, veut dire:
incapable de créer une famille [. . .] Vous qui venez de dénombrer en partie la
descendance de mes grands parents mulâtres, . . . appréciez-vous l'ironie de"

("*Mulâtre* comes from mule, that is to say: incapable of producing a family . . . You who've just counted some of the offspring of my mulâtre grandparents, . . . appreciate the irony of"; 35–36).[62]

Through these passages and verbal plays Lacascade invests Claire-Solange with an agency traditionally denied the exotic Other in literature and science. Unlike canonical exoticist texts in which the woman of color "n'existe que dans le discours de l'homme d'Europe qui parle d'elle" ("exists only in the discourse of the European man who speaks about her"), in *Claire-Solange* the *mulâtresse* heroine speaks and looks back.[63] She invites Jacques Danzel to witness the hairstyling session that spurs his poetic fantasy: "Oh! une idée: voulez-vous venir au spectacle?" ("Oh! an idea: do you want to come to the show?" 48). Indeed, Claire-Solange's insistence on correcting (she is *mulâtresse,* not Spanish), controlling ("Regardez-moi bien"), and staging ("voulez-vous venir au spectacle?") how she is observed seems more reminiscent of feminist film theory than exoticist literature. Her deceptively coquettish invitation to Jacques reads as a literary manifestation of bell hooks's "oppositional gaze," through which black spectators "can both interrogate the gaze . . . but also look back, and at one another, naming what [they] see."[64] Having offered incisive observations about her metropolitan relatives and peers, Claire-Solange turns the lens upon herself. Her accompanying declarations of blackness "emerge . . . as a site of resistance" through which she "resist[s] the imposition of dominant ways of knowing and looking."[65] Unlike the unvoiced object of Thaly's poetry, Claire-Solange seizes upon the "to-be-looked-at-ness" inherent in being a woman of color in 1910s Paris and invites—all the better to control—the gaze of those around her.[66]

What distinguishes Claire-Solange's appropriation of the gaze from mere self-directed voyeurism, what separates post-exoticism from exoticism, is the fact that the character rarely solicits an audience without delimiting the signifiers to be used in properly interpreting the attendant spectacle. Furthermore, Lacascade provides counterdiscourses to both Jeanne and Jacques's misrepresentations of Claire-Solange. Jeanne would have preferred that Claire-Solange pretend to be Spanish, but the text's multiple references to Jewish identity indicate that this substitution of European over African or Caribbean difference might have simply replaced the specter of an Other that is external to Europe with one that is internal to the continent. Writing on the French opera *Carmen* (1875) and drawing on the work of Edward Said, Susan McClary notes that in nineteenth-century Europe Orientalism expanded to encompass a "radical interchangeability of exotic types for the cultural Orientalist: Persian, Greek, Jewish, Spanish, African—all [a]wash together in an undifferentiated realm of Otherness."[67] The sheer range of this Orientalist interchangeability closes the hermeneutic gap between Claire-Solange's "teint doré" ("golden complexion"; 90) being misread as that of a Spaniard and her "wooly" hair being misidentified as that of the Jews of Aden. Always already appropriated by literary stereotype and misrepresentation, Claire-Solange as *mulâtresse* cannot rely upon her unmediated appearance to communicate her racial identity.

In a continuation of Lacascade's intertextual exchange with Baudelaire, the synecdochic relationship between Claire-Solange and her hair reinforces the character's position as an independent, post-exoticist subject: at the intersection of representation, exoticism, and excess, the figurative uncontainability of Claire-Solange's difference mirrors the literal uncontainability of her hair. Whereas Jacques's Baudelairean vision conjures the images of fluidity found in "La Chevelure," a swim leaves Claire-Solange's tresses with "[un] volume anormal" ("[an] abnormal volume"; 127). In response to styling efforts the hair resists, revolts, and "swells" ("gonflent"; 128). Claire-Solange likewise proves to be excessive, more than, inassimilable into various European models of exoticism. She is neither the silenced Baudelairean ideal cherished by Jacques nor the pseudo-Spaniard preferred by Jeanne. An outspoken *mulâtresse* who resists France and Frenchness much as her hair rebels against the waters of the English Channel, Claire-Solange exceeds these representations filtered through literary archetypes. By embracing and speaking her difference, Claire-Solange constructs an alternative self-image that admittedly draws on yet ultimately subverts stereotypes.

Through her inversion and eventual rejection of exoticist representations of the *mulâtresse*, Lacascade recasts the figure's role within Francophone modernist debates of race, nationality, and colonialism. In interwar France and its empire colonial discourse demarcated racial and social difference through semantic difference: while *de couleur* ("of color") signified the highest attainable social level, that of the professional, *nègre* ("Negro" or, alternately, "nigger") connoted the lowest social rung, that occupied by the African cotton laborer or the Antillean cane cutter. *Noir* ("Negro" or "black") functioned as an intermediate category assigned to individuals, such as factory workers, who lacked the educational credentials of the former group but nevertheless occupied a higher social station than the latter.[68] At the time of *Claire-Solange*'s 1924 publication the rejection of this divisive socio-semantic hierarchy was more often associated with representative colored men than with intrepid *mulâtresse* protagonists. Headed by Senegalese militant Lamine Senghor, the Comité de Défense de la Race Nègre (Committee for the Defense of the Black Race, or CDRN) embraced the word *nègre* as a means of forging solidarity between Francophone Africans and Antilleans of all classes: "Ce nom est à nous; nous sommes à lui! Il est nôtre comme nous sommes siens! En lui, nous mettons tout notre honneur et toute notre foi de défendre notre race" ("This name belongs to us; we belong to it! It is ours as we are its! In it, we put all of our honor, all of our pride in defending our race").[69] If Claire-Solange's description of Martinique echoes the verses of exoticist poet Thaly, her professed passion "to defend and to glorify the black race" ("défendre, glorifier la race noire"; 66) foreshadows the words of interwar radical Senghor.

Claire-Solange's linguistic transgressions do not end with the word *noir*. In another scene of self-identification the character embraces the openly controversial *nègre:*

—Alors tu n'approuves pas l'antisémitisme? . . .

[Jeanne] interrompt comme elle peut une conversation qui lui semble risquée.

—Comment vous répondre? Papa a traversé le monde, combattant les préjugés; et pourrais-je mépriser une autre race opprimée, moi qui suis nègre.

—Oh! Oh! Oh! . . . haletait Jeanne en crescendo. Pourquoi te dis-tu nègre? (36)

—So, you don't approve of anti-Semitism? . . .

[Jeanne] interrupted as best she could a conversation which seemed, to her, risky.

—How should I answer you? Papa has traversed the world, fighting prejudice; could I scorn another oppressed race, I, who am *nègre*?

—Oh! Oh! Oh! . . . gasped Jeanne in crescendo. Why do you call yourself *nègre*?

The significance of Claire-Solange's statement far exceeds its capacity to upset Jeanne, who is ever anxious about questions of race. First, the character so brazenly transgressing socioracial boundaries is a woman, *une mulâtresse*.[70] No longer must the examination of mixed-race women in early- to mid-twentieth-century Francophone Caribbean literature begin with the conflicted heroines of Capécia's *Je suis martiniquaise* and *La négresse blanche (The White Negress)* or with Fanon's problematic critique of them. Second, as suggested in the editorial from *La voix des nègres,* Claire-Solange's word choice contradicts the prevailing disposition of her class and dissolves the socially constructed tension within colonial-era racial terminology. In the character's eyes to be *une mulâtresse nègre* (a black mulatta), as opposed to *une mulâtresse blanche* (a white mulatta), is not only possible but desirable. Finally, Claire-Solange's usage of "le gros mot du jour" ("the foul word du jour") comes during a discussion of anti-Semitism, once again situating her assertion of racial consciousness within a broader understanding of European prejudice and racism.[71]

While one might attribute Claire-Solange's declaration of *négritude,* or blackness, to her delight in scandalizing her interlocutors, a subsequent exchange with Jacques suggests an alternative reading, one that foregrounds another important component of Lacascade's post-exoticism: the explicit critique of literature's role in perpetuating false images of the Other and her native "elsewhere."[72] As Claire-Solange speaks to her metropolitan audience, she is also speaking against the disjunction between reality and representation in exoticist rhetoric. The character's explanation of her disappointment with springtime in Paris relies on the inherent instability and problematic oversimplification of exoticism: "Je m'imaginais le printemps, et la France, d'après votre littérature, oui, comme vous vous imaginez les colonies d'après les récits mensongers des explorateurs" ("I imagined springtime, and France, according to your literature, yes, as you imagine the colonies according to the lying accounts of explorers"; 46). Shifting the focus from colony to metropole, the confession challenges the reliability of literary representation, particularly as practiced by those writers invested in recreating the New World.[73] Claire-Solange cannot appreciate Paris because the city does not correspond to what she has read about it. Claire-Solange mocks this disconnect in her refusal to acknowledge the seasonal charms of the French capital, and herein lies the answer to Jeanne's question about Claire-Solange's awareness (and, I would add, opinion) of literary representation as mediation of "tropical" places and peoples.

Reading Claire-Solange's statements within the framework of post-exoticism likewise recasts the penchant for excess exhibited by the protagonist as well as by the novel as a whole. What would happen if one were to consider Lacascade's "grandiloquent à souhait" ("grandiloquent to perfection") rhetoric, as Maryse Condé describes it, the narrative correspondent to the overwhelming presence of darkness around Jeanne's table and the swelling strands of hair on Claire-Solange's wet head?[74] What if, beneath the surfeit of chocolate, hair, and language, one were to locate strategic irony rather than aesthetic disappointment? Describing what he calls "le baroque antillais," Glissant deems flowery, eloquent rhetoric characteristic of a particular strain of Caribbean discourse, one invested in guaranteeing the speaker or writer's assimilation into Frenchness.[75] Lacascade's grandiloquence, her "Caribbean baroque," operates as a means through which Claire-Solange maintains her difference. Her bombastic, oppositional rhetoric—as evidenced by her references to pseudo-cousins, recitation of outrageous childhood stories, and embrace of "foul" words—serves not to incorporate Claire-Solange into French society but to ensure that she will remain outside it. If, in the process, Lacascade does not "destroy" the stereotypes she appropriates in her deployment of post-exoticism, she nevertheless challenges and, consequently, undermines their validity.[76]

The conclusion of *Claire-Solange, âme africaine* more effectively poses the question of how successfully Lacascade counters exoticist discourse. After Jacques Danzel returns from World War I, Claire-Solange professes her love, and the political and theoretical promise of the preceding two hundred pages apparently dissolves into the conventions of the marriage plot, in which the heroine's ultimate goal is domestication, not politicization.[77] Identifying the conclusion as perhaps the most disappointing aspect of the novel, Edwards writes that *Claire-Solange* ultimately "transforms itself into no more than an inversion of the *doudou* myth," with the beautiful Creole winning the Frenchman's hand (in marriage) as well as his heart.[78] Claire-Solange's rhetoric appears to lose all trace of irony as, adopting language used in Jacques's exoticist portrait of her, she resolves, quite literally, to be the sunlight needed to nurse him back to health and to sustain her metropolitan exile: "Je ne verrai plus d'ananas, qu'en conserves; de palmiers, qu'en pots; de vrai soleil, qu'en moi-même" ("I'll no longer see pineapples, except in preserves; no palm trees, except in pots; no real sun, except in myself"; 205). This rather pitiful reflection raises the specter not only of Thaly and Baudelaire, but also of Fanon, who posits racial (if not geographic) exile as an outcome of *lactification.*[79] Lacascade further decontextualizes Claire-Solange by dispensing with the family whose proud, extensive history informed the character's racial consciousness. Étienne, Claire-Solange's father, blesses her union with Jacques, but it remains unclear whether, having just booked two berths on the next ship (for the Caribbean? for Africa?), he intends to stay in France with his daughter and son-in-law. As for Claire-Solange's aunts, Jeanne exits the narrative during the proposal scene, never to be heard from again, and Émilienne, the Duflôt aunt once determined to return her niece to Martinique, makes a similar departure. It is as if Lacascade discards these characters the moment their presence is no longer necessary for Jacques and Claire-Solange's happy ending.

If the novel's conclusion seems tidy or acquiescent when considered with regard to exoticism, setting the marriage of Claire-Solange and Jacques Danzel against the backdrop of interwar politics yields an altogether different reading, one in which the pair's union might be interpreted as a modernist negotiation of the changing relationship between black citizen and white, between colony and metropole. Illustrative of its many paradoxes, the same colonial discourse that distinguished *mulâtre* from *noir* and *noir* from *nègre* also promoted the notion of *la plus grande France* (Greater France); this ideal was reinforced in the aftermath of World War I, when France's colonies, its "overseas mirror image," reaffirmed the battered nation's "status as a world power."[80] During the war France was materially aided by the service of its colonial troops; after the war the nation was ideologically bolstered by the existence of its colonies. Lacascade reflects this shift in colony-metropole relations by shifting the traditional balance of power in the white Frenchman–woman of color relationship. Jacques returns from combat with a maimed left hand and eye and, as Charlotte Brontë's Rochester before him, marries his beloved only after his male bravado and physical power have been neutralized. If we return to Lacascade's inversion of exoticist models (that is, the white Frenchman's identity can be collapsed into that of the metropole just as the woman of color's identity can be collapsed into that of her island), it might very well be Jacques-as-France whom Claire-Solange marries, thus proving herself the statutory equal to her mate.[81] Claudia Tate makes a similar case when writing that African American women's domestic novels "inscribe not merely artificial discursive conventions for depicting an idealized courtship story but strategies for enlarging the social roles for black women and for defining as well as regulating their citizenship as gendered civil performance."[82] When appraising the symbolic register of Claire-Solange and Jacques Danzel's marriage, it is crucial to remember that France's answer to the service of colonial residents in both world wars was assimilation and association, not independence; by novel's end, however, Claire-Solange's goal is no longer to reject Jacques.[83] It is, I would argue, to convince him to recognize her as a marriageable partner rather than a literary stereotype.

For, although *Claire-Solange* reflects some of the revolutionary language of early-twentieth-century colonial politics, like the work of many other Francophone intellectuals at the time it does not advocate the complete revolutionary upheaval proposed by figures such as Étienne Léro and Lamine Senghor.[84] Lacascade uses the marriage plot to allegorize the transformation, not abolition, of the colony-metropole relationship. The departure of Claire-Solange's maternal family from Paris demonstrates as much. Held at the Orsay Station, the farewell party for the Duflôts gathers "îlots humains" ("human islets"; 109) from most corners of Greater France. In addition to members of Paris's Martinican-Guadeloupean community, Senegalese, Réunionese, and Guyanese come to pay their respects to past and present officers—Claire-Solange's grandfather and father, respectively—of the colonial service. The tone of the affair, a virtual diasporic reunion, is largely nostalgic as partygoers recall serving with or under one another at various locations in the French Empire. Aside from a disparaging remark about the white Creole guests, whose condescension and entitlement are attributed to the idiosyncrasies of their caste rather than the racialization of colonial hierarchies, there is no critique of colonialism. Instead, the scene focuses on the expanse and organization of the empire, whose inner workings Claire-Solange explains to Jacques.

As this scene reveals, some aspects of Lacascade's colonial politics are more conservative than activist. Nevertheless, the repeated casting of Claire-Solange in a directorial or instructional role bespeaks an agency that distinguishes the character from the women featured in the work of Lacascade's Guadeloupean contemporaries. Claire-Solange is not the revolutionary *mulâtresse* Solitude, who joined Louis Delgrès's 1802 rebellion against Napoleon's reinstatement of slavery, but neither is she the initially assertive yet ultimately retiring heroine of regionalist literature.[85] Although Oruno Lara introduces his 1923 *Question de couleurs (Blanches et noirs)* with the stated goal of rehabilitating the image of women of color, Nelly Guérin, the novel's primary woman character, must be led to racial consciousness by her male compatriot René Frault.[86] When René first encounters Nelly in Paris and calls her *une négresse* (the feminine form of *nègre*), Nelly insists that he is mistaken because she is a *mulâtresse*. It is only many months and some ninety pages later that Nelly rejects the distinction between *mulâtre* and *nègre*. Moreover, in what Edwards describes as "a bizarrely reactionary vision of a gendered division of labor in the service of racial nationalism," the novel apparently concludes that race pride and romantic love, duty and pleasure, cannot coexist.[87] As if punishing herself for a previous affair with a white man, Nelly professes her love for René but resolves that she will never marry. Instead, she returns to Guadeloupe to devote herself to teaching, to shaping her future students into the men and women of tomorrow. In a farewell letter to René she describes her newfound vocation as "la collaboration de la femme au rêve hardi de l'homme" ("the woman's collaboration in the man's bold dream"; 105). Fully conscientized before her romance, Claire-Solange has no need for surrogate bravado, nor does her interracial relationship signal a denial or denigration of her African heritage. As Valérie Orlando observes, "Out of her own volition, [Claire-Solange] makes a series of choices to which she adheres."[88]

Conversely, Jeanne Randol, the woman of color featured in Renée Lacascade and André Pérye's 1930 novel *L'île qui meurt*, forgoes dreams of politically engaging her compatriots in order to preserve her marriage.[89] Having left Guadeloupe as Jeanne Mareuil, a young woman bound for postsecondary studies in France, she returns as Madame Randol, a university graduate and the wife of the new colonial governor. Jeanne's social range—she has friends among Guadeloupeans of color, white Creoles, and metropolitan French alike—positions her as uniquely qualified to understand the complexities of island society; Jeanne quickly becomes caught, however, between her husband's exercise of metropolitan power and her brother's insistence on local rule. The ensuing power struggle forms the basis of the authors' critique of social stagnation and racial prejudice in 1920s Guadeloupe and leads to the novel's dramatic dénouement: the attempted assassination of Governor Randol and his subsequent recall to Paris.[90] When the paternal Dr. Rozet advises her to remain at her husband's side, Jeanne relinquishes hope of effecting lasting social change: "Qui donc pourrait réussir là où [Jeanne et son mari] avaient échoué si complètement, en dépit de sa profonde tendresse pour son pays d'origine?" ("Who, then, could succeed where [Jeanne and her husband] had failed so completely, in spite of her deep affection for her native land?" 220). The departure seems to mirror Claire-Solange's self-imposed exile in France until one considers that Suzanne Lacascade's protagonist arrives at her decision independent of any male mentor.

Perhaps this is why *Claire-Solange* concludes not with a vision of metropolitan domestic bliss but, rather, with an idealized African pastoral. In a scene reminiscent of René Maran's 1921 novel *Batouala*, Claire-Solange, now settled in France, dreams of a thatched-roof hut occupied by a black man and woman.[91] While the man contentedly chews a kola nut, the woman prepares the day's meal. Instead of returning to Claire-Solange, the novel closes with the sounds of life inside the hut: the chewing of nuts, the swishing of leaves, the rustling of insects. This decontextualized image of African life (assuming that the refreshment of choice for a Caribbean version would have been a stalk of sugarcane) seems to have little to do with Claire-Solange and Jacques Danzel's likely Parisian existence, yet within the context of the novel as a whole the scene reiterates a number of questions central to evaluating Lacascade's post-exoticist discourse. Where does exoticist representation end and modern(ist) appropriation begin? What is the place of Africa the continent and "Africa" the idea in the early-twentieth-century diaspora and Europe? Finally, how does gender inflect these questions? That is, what happens when an imperfect female protagonist replaces the heroic male persona as the presumptive trailblazer from the first question to the second, from exoticism to Negritude?

A QUESTION OF ENGAGEMENT: GENDER, GENRE, AND NEGRITUDE

As critic Joyce Warren notes, it is rare that the periodization of a literary movement depends solely on historical chronology and artistic tenets.[92] The "birth" of Negritude continues to be shifted from one date to the next, but a more or less familiar litany has emerged in accounts of the movement's prevailing themes: the valorization of blackness, the (symbolic) return to Africa, and the engagement of sociopolitical issues.[93] Yet what exactly constitutes "engagement" is less uniformly agreed upon. For Étienne Léro engagement required social upheaval, and the literary role models to be admired were those such as "les deux poètes noirs révolutionnaires" ("the two black revolutionary poets") Langston Hughes and Claude McKay.[94] Echoing Léro's polemical tone, Jack Corzani bluntly states in an early essay that novels featuring any type of romance need not apply for the title of "engaged" literature:

La littérature engagée n'a pas de place pour l'amour sentimental, elle a autre chose à faire, elle laisse cela à Mayotte Capécia ou à René Maran, à ces gens qui passent leur temps à contempler leur nombril, à s'interroger sur les rapports particuliers d'un noir avec une blanche ou d'une noire avec un blanc.[95]

Engaged literature has no room for sentimental love: it has other things to do. It leaves that to Mayotte Capécia or René Maran, to those people who spend their time contemplating their navel, asking themselves about the special relationships of a black man with a white woman or of a black woman with a white man.

To Corzani's credit he avoids the ideological slippage found in Fanon by offering no special dispensation for interracial relationships between men of color and white women. In this particular passage, nonetheless, Corzani echoes Fanon as well as Léro in defining "social relevance" rather narrowly, recalling Warren's argument that many literary periods were neither "designed for [nor] in [the] interests" of "marginalized" or atypical writers.[96] Why must the portrayal of "sentimental love," whatever the racial composition of the couple, preclude political consciousness? If there is no place for such representations in "engaged literature," and Negritude literature involves engagement, is there no room for *Claire-Solange* in Negritude?

To revolt, in a basic literary sense, is to rebel against preexisting modes of thought and to break new expressive ground in the process, and *Claire-Solange* does precisely that, marriage plot, *mulâtresse* protagonist, and all. What Lacascade demonstrates in 1924, and what her successors (among them African American authors Marita Bonner and Dorothy West) show in subsequent years, is that, rather than inherently being a means of avoiding the discussion of "serious" issues such as race and public community, depictions of romance and domesticity can accommodate and even inform such conversations. Maryse Condé encourages just such a reconceptualization in the epigraph with which this chapter opens. Disputing the political grounds on which early Caribbean women's writing has been dismissed, Condé asks, "Qu'est-ce après tout que l'engagement sinon la restitution de quelque aspect de la vérité que l'on a choisi d'illustrer?" ("What is engagement, after all, if not the restoration of some aspect of the truth that one has chosen to illustrate?").[97] When Paulette Nardal raises the question of political consciousness in "Eveil de la conscience de race," she stipulates only that conscientized literature must demonstrate "race pride" ("la fierté de race").[98] I contend that the artistic "truth" that Lacascade has chosen to illustrate is one in which race pride can be articulated through (post-)exoticism, a *mulâtresse* can be *nègre*, and an "African" soul can inhabit the body of a mixed-race, middle-class woman. Likewise, Lacascade challenges the critical "truth" that asserts that an interracial romance cannot test the limits of Negritude. The disparity between the respective positions explored in this and the preceding paragraph, between the interpretive potential foreclosed by narrow definitions of engagement and that facilitated by more expansive understandings, reveals the degree to which the notion of engagement has been shaped by gender and genre as much as—if not more than—by content and period. Should one choose to look beyond Lacascade's navel, one might find *Claire-Solange, âme africaine* an intriguing text that challenges notions of engagement and literary periodization in important ways.

The easiest point at which to begin the examination of Lacascade's engagement is her realization of Caribbean Negritude's primary inventive impulse: the recreation of "Africa."[99] Within the context of Claire-Solange's logic of identification most of the character's major actions, from her rejection of exoticist stereotypes to her embrace of blackness in spite of her interracial parentage and marriage, can be traced to a knowledge of and investment in her African heritage. To be *mulâtresse* is to be *nègre* and to be *nègre, africaine:* Claire-Solange declares her Africanness three chapters after her first use of *nègre.*[100] In a departure from the persona of Aimé Césaire's *Cahier d'un retour au pays natal,* Claire-Solange's link between blackness and Africa does not grow out of "an Africa of the [h]eart," a phrase used to describe a relationship with the continent that is metaphorical rather than experiential.[101] For Lacascade's protagonist Africa is as intensely personal and immediate as that of Césaire's figure is majestically symbolic and distant. The African past that Claire-Solange evokes is not reminiscent of the collective yet anonymous "vomissure de négrier" ("vomit of slave ships") conjured in the *Cahier* but populated by identifiable ancestors from particular tribes and regions (Césaire 60/61). Moreover, whereas the ancestors of the Césairean hero were "jamais . . . Amazones du roi du Dahomey, ni princes du Ghana avec huit cents chameaux" ("never . . . Amazons of the king of Dahomey, nor princes of Ghana with eight hundred camels"; 60/61), Claire-Solange traces her diasporic identity through a royal-born great-great-great-grandmother. Writing decades before a similar perspective appeared in Senghor's "princely" African Negritude, Lacascade presents a Caribbean protagonist whose relationship to Africa is contemporaneous as well as royal: the home that Claire-Solange's maternal family maintains in West Africa is "cette maison sénégalaise où, au XVIIIe siècle, l'aïeul avait installé sa princesse Tsin-Saloum" ("that Senegalese house where, in the eighteenth century, the ancestor had installed his princess Tsin-Saloum"; 105).[102] Africa is just as much a part of Claire-Solange's material reality as it is of her diasporic imagination. Whereas exoticism reduced Africa to the source of corporeal passion, Lacascade presents the continent as the source of a regal heritage; whereas colonial discourse excised Africanness from the language with which Antilleans identified themselves, Lacascade privileges blackness in her protagonist's multiracial identity.

And, whereas canonical Negritude largely reads as masculinist, Lacascade's valorization of blackness is decidedly matrilineal. If the Negritudes articulated by Aimé Césaire, Léon-Gontran Damas, and Léopold Sédar Senghor highlighted the figure of "woman," that figure was often an idealized, feminized representation of Africa through whom the writers authenticated their blackness.[103] Lacascade, in contrast, authenticates Claire-Solange's blackness by having the character deny a male figure that represents Europe and whiteness: her father. Although this denial is never voiced (Claire-Solange toys with the idea of renouncing her white grandmothers, but not Étienne), the novel's general obfuscation of paternal heritage effectively de-emphasizes Étienne and his racial identity. The African genealogy that Lacascade delineates for Claire-Solange is almost exclusively feminine, and the lone male ancestor highlighted in the Duflôt family history appears briefly, goes unnamed, and, as noted earlier, fulfills the narrative function of explaining the relocation of his royal wife. The result is an account rich in detail but devoid of significant male figures. While this strategic gendering of Claire-Solange's African past reflects another element of the novel's 1920s modernist feminism, the erasure also reflects a racial essentialism that conforms to more than contests canonical Negritude.

Claire-Solange's Negritude essentialism involves not only the dismissal of her paternal line but also the selective representation of her maternal history. Although such declarations are meant to clarify the character's identity, they tend to elide the racial complexity of her background. When Claire-Solange contemplates denying the aforementioned white grandmothers, it is unclear whether she would include those in her mother's family, which is mixed-race and thus also descended from white ancestors. Claire-Solange's maternal line also includes "grand'mères caraïbes" ("Carib grandmothers"; 67), yet she introduces them only briefly and then to criticize their passivity. These actions, which seem contradictory to the character's goal of encouraging careful, nuanced readings of the Caribbean in general and of Caribbean women of color in particular, reveal one of the paradoxes of essentialism in the service of racial valorization: the privileging of Africa at the expense of the other regions in which diasporic identities have been forged.[104] Glissant offers one possible explanation for this essentialism-valorization interrelation in his concept of *détour* (diversion):

> Le détour est le recours ultime d'une population dont la domination par un Autre est occultée: il faut aller chercher *ailleurs* le principe de domination, qui n'est pas évident dans le pays même: parce que le mode de domination (l'assimilation) est le meilleur des camouflages.

> Diversion is the ultimate resort of a population whose domination by an Other is concealed: it then must search *elsewhere* for the principle of domination, which is not evident in the country itself: because the system of domination [(assimilation) is the best of disguises.][105]

One might argue that, with the reality of their "native lands" obscured by assimilationist policies as well as by exoticist narratives, Caribbean Negritude writers turned away from the archipelago and toward Africa—their "elsewhere"—as a means of better negotiating the racial difference that the French attempted to elide. Thus, after an opening section that explodes myths of unspoiled island paradises, Aimé Césaire's *Cahier* reverses the Middle Passage, sending its persona back to an ancestral land that allows him to embrace "la 'part africaine' de [son] être, si longtemps méprisée, refoulée, niée par l'idéologie en place" ("the 'African element' of [his] past for so long scorned, repressed, denied by the prevalent ideology").[106] Lacascade charts a different path for her protagonist, one in which Diversion entails finding a genealogical elsewhere relatively free from signs of Claire-Solange's *créolité,* or "Creoleness."[107] The character has no difficulty incorporating the African element of her past into her self-determined, racially conscious identity; it is the European and American elements that give her pause. In other words, the domination that she must face is the colonial practice that long preceded the policy of assimilation: miscegenation. Valérie Orlando argues that Claire-Solange manages this ambivalence by imagining her beloved father *"is and isn't* white"; as a *métropolitain,* Étienne is white, but he is "not implicated historically as a *colon,"* or *béké,* and can thus be rehabilitated as the defender of personal liberty his daughter so admires.[108]

Whereas Lacascade's writing evokes (if it does not exactly mirror) the racially essentialist diversion of the Negritude poets, her engagement of gender more closely corresponds to *retour* (Reversion), the concept Glissant pairs with *détour.* In Glissant's formulation the transition from *détour* to *retour* ideally engages the complexity once obscured by domination; its purpose is not to produce a hegemonic counterdiscourse. Yet it is just such a discourse that the masculinist perspectives of canonical Negritude suggest. Lacascade, in contrast, negotiates an important "point of entanglement" in early-twentieth-century literary and artistic discourse: the intersection of colonial exoticism and modernist primitivism in representations of black women.[109] Exoticism's positing of woman-as-cultural-embodiment, its representation of the woman of color "as an easy reservoir of immediately recognizable tropes to inscribe the 'wonderful islands' and to propel textual desire," found an analogue in primitivism's drive to escape the anxiety and alienation of modern warfare and society.[110] In the post–World War I *tumulte noir* the perceived simplicity and spontaneity of Africans seemed an ideal antidote to the technology and rationality of European life. Being precise about who exactly was "African" was a minor concern. Whether citizen (Antillean), colonial (African), or expatriate (African American), all diasporic individuals were potential screens onto which the French could project their impressions of primitive, redemptive African sensuality. Thus, however inexplicable Claire-Solange's *mulâtresse-nègre-africaine* association might have been to her bourgeois peers, it would have been quite comprehensible to the Negrophiles and Negrophobes of Jazz Age Paris. It was a sociocultural climate that saw the casting of African American entertainer Josephine Baker as sexualized figures from everywhere but the United States and the re-emergence of the Caribbean *mulâtresse* as "a highly eroticized figure in the French imagination."[111]

The penchant for a feminized, decontextualized primitivism marked African and African diasporic modernism as well as European literary and popular culture. Condé argues that a number of black male writers, no less attentive to the symbolic value of primitivism, relegated black women to the role of modernist icon:

De façon contradictoire, on lui [la femme noire] demande de rester la détentrice des valeurs traditionnelles et de représenter le rempart contre l'angoissante montée du modernisme alors que la société tout entière est engagée dans la course au progrès.[112]

In a contradictory fashion, one asks [the black woman] to remain the keeper of traditional values and to represent the rampart against the agonizing rise of modernity while the rest of society is engaged in the race for progress.

Although celebrated as a cultural repository within this matrix, the black woman still functions as a symbol of or conduit to cultural vindication: she is not presented as an agent of change. The subsequently circumscribed representations of women of color thus recall—even as they hypothetically reject—the objectification of the black woman by white artists, writers, and audiences. It is in this context that Lacascade's novel begins to seem less assimilationist and emerges more fully as a call to arms against the relegation of black women to either celebratory or derogatory iconic status. Rather than answer such images with an equally noble and silenced ideal woman, Lacascade counters with her brash, independent protagonist. Indeed, Claire-Solange's active representation of herself as a thinking subject instead of an ideal object, an "African soul" (âme africaine) instead of an African idol, causes even Jacques Danzel to temper his doudouiste reflections long enough to admire her political literacy.[113]

The importance of such a pause, however momentary, is that it invites one to shift the grounds of comparison from Lacascade and the bards of Negritude (or, for that matter, exoticism) to Lacascade and other women intellectuals such as Paulette Nardal, Suzanne Césaire, and Maryse Condé. A comparison built around Lacascade and Nardal, for example, contests the masculinist dynamics of Negritude origin stories as well as launches a critical *retour*, an unraveling of the silence that once surrounded early Francophone Caribbean women's writing.[114] As in my earlier discussion of engagement, entangled in this silence are questions of artistic merit and social consciousness: in other words, is this writing sophisticated or progressive enough to warrant inclusion in the African diasporic literary canon? I raise this discomfiting inquiry to indicate the constraints that such keywords place upon the study of black modernist women writers. Lacascade's articulate protagonist owes her perspective in part to class privilege: Claire-Solange's maternal family is as comfortably situated in the Martinican bourgeoisie as her paternal family is in the metropolitan middle class. Writing out of a similar social milieu, Nardal earnestly expresses her debt to European culture:

Faut-il voir dans les tendances que nous exprimons ici une implicite déclaration de guerre à la culture latine et au monde blanc en général?

C'est une équivoque que nous nous en voudrions de ne pas dissiper. Nous avons pleinement conscience de ce que nous devons à la culture blanche et nous n'avons nullement l'intention de l'abandonner pour favoriser je ne sais quel retour à l'obscurantisme. Sans elle, nous n'eussions pas pris conscience de ce que nous sommes. (31)

Should one see in the tendencies here expressed a sort of implicit declaration of war upon Latin culture and the white world in general? It is our duty to eliminate such an error. We are fully conscious of our debts to the Latin culture and we have no intention of discarding it in order to promote I know not what return to ignorance. Without it, we would have never become conscious of our real selves.

One could stop reading with these words, which in isolation suggest that Nardal exemplifies the intellectual corruption condemned by Léro, or one could continue to the next sentence, which reveals Nardal's ultimate goal of "dépass[ant] le cadre de cette culture" ("go[ing] beyond this culture"; 30). For that reason economic and/or social privilege should make the work of Lacascade and Nardal fair game for critical discussion, not dismissal. In neither case should their avowed or implied economic circumstances be used to discount the ingenuity and foresight with which both writers address metropolitan racializations of femininity and womanhood.

Let me conclude this discussion of Lacascade's literary engagement by neither excoriating nor excusing her limited interrogation of class but by contextualizing the limitation and thus attempting to address it constructively. J. Michael Dash describes the Caribbean writer's response to reductive modernist representations as "a sustained, creative struggle for self-definition within a modernist poetics," and I would argue that this struggle is internal as well as external.[115] That is, in addition to confronting how metropolitan writers reify "Otherness" through modernist primitivism, the Caribbean writer must also contend with her position vis-à-vis the sociocultural system out of which that primitivism has grown. In the interwar period during which Lacascade wrote, the French "civilizing mission" was inflected with philosophies such as "colonial humanism," which advocated the alignment of France's "colonial policy [with its] tradition of liberal humanism."[116] According to historian Gary Wilder, the bureaucratic face of this philosophy was Minister of Colonies Albert Sarraut, but his position was shared by members of the Francophone intelligentsia within and outside of the colonial service. This politically moderate stance criticized France for failing to live up to its revolutionary ideals of liberty, equality, and brotherhood but did not advocate the independence of the nation's colonies.[117]

I have chosen to address the class dynamics in *Claire-Solange* in political rather than economic terms for two reasons: (1) the protagonist's class status is indicated primarily through her family's participation in the colonial service; and (2) the oxymoronic nature of the phrase *colonial humanism*—can colonialism ever be humane or in any way indicative of humanist principles?—foregrounds the struggle that Lacascade alludes to yet does not resolve: how to reconcile Claire-Solange's privilege with her politics. Take, for example, the character's acerbic remark about an excursion to the zoo: "Dites vite, nous partons au Jardin des Plantes, rendre visite aux bêtes de chez nous" ("Say it quickly. We're leaving for the Jardin des Plantes to visit the animals from home"; 86). Like Claire-Solange's observation about Parisian poverty, the comment critiques French policy, in this case the capture and display of colonial plunder, without examining how Claire-Solange's family, through its occupational choices, is implicated in that policy.[118] It is a contradiction resonant with Nardal's simultaneous advocacy of race consciousness and association of non-European culture with ignorance and Renée Lacascade's simultaneous complication of Guadeloupean society and infantilization of the Guadeloupean people.[119] To return to a point with which this chapter opened, rather than falling neatly into predetermined categories, much of early Francophone Caribbean writing is enigmatic, and class is just one of the lenses through which to negotiate this historically and politically illuminating, if at times perplexing, body of literature. Given the many paradoxes of interwar Francophone culture and society, if one were to challenge the validity of the aforementioned women writers on the basis of class alone, then surely one would also have to dismiss the Negritude "fathers" for their less-than-progressive gender dynamics.

Claire-Solange, âme africaine demonstrates that the valorization of blackness is not the exclusive province of men, radicals, or radical men. It is an engaged, groundbreaking novel in its dissection of exoticist paradigms, control of the European gaze, and embrace of the term and identity *nègre*. Suzanne Lacascade and *Claire-Solange* should be reread as black modernist intellectual and text, respectively, not in spite of the incongruence between Lacascade's post-exoticist figure and the heroic persona of canonical Negritudes but because of this disjunction. The result is a more nuanced, more comprehensive genealogy of Francophone modernism, one that acknowledges the potential slippage between exoticism and Negritude, *doudou* and revolutionary. It is also a genealogy that, to return to Glissant, accommodates a poetics of the fallible, but nonetheless instructive, black woman subject.

If the biography of Suzanne Lacascade is an enigma, the literary pedigree of her novel need not be. Endowing its title character with "une vivacité de langage singulièrement acide" ("a vivacity of language that is uniquely acid"), *Claire-Solange* borrows from the twilight of exoticism as it gestures toward the Negritude to come.[120] The novel's play on canonical exoticism is sometimes risky, often undermining the figure's agency and casting doubt on the veracity of her proclamations. Is Claire-Solange intellectually invested in her professed political and social beliefs, or is she merely succumbing to the influence of her double heredity, the "passion [that] is [her] birthright, an inheritance from her *sang africain*"?[121] Lacascade treads an equally delicate line with other exoticist tropes explored in the novel. While the botanically resplendent Martinique vaunted by Claire-Solange serves as an effective foil to the metropole that she is intent on disliking, the island's material realities risk being dissembled by the very beauty Claire-Solange celebrates.[122] Likewise, the representation of Claire-Solange's decision to marry Jacques Danzel as an exchange of colonial warmth for metropolitan love recapitulates the Caribbean-Europe dichotomy that is a staple of exoticist discourse. The care with which Lacascade stages her protagonist's encounter with the metropole, however, moves her writing from the pedestrian fray of exoticism to the more provocative realm of post-exoticism. Claire-Solange's excessive rhetoric lends an air of surreality to many of her metropolitan encounters, and Lacascade uses this quality to question representation within the *négritude* Claire-Solange embraces as well as within the exoticism the character rejects. As embodied by the apparent disconnect between the novel's concluding scene and the resolution of its key plot points, the Africa imagined by the newly married Claire-Solange seems as incommensurable with her daily existence as the explorers' "lying" accounts of the Caribbean were with her life in Martinique.

Whereas Lacascade falters in mapping her character's exploration of race and identity onto concrete locales, she excels in interrogating the human geography of these issues. Claire-Solange's *négritude* emerges most effectively through her awareness and manipulation of her "to-be-looked-at-ness." When Claire-Solange implores viewers to discern the blackness behind her mystifying difference, she provides a counternarrative that opposes both metropolitan and

Francophone objectifications of the woman of color. The eerily placid or uncontrollably fiery Creole beauties and primitive icons of literary master narratives rarely speak back, yet that is precisely what Claire-Solange does in order to prevent the misinterpretation or misappropriation of her identity. Whether imagined to embody an idealized paradise or to restore a lost mother(land), the woman of color is silenced when cast as a symbol, reduced to one dimension through her elevation to iconic status. By giving voice to the paradox-embracing character who counters this iconicization—and encouraging others to look at Claire-Solange carefully—Lacascade relieves the modern woman of color of the passive roles of exotic Other or Negritude muse and recasts her, instead, in the active position of black modernist protagonist.

A Negritude heroine, Claire-Solange is not; she is outspoken, *mulâtresse*, and, by novel's end, married to a white man. Neither is Lacascade's work the exemplary Francophone modernist woman's text. I concur with Sharpley-Whiting's assertion that "*the* oppositional text of black female representation" does not exist because women's writing tends to "reflect the range and diversity of black female subjectivities rather than monolithic, homogenizing constructions of black femaleness."[123] What I would posit *Claire-Solange, âme africaine* as is a paradigm-shifting text through which the limits of diasporic male heroism can be exchanged for the study of black modernity across categories of race, class, and gender. If the hermeneutic possibilities of such a shift are foreshadowed in Lacascade's 1924 novel, one year later they would emerge fully realized in the literary debut of African American writer Marita Bonner.

Portrait of Marita Bonner from the Radcliffe
College yearbook, class of 1922
The Schlesinger Library, Radcliffe Institute,
Harvard University

2 The Limits of Exemplarity

Marita Bonner's Alternative Modernist Landscapes

There are all the earmarks of a group within a group. Cut off all around from ingress or egress to other groups. A sameness of type. The smug self-satisfaction of an inner measurement; a measurement by standards known within a limited group and not those of an unlimited, seeing world. . . . Like the blind, blind mice. Mice whose eyes have been blinded.
—MARITA BONNER, "On Being Young—a Woman—and Colored" (1925)

As detailed as Suzanne Lacascade's is vague, the biography of Marita Bonner (1899–1971) reads as a virtual primer of New Negro success. Her personal history positions her squarely within the cultural and intellectual traditions that shaped many an early-twentieth-century African American luminary: Bonner was raised along the U.S. eastern seaboard in Brookline, Massachusetts; took an undergraduate degree in English and comparative literature in 1922 from the prestigious Radcliffe College; and was fluent in a foreign language, German.[1]

In 1924 Bonner followed in the footsteps of Anna Julia Cooper and Jessie Redmon Fauset, both of whom spent part of their careers teaching in the nation's capital, and began teaching at Washington's Armstrong High School.[2] Bonner also participated in Georgia Douglas Johnson's "S" Street Salon and, from 1925 until 1941, contributed regularly to *Crisis* and *Opportunity*, two of the premier showcases for Harlem Renaissance literary talent. Bonner interrupted her career in 1930 to marry Brown University alumnus William Occomy and relocate to Chicago, where she spent most of the 1940s focused on wife- and motherhood before eventually returning to teaching. If one pauses here, these personal and professional achievements seem the very hallmarks of W. E. B. Du Bois's "Talented Tenth," the black "aristocracy of talent and character" poised to educate and uplift "the masses of the Negro people."[3]

Yet, however much Bonner's biography corresponds to model African American modernity, her work reveals rather than relishes the limits of exemplarity. Whereas Du Bois argues that the Talented Tenth will assist "all that are worth the saving up to their vantage ground," Bonner questions the desirability and stability of said ground.[4] Whereas Alain Locke contends that improved race relations must begin with "the carefully maintained contacts of the enlightened minorities of both race groups," Bonner disputes the blanket applicability of the term *enlightened* to any elite, white or black.[5] And, finally, whereas Elise Johnson McDougald advocates the subsumption of gender equity to the greater good of "the race," Bonner demonstrates how race cannot be discussed independently of gender. From her first published essay to her final short story Bonner critiques reductive expressions of intraracial solidarity, cracks facades assumed for the purpose of group preservation, and creates narrative landscapes in which despair and struggle often trump hope and success. While in her nonfiction Bonner writes from a position of privilege that she alternately finds liberating and stultifying, in her drama and fiction she moves from anonymous wastelands to finely appointed black bourgeois homes, and, finally, to cramped urban tenements, sparing no group or locale in her critique of restrictive conceptions of race and belonging. Shifting skillfully between sites, voices, and perspectives, Bonner problematizes the utopian spirit of the Talented Tenth and New Negrohood and maps in its stead an alternative African American modernism, one that turns on, rather than away from, the tension between individual concerns and communal solidarity.

Bonner explored and refined these themes in a body of work spanning two essays, three plays, and twenty short stories, five of which were published posthumously. Bonner's admirers included some of the Harlem Renaissance's most discriminating readers: her work garnered numerous awards in the leading African American cultural arts competitions of the 1920s and 1930s. The essay "On Being Young—a Woman—and Colored" placed first in the 1925 *Crisis* literary contest, the one-act play *The Purple Flower* received the 1927 *Crisis* award for drama, and the short story "Tin Can" won *Opportunity*'s 1933 fiction prize.[6] *Frye Street and Environs: The Collected Works of Marita Bonner,* the first and to this date only comprehensive Bonner anthology, was published in 1987 and brought yet another accolade: the 1988 Boston Globe Literary Press Prize.[7] Decorated with laurels in not one but three genres, Bonner's publishing record is as impressive as it is extensive.

Far from being a question of literary talent, the discrepancy between this prolific and prize-winning career and the uneven critical attention it has received can be attributed to the gender, political, and geographical typecasting of canonical African American modernism. Neither Nathan Irvin Huggins's *Harlem Renaissance* (1971) nor David Levering Lewis's *When Harlem Was in Vogue* (1981), two early landmark studies in the field, mentions Marita Bonner, and, although Lewis devotes more attention than Huggins to African American women modernists, his cultural history, by virtue of its genre, focuses on the mechanics of the Renaissance over its poetics.[8] As Deborah McDowell notes in "Regulating Midwives," if such an emphasis still leaves male figures such as Howard University professor Alain Locke positioned as Renaissance impresarios, it often results in women such as *Crisis* literary editor and essayist/novelist/poet Jessie Fauset being remembered as mediators more than as independent, innovative intellectuals.[9] Such narrowly drawn literary historical parameters leave little to no room for figures such as Bonner, whose stance toward New Negro ideals was as openly antagonistic as Fauset's was subtly critical. Indeed, it has only been within the last twenty-five years that, with the efforts of critics such as McDowell and Cheryl Wall, author of *Women of the Harlem Renaissance* (1995), Bonner's work has figured more prominently in African American modernist studies.[10]

One of the ways in which Bonner's literary practice differed sharply from mainstream New Negrohood was in her extended, nuanced discussions of gender. Wall argues that, in the modernist era, "a woman who persisted in raising such concerns [about sexism] might see them dismissed as irrelevant or trivial; she herself might be perceived as disloyal to the race."[11] Even as Locke criticizes those who would ignore the complexities of African American society by "treat[ing] the Negro *en masse*," his New Negro composite remains uncomplicated by questions of gender difference.[12] Perhaps because acknowledging the lingering impact of racial stereotypes on women would detract from his optimistic vision, Locke focuses instead on the social advances made by the implicitly masculine New Negro and the accompanying artistic strides of male writers.[13] Initially, McDougald's "The Task of Negro Womanhood" (1925), included in Locke's anthology, seems poised to fill the gaps left by "The New Negro": whereas Locke posits his New Negro "as an augury of a new democracy in American culture," McDougald offers the generic figure of woman as the "weather-vane" of social conditions and the specific figure of "the Negro woman" as the marker of African American social progress.[14] Yet, even as McDougald acknowledges intraracial and intra-gender differences, she nonetheless avoids the challenge of incorporating gender into her discussion of racial justice. Not surprisingly, then, in dispassionate phrasing characteristic of her sociological framework, McDougald concludes that the Negro woman has responded to this political quandary by subsuming her "feminist efforts" to the "realization of the equality of the races."[15] For the sake of racial unity the representative (New) Negro woman—in this case McDougald as well as her subject—must fold herself back into the ostensibly gender-neutral New Negro.

For in the eyes of many of Bonner and McDougald's contemporaries the fissures beneath the Harlem Renaissance project of achieving social advancement through artistic production were not to be discussed openly, much less in print. Locke and *Opportunity* editor-in-chief Charles S. Johnson, for example, viewed the political and social climate of the early twentieth century as a prime opportunity for integrating the African American subject into the American national fabric. Johnson, a sociologist by training, considered the arts a means of "speed[ing] up the movement of the race relations cycle," of forging social change through a path of "high visibility and low vulnerability."[16] In brief the arts would allow African Americans to improve their social profile with little risk of offending current white patrons and potential white allies. Philosopher and cultural broker Locke held a similar view: "The especially cultural recognition [African American artists] win should in turn prove the key to that revaluation of the Negro which must precede or accompany any considerable further betterment of race relationships."[17] Reinforced by the institutionalization of the New Negro movement through prizes and publications, these ideas situated early-twentieth-century African American cultural work as an ideological front, a key site in the battle for racial justice and citizenship rights: in

September 1925 Johnson announced the creation of the *Opportunity* literary prizes; the NAACP organ the *Crisis,* headed by editor-in-chief Du Bois and literary editor Fauset, began its own cultural arts competition in the same year.[18] If African Americans could not assert their rightful place in society through the power of the sword or of the ballot, they might be able to do so—in keeping with Frances Ellen Watkins Harper's description of the pen as "the weapon of civilization"—through the power of the printed word.[19]

As Johnson, Locke, and others invested Harlem Renaissance artists—whatever the artists' awareness of or commitment to such an agenda—with the responsibility of recreating African America for the benefit of the nation at large, the art itself became a facade onto which redeeming images of African Americans and their communities were to be projected, or re-presented, for public viewing. This concerted effort to change society through art contributed to, if it did not create, what David Levering Lewis identifies as the "Renaissance intramural competition" between the "primitive" and "genteel" schools of early-twentieth-century African American literature.[20] While "primitive" literature focused on exploring the lives and social concerns of the African American folk, the "genteel" tradition focused on putting the race's collective best foot forward by portraying the lives of the black bourgeoisie. Unfortunately, the emphasis of this literary "competition" soon shifted from focus to exclusion, with artists of the primitive camp identifying the popular masses as "the source of cultural renewal for the African of the diaspora," those of the genteel school charging the cultivated elite with the diaspora's social renewal, often with neither side willing to acknowledge the positive attributes of the other.[21] For every Langston Hughes criticizing the black bourgeoisie for its "Nordic manners, Nordic faces, Nordic hair, Nordic art (if any), and . . . Episcopal heaven," there was a W. E. B. Du Bois claiming that primitive novels such as Claude McKay's best-selling *Home to Harlem* (1928) left him "feel[ing] distinctly like taking a bath."[22] Although written from opposite sides of the ideological fence, the Hughes and Du Bois comments share a verve and venom that (1) speak to how the artistic and political stakes of Harlem Renaissance literary production were often indistinguishable; and (2) suggest how such inseparability could discourage writers—whether popular or bourgeois—from pursuing their right "to express [their] individual dark-skinned selves without fear or shame."[23]

Even the typically unflappable Locke at times seemed unsure of which tradition to embrace. He celebrates the folk aesthetic in "The New Negro" but primarily as a remnant of the past. Similarly, while he praises primitive school artists such as McKay in "Negro Youth Speaks," Locke also posits "the folk-gift" as that which young African Americans will elevate "to the altitudes of art."[24] In the latter essay the folk aesthetic constitutes the foundation but not the re- alization, of African American artistic expression. This ambivalence results, I would argue, from Locke's desire to elide more so than deny social and cultural difference among African Americans. In keeping with racial uplift ideology, which "promot[ed] bourgeois morality, patriarchal authority, and a culture of self-improvement, both among blacks and outward, to the white world," Locke felt that New Negro voices should be enriched, but not dominated, by the folk experience.[25] Thus, while African America's new place in U.S. society was thought to be dependent upon the recognition of its singular artistic gifts, this singularity was to be highlighted judiciously as part of the larger goals of as- similation and integration.[26] It is a somewhat progressive, somewhat regressive stance not unlike that taken by many members of the early-twentieth-century Francophone bourgeoisie as depicted in Suzanne Lacascade's *Claire-Solange, âme africaine;* indeed, it is probably just the stance that Claire-Solange's aunt would have liked her niece to adopt if the topic of race had to be addressed at all.

If Lacascade tenders a narrative olive branch with the happy resolution of *Claire-Solange*'s marriage plot, Marita Bonner offers no such appeasement in her writing. In her first published essay, the autobiographical "On Being Young—a Woman—and Colored" (1925), Bonner boldly outlines a blueprint for an alternative African American modernism. From the outset she describes a relationship between individual and community that is as fraught with intra- racial conflict as it is with interracial tension. Remarkable for a skepticism that departs from the respective enthusiasms of Du Bois, Locke, and Hughes, "On Being Young" envisions no fundamental accord or connection either between the speaker and members of different classes or between the speaker and mem- bers of her own social milieu. Armed with an education ranging "from kinder- garten to sheepskin covered with sundry Latin phrases" (3), the speaker opens with a commentary on racial uplift that is at once perplexed and cynical: "All your life you have heard of the debt you owe 'Your People' because you have managed to have the things they have not largely had. . . . So you find a spot where there are hordes of them—of course below the Line—to be your catnip field while you close your eyes to mice and chickens alike" (3). This ambiva- lence begs the question of what, in the absence of personal motivation or no- blesse oblige, can produce enduring ties across the spectrum of African American experiences. More interested in race as a source of inherent instability than of collective identity, Bonner expands the Du Boisian notion of "double consciousness" to articulate a multiply inflected consciousness.[27] Whereas Du Bois argues that the African American "ever feels his two-ness,—an American, a Negro; two souls, two thoughts, two unreconciled strivings, two warring ideals in one dark body," Bonner introduces a figure whose sense of self is informed by class, gender, and geography as well as by race and citizenship.[28] Thus, while initially suggestive of the Mason-Dixon Line's division of the United States between slaveholding states and free, over the course of "On Being Young" the aforementioned "Line" begins to signify numerous demarcations, including those separating men from women, middle class from working class, whites from blacks. For Bonner these lines shift rather than remain stable, sometimes paralleling each other, occasionally intersecting, and often colliding.

Central to Bonner's project is an interrogation of the geographic limitations of New Negrohood. The interchangeability of the modifiers *Harlem* and *New Negro* in scholarly and popular discussions of the early-twentieth-century renaissance in African American arts and letters speaks to one such limit: at the same time that this wordplay communicates the remarkable concentration of black writers and artists in 1920s and 1930s New York City, the critical slippage it has engendered positions upper Manhattan as *the* cradle of African American modernism. The latter move is not without its Renaissance-era precedents, the most famous being Locke's positing of Harlem as a nascent "race capital" that "has the same rôle to play for the New Negro as Dublin has had to play for the New Ireland or Prague for the New Czechoslovakia."[29] While the speaker of "On Being Young" recognizes New York "as a site of the . . . cultural sublime," she also laments the city's inaccessibility to those without the full range of New Negro mobility: "You hear that up at New York this is to be seen; that, to be heard. [Yet] you know that—being a woman—you cannot twice a month or twice a year, for that matter, break away to see or hear anything in a city that is supposed to see and hear too much . . . That's being a woman. A woman of any color" (4–5).[30] While this particular passage focuses on gender, one cannot help but imagine that the pleasures of New York would be no more accessible to the underprivileged masses invoked at the beginning of the essay.

This association is borne out in Bonner's decision to carry the theme of restricted mobility through to a discussion of residential segregation: the social constraints the speaker faces because she is a woman parallels the spatial confinement experienced by African Americans whose housing options are limited by economic status, discriminatory real estate practices, or both. The speaker describes the "Black Ghetto" as a site where inhabitants have been "cut off, flung together, shoved aside in a bundle because of color and with no more in common" (4), and she is skeptical that such cohabitation, along with the inhabitants' shared racial identity, will lead to cooperation. In fact, the speaker imagines ghetto residents "milling around like live fish in a basket. Those at the bottom crushed into a sort of stupid apathy by the weight of those on top. Those on top leaping, leaping; leaping to scale the sides; to get out" (4). Despite their shared plight, nowhere is there mention of "those on top" reaching back to help "those at the bottom." In this dismal view of the black enclave it would seem that survival supersedes solidarity. As Bonner's later writing reveals, however, this pessimism stems not from any conviction of the impossibility of human connection but, rather, from the assumption that "color"—in other words, race—and not other, more substantial ties should be the sole catalyst for conscientious and sustained social interaction.

This distinction is underscored when the speaker holds her own, more rarefied social milieu to the same level of scrutiny. Indeed, the world of the black elite seems to be as stifling and unsatisfying as the Black Ghetto: "Parties, plentiful. Music and dancing and much that is wit and color and gaiety. But they are like the richest chocolate; stuffed costly chocolates that make the taste go stale if you have too many of them" (4). These words foreshadow the fictional experiences of Helga Crane and Janie Starks, the protagonists of Nella Larsen's *Quicksand* (1928) and Zora Neale Hurston's *Their Eyes Were Watching God* (1937), respectively; both Helga and Janie become the subject of gossip and criticism when their interests exceed the pursuits that their societies deem appropriate for women of their class.[31] Far from the cheerful prosperity highlighted in Elise Johnson McDougald's litany of "well-appointed homes, modest motors, tennis, golf and country clubs, [and] trips to Europe and California," the analogous environments in Bonner, Larsen, and Hurston conjure images of entrapment and stagnation.[32] The result is a social claustrophobia that Bonner's speaker openly resents but which McDougald and Alain Locke, who declares that the New Negro is "inevitably moving forward under the control largely of his own objectives," clearly do not envision.[33]

Gender remains at the forefront when the essay encourages yet another comparison, this time between the aforementioned residential and social segregation and the rhetorical imprisonment of African American women through stereotypes. Once again, the target of the speaker's disdain is not blackness but the manner in which the fundamental racial solidarity championed by black intellectuals could quite easily lead to problematic racial essentialism. Like Suzanne Lacascade before her, Bonner counters reductive depictions of black womanhood by shifting the focus from the stereotype's object to its producer/consumer:

Why do they see a colored woman only as a gross collection of desires, all uncontrolled, reaching out for their Apollos and the Quasimodos with avid indiscrimination?

Why unless you talk in staccato squawks—brittle as seashells— unless you "champ" gum—unless you cover two yards square when you laugh—unless your taste runs to violent colors—impossible perfumes and more impossible clothes—are you a feminine Caliban craving to pass for Ariel? (5)

As if in recognition of Western civilization's equation of normative womanhood with whiteness, the speaker builds her critique around masculine rather than feminine icons. She begins with two extremes of Eurocentric understandings of male beauty—Apollo, the handsome god of Greco-Roman mythology, and Quasimodo, the grotesque antihero of French fiction—and concludes with Shakespeare's *Tempest* and its opposing models of "colored" personhood, the rebellious slave Caliban and the cooperative sprite Ariel.[34] Through these allusions Bonner demonstrates a command of cultural capital for which these stereotypes do not allow: she writes as an African American woman in control of her intellect as well as of her desire. Her speaker forgoes the timidity of Miranda for the candor of Anna Julia Cooper and in so doing rejects any stock role to which one might presume to assign her, be it that of loyal "race woman" or stereotypical black nursemaid/harlot. Impressive in its simultaneous sweep and economy, the move is but the beginning of Bonner's emergence "as a modernist artist . . . developing a bold combination of sociological detail, allegorical patterning, and stream-of-consciousness to represent the experience of urban African Americans."[35]

The abstract collectivity of "The Young Blood Hungers" (1928), the second of Bonner's two major essays, may seem an unexpected departure from the specific, almost defiant individuality of its predecessor. While "On Being Young— a Woman—and Colored" encourages the reader to link the speaker's predicament to the plight of others, the speaker herself indicates little desire to collapse her hard-won *I* into a plural *we*. In the three-year span between the first essay and the second, however, Bonner's continuing dissatisfaction with oppressive social conventions yields a piece written in the first person but punctuated by the refrain "I speak not for myself alone" (9). Equally rich with intertextual citations, Bonner's approach in "The Young Blood Hungers" differs from that found in "On Being Young" in two additional ways: (1) she refracts her critique principally through religion rather than gender or class; and (2) she stages the essay primarily as an in-group conversation rather than as an exchange between the speaker and society at large. As represented by the speaker, the eponymous, racially unmarked "Young Blood" demands to be acknowledged by the "Old Blood," to have its youthful malaise recognized as a profound discontent with group leadership and not misdiagnosed as a morally deficient character. The centerpiece of this conflict is religious faith, which the Old Blood prescribes as a panacea to be taken blindly. The Young Blood, in turn, refuses the Old Blood's representation of God as a remote, wrathful being who responds to human suffering by "offering a heavenly reward for an earthly Hell" (10). It is unable to accept the admonition to be complacent, much less at the behest of elders whose "hands [are] not always too free from blood" (12). Ultimately unable to reconcile the Old Blood's vision with its hunger for critical spiritual engagement, the Young Blood sets out to define its own spirituality.

Despite its emphasis on religion and lack of explicit racial markers, "The Young Blood Hungers" recalls many of the metaphors introduced in "On Being Young," particularly those relating to sight and blindness. Bonner's attribution of the qualities of passivity and engagement to the Old and Young Blood, respectively, suggests Alain Locke's differentiation between Old Negro and New; Locke characterizes the former as a figure who "has been more of a formula than a human being—a something to be argued about, condemned or defended, to be 'kept down,' or 'in his place,' or 'helped up.'"[36] Lest one misconstrue this similarity as a reversal on Bonner's part, an endorsement (of the New Negro) that counters the perspective of her earlier essay, her play on a second Du Boisian metaphor reasserts her opposition to consolidated visions of African American community: "The Young Blood hungers and searches somehow. The Young Blood knows well that Life is built high on a crystal of tears. A crystal of tears filled with Illusory Veils of Blind Misunderstandings and Blunderings. Enough filmy veils wet with tears, stamped down hard beneath your feet to let you rise up—out—above—beyond" (10). As students of *The Souls of Black Folk* well know, Du Bois presents the veil as that which separates the African American subject from those outside of his racial group: "Then it dawned upon me with a certain suddenness that I was different from the others; or like, mayhap, in heart and life and longing, but shut out from their world by a vast veil."[37] Bonner, in contrast, asserts that the "Blind Misunderstandings" lamented by the Young Blood are not simply a divider between the African American and non–African American worlds. Here the veils also symbolize intraracial divisions between duplicity and integrity, artifice and substance. They engage, not excuse, the idealized racial identity represented by Locke's New Negrohood. Thus, as mirrored in the essay's structure, the obstacles posed by the "Illusory Veils" are to be phased out along with the dated practices of the Young Blood's elders: as Bonner introduces the veil metaphor and its subsequent transformation from impediment to instrument, so she ceases to use the phrase *Old Blood.*

Through "On Being Young—a Woman—and Colored" and "The Young Blood Hungers" Bonner launches theories of identity and community that she would go on to develop over the next sixteen years. Foreshadowing late-twentieth-century discussions of African diasporic identities, Bonner posits race as a contested, conditional identity that is complicated, not clarified, by gender, class, and religious affiliations. Bonner's nonfiction personae reject "African Americanness" not as an identity but as a singularity that recalls the "anti-essentialist essentialism" that, Paul Gilroy argues, attempts "to explore critically and reproduce politically the necessary ethnic essence of blackness."[38] Whether under the aegis of the New Negro or the cloud of negative stereotypes, this "essence" entails a loss of critical nuance and an attendant elision of identities that Bonner is unwilling to accept. Instead, she seizes upon and highlights the myriad divisions underlying notions of racial unity. Although firmly ensconced in the middle class, Bonner produced work that, to paraphrase Werner Sollors, is neither primitive nor genteel yet both.[39] Although sensitive to the force that race is in U.S. social dynamics, Bonner proposes that sometimes the most effective means of addressing the problems of racialized communities is to inflect examinations of their constitution and cohesion—or lack thereof—with discussions of gender, age, class, nationality, and geography. Introduced in her nonfiction and subsequently developed in her drama and fiction, these bold assertions elevate Bonner's work from the limits of racial exemplarity to the possibilities of multiracial, multiethnic modernisms.

The Purple Flower: Modernist Revision through Expressionist Abstraction

The dramatic subgenre of expressionism, with its "de-emphasis of the individual" and presentation of generic rather than specific characters, does not immediately read as the most effective means of countering exemplarity.[40] Indeed, names such as "Finest Blood" and "Cornerstone," found among the dramatis personae of Bonner's 1928 expressionist play *The Purple Flower*, seem to echo more than eschew the archetypal blackness represented by the New Negro and his feminine counterpart. Contrary to the representational impetus of canonical African American modernism, however, expressionism rejects "the confines of verisimilitude" and through this rejection seeks to explore the interiority absent in realist drama.[41] Hailed by Joyce Flynn as "Bonner's . . . dramatic masterpiece," *The Purple Flower* joins the introspection of "On Being Young— a Woman—and Colored" to the abstraction of "The Young Blood Hungers" to produce a searing critique of in-group and intergroup relations.[42] Within early-twentieth-century African American drama the stunning play troubles the key artistic parameters advanced by intellectuals such as Alain Locke and W. E. B. Du Bois and, more broadly, soundly dispels notions that either radical politics or experimental art were anathema to middle- and upper-middle-class black women modernists.

Although in keeping with their larger New Negro–era visions of art's transformative potential, Locke's and Du Bois's respective views on the nature and content of African American drama were also influenced by the output of Anglo American playwrights.[43] Chief among these was Eugene O'Neill, who was widely hailed as "America's most important practitioner of expressionism" and who began to garner praise with his 1920 play *The Emperor Jones*.[44] When produced, the work not only introduced American audiences to expressionism but also integrated the Broadway stage by featuring an African American actor in the lead role. A portrait of the decline of the titular character, a transplanted African American who has seized power of an unnamed Caribbean island, *The Emperor Jones* explores the psychological fallout of violence, racism, displacement, and colonialism. Unfortunately, as noted by critic Shannon Steen, O'Neill's drama also evokes many of the racialized stereotypes of modernist primitivism: "The patois, the rolling eyes, the desperate prayer to 'Lord Jesus' to save him from the Crocodile God combine to render Brutus Jones an outrageous vision of blackness."[45] In response to this and other dramatic renderings of black atavism, Du Bois, Locke, and Montgomery Gregory, Locke's Howard University colleague, promoted "native" dramas that would depict African American life more accurately. While Du Bois championed "propaganda" plays, which addressed racism directly, Locke and Gregory favored "folk" plays, which "sought to depict the black experience without focusing on the oppressive issues blacks faced daily."[46] Perhaps to emphasize the importance of cultural accuracy to native drama, both Du Bois and Locke advocated formal realism over experimentation.[47]

From the outset of Bonner's *Purple Flower* it is clear that realism is not the artistic order of the day: the play is set during "The Middle-of-Things-as-They-are" in a location that "might be here, there or anywhere." The plot turns on the mounting frustration of the "Us's" with their subordination to "Sundry White Devils," and the fluidity of its temporal and geographic moorings is mirrored in the unstable identities of the two groups. While Bonner clearly marks the color of the White Devils, she undermines assumptions about their humanity by describing them as "artful little things with soft wide eyes such as you would expect to find in an angel" and "soft hair that flops around their horns." Some thirty years before the Nation of Islam jarred American audiences with its indictment of "the devil white man," Bonner's description deftly combines popular associations of whiteness with purity and political associations of whiteness with evil.[48] Conversely, while the Us's are recognizably human, their color is not always distinctly "Other": the list of dramatis personae reveals that the Us's "can be as white as the White Devils, as brown as the earth, as black as the center of a poppy" (30). They are as varied as the multihued panorama around Jeanne Hucquart's Parisian table in Suzanne Lacascade's *Claire-Solange.* It is only fitting, then, that, in explicating the conflict between the two groups, the stage directions articulate difference not through their skin color but through their respective access to the coveted object from which the play takes its name: "*The* WHITE DEVILS *live on the side of the hill. Somewhere. On top of the hill grows the purple Flower-of-Life-at-Its-Fullest. This flower is as tall as a pine and stands alone on top of the hill. The Us's live in the valley that lies between Nowhere and Somewhere and spend their time trying to devise means of getting up the hill. The* White Devils *live all over the sides of the hill and try every trick, known and unknown, to keep the Us's from getting to the hill. For if the Us's get up the hill, the Flower-of-Life-at-Its-Fullest will shed some of its perfume and then there they will be Somewhere with the* WHITE DEVILS" (31). The struggle over the flower forms the locus of Bonner's "paradoxical suggestion that race is both an illusion *and* a primary determinant of social identities in the United States."[49] For, whatever the hypothetical interchangeability of the White Devils and the Us's, in the Middle-of-Things-as-They-are life revolves around the former reveling in their privilege—epitomized by their gleeful dances on the "Thin-Skin-of-Civilization" (30)—while the latter plot to dismantle it.

Bonner characterizes the Us's through a series of figures who evoke the interrelation between systemic racism, internalized racism, and idealized African Americanness; the comportment and self-perception of each are inextricably tied to both the group's relationship to the White Devils and its quest for the Purple Flower. While Old Lady, an unsuccessful seeker of the flower despite years of hard work, personifies the long-suffering elder, the stereotype of the lazy African American appears in the character Another Us, who vows to storm the White Devils' hill right after he takes a nap. Average, the male head of the play's model black family, believes that this indolence is precisely what has kept the Us's from the flower and chastises his peers for indulging in frivolous pursuits: "Look at that! Dancing!! The Us will never learn to be sensible!" (35). His perspective, in turn, is countered by others, most notably that of Cornerstone, his wife and an admirer of the dancers. The presence of a conscientized younger generation rounds out the roster of core characters. If Average and Cornerstone represent the skeptical man-on-the-street and the affirmative woman-as-community-pillar, respectively, their children, son Finest Blood and daughter Sweet, suggest hope for a future in which the Us's may reach Somewhere. When their elders question the utility of yet another conversation about their collective plight, Finest Blood and Sweet volunteer to continue the discussion. Not yet discouraged and disillusioned, the siblings possess the initiative and energy of which perpetual struggle has robbed older members of the community.

Although a source of disagreement within the play, this lack of unified fronts among the Us's serves the metanarrative function of transforming Bonner's generic characterization from archetypal reduction to political engagement. As their ongoing debate evolves, the Us's contemplate not only the efficacy of their individual approaches to reaching the Purple Flower but also that of the strategies proposed by various community leaders. Old Lady echoes Booker T. Washington—and his critics—when she complains: "But that's what the Leader told us to do. 'Work,' he said. 'Show them you know how.' As if two hundred years of slavery had not showed them!" (32). In contrast to Washington's prediction that African Americans "shall prosper in proportion as [they] learn to dignify and glorify common labour," Old Lady's failed attempts to see the flower disprove the notion that industry alone will propel social change.[50] Newcomer joins the conversation with a similar complaint. However impressive, his wealth cannot reverse the White Devils' refusal to "sell [him] even a spoonful of dirt from Somewhere" (39); his bags of gold are useless when he is denied access to circuits of economic exchange. The Us's dissatisfaction with the advocacy of advancement through erudition is equally palpable. In "The Talented Tenth" Du Bois argues that "from the very first it has been the educated and intelligent of the Negro people that have led and elevated the mass," yet in *The Purple Flower* the "educated and intelligent" are just as frustrated as their working-class peers.[51] Average complains that eloquent rhetoric does little to move the Us's any closer to Somewhere, and Young Man opts to discard his books, claiming that their authorship renders their content useless to the Us's struggle: "The White Devils wrote the books themselves. You know they aren't going to put anything like that [how to get Somewhere] in there!" (37). Across the socioeconomic spectrum neither bootstrap nor book has enabled the Us's to integrate or overthrow the White Devils.

The futility of the Us's efforts also leads them to reconsider the utility of religion and its role in their lives. When an Old Us cries that he has been waiting for God's help for seventy years, the Young Us's retort that this strategy has left him exactly where he began, "sitting on the rocks in the valley" (37). With its debate framed in terms of elder versus youth, Old Testament versus New, the exchange is reminiscent of "The Young Blood Hungers." The Young Us's see God much as their nonfiction counterparts do: as "a friendly father who [desires] cooperation and thanksgiving as much as He want[s] supplication" (10). Consequently, they believe that religion has not paved the way to the Purple Flower because the Old Us's have built their faith solely on pleas and submission. Bonner uses this intergenerational disagreement both to continue her ongoing commentary on religion and to develop the larger theme of collaboration. Just as divine intervention works best in concert with rather than in place of human initiative, so the Us's should consider religion one tool among many in their quest for the coveted flower. Ultimately, the faith that will enable the Us's to reach the prize will be proactive, not passive.

Drawing on this spirit, Bonner locates the Us's best hopes for progress in the combined efforts of the two generations. Old Man, who emerges as the group's senior elder, proposes an as-yet unexplored option: the rebirth of society through the figure of the "New Man" (44). Initially, the conditions for this birth are the familiar, if previously rejected, hallmarks of community revitalization, and the Us's willingly follow Old Man's directions to pool their resources—symbols of their labor (dust), capital (gold), and education (books)—in an iron pot. If the approach seems an amalgam of New Negro, black self-reliance, and racial uplift philosophies, Old Man's final request disabuses the reader of this impression and stuns the Us's into silence:

> Old Man
> Now bring me blood! Blood from the eyes, the ears, the whole body! Drain it off and bring me blood! *(No one speaks or moves.)* Now bring me blood! Blood from the eyes, the ears, the whole body! Drain it off! Bring me blood!! *(No one speaks or moves.)* Ah hah, hah! I knew it! Not one of you willing to pour his blood in the pot! (41–42)

Only when the appropriately named Finest Blood volunteers his life does the Old Man reveal that his intent is not self or group sacrifice but direct confrontation with the White Devils, a revelation Bonner foreshadows with Old Lady's recounting of her dream of a White Devil's dismemberment. In a provocative revision of the biblical story of Abraham, Old Man sends Finest Blood to capture the White Devil who has attacked his sister. In the Bible God tests Abraham's faith by commanding that he sacrifice Isaac, his only son; when Abraham is about to kill the child, God rewards his servant's faithfulness by providing a ram in the bushes to be sacrificed instead.[52] In *The Purple Flower* Bonner places Finest Blood in the role of Abraham and identifies the White Devil, who assaults Sweet while "sitting in the bushes," as the sacrificial animal (38). The play concludes with Finest Blood proclaiming his intent to fulfill his mission : "White Devil! God speaks to you through me!—Hear Him!—Him! You have taken blood: there can be no other way. You will have to give blood! Blood!" (46). Finally commanding the attention of the White Devils, Finest Blood forgoes the patriotic, almost utopian integration sought by Locke's New Negro, announcing instead what Nellie McKay calls "the inevitability of race war."[53]

 The Purple Flower's dramatic conclusion precedes a second, narrative ending that speaks not only to the play's immediate context but also to the work's broader significance within Bonner's oeuvre and the African American dramatic tradition. Echoing Finest Blood's assertion that social change will not be wrought in hesitant, incremental steps, the final stage directions reiterate the need for radical action by conscientized individuals: *"Let the curtain close leaving all the Us [sic], the White Devils, Nowhere, Somewhere, listening, listening. Is it time?"* (46). Provocative, interrogative, and open-ended, these lines forcefully challenge the reader to contemplate her allegiance and positionality (with the Us's or the White Devils? Nowhere or Somewhere?) as well as her readiness for the coming insurrection. By privileging revolution over representation, Bonner bypasses the propaganda and folk play variants of early-twentieth-century African American drama to portend the "black revolutionary drama" of the 1960s and 1970s.[54] And, by privileging questions over answers, she implies that notions of success or failure, gentility or primitivism, are far more complex than archetypal articulations of black modernism acknowledge. That Bonner makes this claim in an expressionist play, that she uses dramatic abstraction to address the realities of economic, social, and racial exclusion in the United States, attests to her skill as both creative writer and cultural critic.

Gender, Class, and New Negro Claustrophobia

In "On the Altar" (1937–40) and "Hate Is Nothing" (1938), short stories situated in upper-middle-class black communities, Bonner replaces the expressionist wasteland of *The Purple Flower* with the insular, stifling bourgeois world alluded to in "On Being Young—a Woman—and Colored."[55] The "Thin-Skin-of Civilization" explored here is not that separating Us's and White Devils but that separating African Americans from each other. In a further departure from the "genteel" tradition of lionizing the African American elite, Bonner's stories become a means of revealing the intraracial segregation often promoted by this "group within a group" and its ever-shifting membership rules. If a shared sense of exceptionality consolidates the black elite of "On the Altar" and "Hate Is Nothing," its members are also joined by acts of self-interest and duplicity designed to maintain an existence that Bonner criticizes for being more artifice than substance. She depicts this elite not as African American paragons of wealth, culture, and virtue, the "Men of the Month" and "Washington, D.C. Children" gracing the pages of *Crisis* and *Opportunity,* but, rather, as the "blind, blind mice" cited in this chapter's epigraph: middle- and upper-class African Americans whose inability or unwillingness to look beyond their hermetic, homogeneous communities impedes social progress and connotes "smug self-satisfaction" and internalized racism (4).[56]

Although the internally defined segregation of the black middle class mirrors the externally determined isolation of the black working class, the play on the nursery rhyme "Three Blind Mice" reveals a crucial element of Bonner's social critique: despite such similarities, the former group would be reluctant to acknowledge this or any other link between itself and its less fortunate "brothers" and "sisters." Indeed, E. Franklin Frazier argues that, in the face of diminishing or precarious economic circumstances, most members of the early- to mid-twentieth-century black bourgeoisie sought to cement their social positions by distinguishing themselves from "the great mass of the Negro population"; the folk provided a human base upon which the black bourgeoisie built its status in the absence of stable socioeconomic foundations.[57] This dependence reflects the no less problematic relationship between the black elite and the "white bourgeois world" through which it seeks valorization and acceptance, and Frazier concludes that the only way the black bourgeoisie can reconcile these contradictions is by residing "largely in a world of make-believe" in which intraracial difference is magnified and interracial difference masked.[58] Frazier's sociological commentary finds a creative precursor in Bonner's short stories, in which substantive exchange between the African American elite and their working-class peers is few and far between and racial uplift, when practiced at all, veers between reluctant altruism and patronizing charity.

The elitist antagonists of Bonner's short fiction maintain intraracial borders by coating themselves with a veneer of exclusivity, most notably manifested through the promotion of a pigmentocracy, or color hierarchy. Gran, the powerful matriarch and pillar of the "fair-skinned" black bourgeoisie in "On the Altar," objects to the secret marriage of her high school–age granddaughter not because of Beth's youth but because of her choice of husband.[59] When investigating rumors that Beth has been sighted in the company of classmate Jerry Johnson, "a tall black boy," Gran concludes that "none of their group had tall black sons" (230).[60] The wry yet powerful statement communicates the incongruity of such an alliance to Gran's social circle: it is not that no one in the circle has sons but, rather, that those sons do not have dark skin. That this distinction is rooted in a legacy of enslavement and concubinage apparently escapes Gran and her kind, who seem oblivious to the past legal and social subordination on which they base their privilege. Only the omniscient, third-person narrator appreciates the tragic irony of Gran's expeditious annulment of Beth's marriage. To verify and void the union simultaneously, Gran enlists the aid of "an old judge who was related to her by a blood that never recognized the tie" (236). Just as her white relative refuses to acknowledge their biological relationship, so Gran denies the validity of Beth's love for her husband. The most jarring consequence of this internalized prejudice is the forced termination of Beth's first pregnancy, a termination ordered after Gran's calculation that the infant's chances of being "a tar-kettle" far outweigh the value of its life (237). Through these examples Bonner stages a narrative confrontation with the past and with the politics of representation that her black bourgeois matriarch, however imperious, dares not undertake.

This internalization of color and caste prejudice, at once uncritical and calculating, feeds yet another means of consolidating black bourgeois facades: conspicuous consumption. "Front A," the first vignette of Bonner's story "Black Fronts" (1938), follows one couple's descent into financial ruin and emotional despair. Big Brother and his wife Rinky's pre-1929 pursuit of middle-class success initially appears to be a case of misplaced priorities, the overeager social drive of young, ambitious newlyweds: he, a lawyer; she, a business college graduate. After the stock market crash the couple's inability to break a cycle of excessive consumption leaves Big Brother and Rinky destitute and isolated, estranged from both the family whose sacrifice their selective memory has forgotten and the "friends" for whose benefit they throw "splashing part[ies]" in spite of mounting debts (152). The vignette concludes with an internal monologue in which Rinky contemplates the horror of having gambled her future on a lifestyle she can no longer endure: "She did not dare think forward . . . There was nothing to which she could think back . . . Nothing . . . So—she could only cover—hide herself—away from life—beneath her front" (153). The consumption once adopted to broadcast the couple's prosperity now serves little purpose other than masking their financial and emotional bankruptcy.

If I have indulged in this brief detour from "On the Altar," it is to demonstrate how Bonner's critique of misplaced middle-class priorities is a sustained project rather than a passing fancy. Gran is blinded by the obsessive pursuit of self-preservation through materialism just as Rinky and Big Brother are. Although Gran's social rank—as confirmed by her majestic name, Mrs. Blanche Kingsman Breastwood—is indisputable, she nonetheless liquidates her investments to finance the rehabilitation of Beth's and, by extension, the family's image. In Gran's estimation the social price of welcoming the dark-skinned Jerry into the family is less palatable than the economic cost of removing the "stain" left by his marriage to her granddaughter: "With a talking program safely started, Gran outfitted Beth and herself, had an itemized list of each outfit printed in the society column of the colored newspaper and rounded up a few old cronies to see them off exactly one week after graduation" (232). After Gran's death Beth's mother assumes responsibility for preserving the family name. She parades Beth in a mourning ensemble that restyles the teenager's unhappiness as "subdued devilment rather than entirely dead lack of love of living on any level" (239–40). At Beth's second wedding, at which "[her mother's] good taste in dress" leads the congregation to misread the bride's despair as breathtaking beauty (243), external perfection again masks internal turmoil and, as with Rinky in "Front A", augurs emotional death.

A literary warning that offsets the photographic celebration of New Negro affluence, Beth's tragicomic nuptials warrant closer attention. The economic folly of Gran's personal public relations campaign pales before the human tragedy set in motion by her actions. Unlike the biblical story of Abraham and its parallel in *The Purple Flower,* in which Finest Blood is spared death, the elders of "On the Altar" are more than willing to sacrifice their progeny for the "greater good" of their collective reputation. Beth's stillborn child is but the first victim, as Beth herself is eventually sacrificed through marriage to Dr. Cliff Robertson, a mercenary, thrice-married bachelor handpicked by her mother:

> Everyone who was anyone or who thought he was anyone was bidden to the colored Episcopal church.
>
> Up the aisle came flower girls and ring-bearers.
>
> Close on their heels followed twelve bridesmaids and a matron and maid of honor.
>
> Parallel to them came the cream of the race, the hope of tomorrow—the ushers.
>
> Everyone was truly lovely to look at for there is no beauty or distinction to be found anywhere as truly exciting as in a group of these latter-day Negroes. (243)

Described in language reminiscent of the stage directions from Bonner's plays, this extravagant, funereal affair dooms Beth to an existence as "a woman whose poise forever was merely to be a frozen agony and a derisive sneer at living" (244). Her fate reflects the black bourgeoisie's replication of "the problems of subordination and oppression [of] the larger society in which [it] live[s]."[61] For the fundamental purpose of this wedding, as of Beth's "coming-out-round-the-country tour," is not the affirmation of individual will or desire or even the celebration of family. It is, on the contrary, the restoration and consolidation of communal order. The soundtrack of such an event, then, may very well be what Ann duCille deems the "bourgeois, wedding bell blues."[62] DuCille contends that in the novels of Bonner's contemporaries—namely Zora Neale Hurston, Nella Larsen, and Jessie Fauset—"marriage ceases to be celebrated . . . as the quintessential signifier of civil liberty and becomes instead the symbol of material achievement."[63] If one extends duCille's claim to include social triumph, the spectacular, excessive production of Beth's sanctioned wedding at once permits the dismissal of her relationship with Jerry as a youthful indiscretion and engineers her subsequent return to the folds of the fair-skinned black bourgeoisie. Appropriated by her grandmother, her mother, and, finally, her community, Beth's life is drained of all value save its currency in "the game of social advancement."[64]

If the group emerges victorious in "On the Altar," personal conviction prevails in "Hate Is Nothing," in which Lee eventually breaks free from her mother-in-law's repressive presence in order to reimagine herself and her community. Bonner locates the beginnings of Lee's psychological liberation in physical flight, for it is as an intrusive physical presence that Mrs. Sands makes her first entrance in the story and encroaches on Lee's personal space:

> "Hey, ole Injun!" [Lee] started to greet [Roger], but a door creaked open somewhere toward the back of the house.
> That meant her mother-in-law was listening.
> That meant her mother-in-law was standing somewhere between the kitchen and the inner hall.
> In the shadow.
> Listening. (158)

Cast by Bonner as the voice of black bourgeois social mores, Mrs. Sands converts Roger and Lee's spacious, well-appointed home into a familial Panopticon, with daughter- and mother-in-law drawing the lines of authority and supervision around the neutral husband-son through whom they are related.[65] Consequently, despite the expansive material comfort in which she lives, Lee finds herself, like the persona of "On Being Young—a Woman—and Colored," confined to a ghetto, in this case her tastefully decorated sitting room. Rather than sparking expressive liberation, this "room of [her] own" instead engenders what one might call New Negro claustrophobia.[66]

As in "On the Altar," Bonner disputes the assertion of skin color as either a mantle of moral distinction or marker of racial solidarity. Lee's intrusive mother-in-law considers the terms *pigmentocracy* and *aristocracy* synonymous, rendering pedigree in the absence of whiteness, or near-whiteness, moot: "[Her son Roger] had raised her hopes to great heights . . . and then he had dashed her sensibilities by bringing home a brown-skinned wife whose only claim to distinction was good breeding. . . . Not that Mrs. Sands conceded good breeding to Lee. To her the most necessary ingredient for anything that set a person apart was the earlier or later earmarks of bastardy" (164). Whereas Gran engineers an abortion against her granddaughter's will, Mrs. Sands fetishizes illegitimate, interracial offspring, and because neither woman is genuinely concerned about the welfare of her respective family member, the behavior of each calls the moral character of the African American elite into question. Although she does not protest as readily or as vociferously as Claire-Solange, Lee does recognize the incongruity of her mother-in-law's internalized racism. Mrs. Sands's disquieting remark praising family friends able to "trace their name back to the old aristocrat who owned their grandmother" is met by the silent protest of Lee's internal monologue:

> ("The man who owned their grandmother." Lee's mind echoed. "Aristocratic!") . . .
> ("The *man* who owned their grandmother! The Brewsters trace their *aristocratic* names to him. Now—! those *ordinary* Negroes!" Lee repeated this all to herself.) (170, 171)

Bonner's emphasis counters Mrs. Sands's simultaneous reification of slave owners and denigration of African Americans unable to trace kinship to them. Bonner suggests that in order for this hypocrisy to be revealed, in order for Lee to escape the tragedy of "On the Altar," the younger woman must learn to voice her opposition. She must, in other words, dispense with the propriety that facilitates the maintenance of black bourgeois fronts and openly challenge her mother-in-law.

Lee's reeducation begins not in a New Negro drawing room but in another of Bonner's alternative modernist landscapes. The character flees the confinement and representative African Americanness of her bourgeois enclave through a midnight journey to Tootsville, "the little colored settlement" on the outskirts of town: "Deep yellow streaks were showing to the east where the sun was coming up out of the river mists. The tar-paper and tin houses of Tootsville looked so inadequate and barren of any beauty that Lee began to wish that she had driven in another direction. . . . But what was the need of trying to leave ugliness? It had to be seen through—and lived through—or fought through— like her own troubles" (165). Bonner uses this semirural wasteland to exteriorize Lee's problems and enable the character to link the events unfolding before her to the world she has temporarily left behind. With a physical barrenness reminiscent of *The Purple Flower*, Tootsville becomes a site where Lee can situate her struggle with Mrs. Sands within the context of earlier tragedies: the premature death of her parents, the annulment of an unhappy first marriage, and the death of her former husband in a drunk-driving accident. Through this process of dislocation, reflection, and reorientation, Lee begins to escape the oppressive reach of Mrs. Sands and the black bourgeoisie she embodies.

The defining moment of Lee's excursion comes with another thematic return, here to that of marriage as calculated, often unholy wedlock. Drawn to help a harried mother whom she encounters in the road, Lee finds herself the unwitting facilitator of and witness to the marriage of the woman's teenage daughter, Annie Mae, and the boyfriend with whom she has been arrested on a morals charge. The ensuing jailhouse nuptials not only echo the unceremonious tenor of Lee's first wedding but also present another example of marriage as the strategic restoration of social order: it is unclear whether Annie Mae's mother is more concerned about her daughter's premarital sex or about the gossip that sex will generate. The conditions of the teenager's marriage situate her midway between the youthful romanticism that propelled Lee into her ill-advised first marriage and the tragicomic dimensions of the matrimonial spectacle in "On the Altar." Whatever the role of individual passion in the indiscretion for which Annie Mae is arrested, her mother's insistence propels the ceremony intended to sanction it. Bonner's depiction of all three cases—Beth's, Lee's, and Annie Mae's—evokes "a profoundly political, feminist urge to rewrite [the] patriarchal strictures" of the Victorian ideals of marriage and true womanhood.[67] However much marriage as social contract may bolster caste, class, or race, the benefits of such arrangements to Bonner's characters, particularly the women, are often debatable.

In this regard Lee's struggle with Mrs. Sands is not simply a matter of daughter against mother-in-law but also one of individual will against communal orthodoxy. Although Lee suppresses the impulse to stop Annie Mae's wedding, the experience provides her with a greater awareness of her place—and agency—within the cycle of women sacrificed to and circumscribed by notions of duty, honor, and propriety. When Mrs. Sands loans her daughter-in-law's heirloom china to the "aristocratic" Brewsters, the post-Tootsville Lee is at last able to dispute her mother-in-law's specious front of exceptionality and contingent claims of community: "There are some things in your son's house— (which happens to be my house too)—that do not belong to your son! That tea set was mine! You had no right to touch *one thing* in here without asking me!" (174). In reclaiming the tea set, a sign of bourgeois mores as well as of personal history, Lee performs the double move of asserting her position in the class that Mrs. Sands polices and reclaiming her identity as an independent being who is more than her husband's appendage. Lee's rejection of her mother-in-law's invasive presence reinforces her rejection of the older woman's exclusionary vision of community. Breaking the literal and figurative silence enveloping other Bonner protagonists, Lee finally demands a self-defined existence free from the psychological and spatial restrictions set by others. She refuses to inhabit any "Black Ghetto," be it a nicely decorated refuge within her own home or a socially stifling atmosphere within her community.

It is important to note that Bonner uses Lee's transformation to assess the possibilities as well as the problems of the social milieu from which the character flees. Upon returning home, Lee views her surroundings with a fresh perspective and, for the first time in her ongoing battle with Mrs. Sands, reconsiders her husband's position within their contentious household: " 'Why—*he* has seen how hatefully highhanded his mother can be—before this!' Shot swiftly through Lee's mind" (175). In positioning Lee's spouse as a potential ally, Bonner reinforces her critique of the values represented by Mrs. Sands and destabilizes monolithic notions of the black bourgeoisie. In their united stand against the hypocrisy and snobbery of an older generation, Lee and her husband, like *The Purple Flower*'s Sweet and Finest Blood, suggest the promise of a younger, more progressive generation, one to which the self-aware persona of Bonner's "On Being Young—a Woman—and Colored" and "The Young Blood Hungers" might belong. Rather than depend on rigid nineteenth-century social dictates as Gran and Mrs. Sands do, these alternative modernist figures instead tap into early-twentieth-century currents of social change and self-determination.

Similarly, Bonner also avoids romanticizing the working-class setting that prompts Lee's reevaluation of her past. There are no rural (African) pastorals as one finds in Lacascade's *Claire-Solange.* On the contrary Bonner, presenting the Tootsville characters as mere mortals whose very real, very human failings force Lee to examine her own foibles, refuses to portray Annie Mae and her mother as the noble poor leading a conflicted bourgeois heroine to redemption. Tootsville seems strikingly familiar to Lee because the same preoccupation with representation that drives her from Mrs. Sands drives Annie Mae's mother to see her daughter married: "The reverend he gonna marry them two right in the lockup so when some of these nosey niggers says to me long about next week—'Seems like I heard somebody say your Annie Mae was in the lockup lass week!'—Then I can bust right back and say, 'You liable to hear 'bout anything child! Meet Annie Mae's husband!' Then they'll heish! See?" (166–67). This plan to circumvent neighborhood gossip leaves Lee just as uncomfortable as Mrs. Sands's adulation of the "aristocratic" Brewsters, but this familiar discomfort serves to dispel any notion that Lee's transformation turns on some automatic or essential racial solidarity. Annie Mae's present resonates with Lee's past not because of a shared biological essence but because of the similar circumstances under which the two women enter their respective first marriages. The problematization of wedlock and the restrictive morality that it reinforces, not a superficial interest in racial uplift, spurs Lee's investment in the events in Tootsville. Consequently, Lee's excursion ends not with her rescuing Annie Mae from the altar but with her returning home to confront her own problems. Only then can Lee articulate a critical voice for the first time and, in so doing, reconstitute her marriage as a communicative, mutually considerate partnership.

As "On the Altar" and "Hate Is Nothing" demonstrate, the "game of social advancement," or at least of social preservation, transcends class lines in Bonner's fiction. There is little to no room for idealized mothers or daughters of "the race." Both Gran and Ms. Smith (Annie Mae's mother) are willing to endure economic hardship in exchange for the protection of their families' reputations. Where Beth's traveling ensemble is selected to erase the memory of her mésalliance, Annie Mae's marriage is orchestrated to overshadow the stigma of her premarital indiscretion. In Gran's world the forum of choice is the press; in Ms. Smith's Tootsville it is the street. Frazier would attribute Gran's reliance on publicity to a need "to create a world of make-believe into which the black bourgeoisie can escape from its inferiority and inconsequence in American society," but Bonner attributes this need to Ms. Smith as well.[68] If Gran's caste seeks to escape "inferiority and inconsequence" in mainstream (read white) society, then one may very well argue that Ms. Smith's efforts are designed to counter the double invisibility of a black working class deemed inconsequential not only by the wider world but also by African American communities headed by the likes of Gran and Mrs. Sands. In effect, at the intersection of social and economic currency it is intraracial difference that joins Bonner's working- and middle- to upper-class characters as much as, if not more than, any fundamental racial similitude. If Bonner's nuanced exploration of these themes—mobility and confinement, community and contention, modernity and tradition—begins in the anonymous locales of works such as "On Being Young—a Woman—and Colored," *The Purple Flower,* and "On the Altar," it culminates in the richly detailed imagined Chicago community she calls Frye Street.

Multiethnic Space and/as Alternative Black Modernism

For subjects whose experiences of race, gender, and class are not found in representations of model modernity, Bonner's work proposes an alternative modernist cartography, one that (1) destabilizes Harlem's place as "the topographical center of African-American modernism"; and (2) replaces the "newly emergent 'race' or 'nation'" that Houston Baker reads in Locke's *New Negro* with a multiethnic space shaped by but not limited to the borders of the continental United States.[69] This space emerges in a series of short stories that Bonner wrote between 1926 and 1941 and used, I would argue, to shift the discussion of modernity and its discontents from the eastern seaboard, African American middle-class milieu of "On Being Young—a Woman—and Colored" to a fictional, multiethnic, working-class Chicago neighborhood named Frye Street.[70] At once singular and familiar Frye Street is a site where races, nationalities, and languages come together. As the narrator of the 1933 story "A Possible Triad on Black Notes" observes, "There is only one Frye Street. . . . All the World is there" (102).

Bonner foregrounds this cosmopolitan familiarity from the opening page of "Nothing New" (1926), the story in which she introduces Frye Street: "You have been down on Frye Street. You know how it runs from Grand Avenue and the L to a river; from freckle-faced tow heads to yellow Orientals; from broad Italy to broad Georgia, from hooked nose to square black noses. How it lisps in French, how it babbles in Italian, how it gurgles in German, how it drawls and crawls through Black Belt dialects. Frye Street flows nicely together" (69). Initially, Bonner's interpellation of the reader through direct-address narration reads as somewhat idealistic, if not essentialist: Italy and Georgia may be joined by the modifier *broad,* but a "hooked nose" is not to be confused with its "square black" counterparts. When considered alongside the other Frye Street stories, however, the passage draws attention for its depiction of a community that has, to return to Martinican theorist Édouard Glissant, "[fit] irruption dans la modernité" ("irrupt[ed] into modernity").[71] While fluid, unlike the various black enclaves of "On Being Young—a Woman—and Colored," "Hate Is Nothing," and "On the Altar," Frye Street is no less contentious. Instead, in a manner recalling Glissantian modernity, it is a site of struggle and love, communion and conflict.[72] Bonner populates this dynamic landscape with characters who embody the very contradictions that archetypal blackness often denies.

Although one might be tempted to trace Bonner's choice of setting solely to her 1930 move to Chicago with husband, William Occomy, the publication of "Nothing New" (1926) four years before the couple relocated suggests that other factors were also at play. There was much to recommend early-twentieth-century Chicago as an inviting if challenging canvas for the reconceptualization of American modernity in general and African American modernity in particular. "From newly created frontier in 1803 to world metropolis in 1890," explains Carla Cappetti, "Chicago traveled the route of other American cities at twice the speed."[73] The city was indelibly changed by the transition from a rural agrarian economy to an urban industrial one as well as by the influx of European immigrants and African American migrants, and, as the nineteenth century became the twentieth, Chicago "seems to have telescoped and grandly reproduced" the history of the United States.[74] Because of the national resonance of its particular experience, the city became a test site for new ways of understanding and mediating modern social relations. While comprehension was the primary concern of the early "urban theorists" who founded the Chicago school of sociology, intervention and reform were the chief pursuits of Jane Addams, who introduced the settlement movement (and its principles of collective living and social activism) to the United States with Hull-House.[75]

Chicago, then, provides a fruitful inspiration for Frye Street not simply because of its midwestern location, its status as "not-Harlem." Judith Musser observes that, in shifting from nonfiction and drama to fiction, Bonner trades the "symbolic images, subjective elements, and expressionism" of her earlier work for "realism."[76] In concert with the interests of academics and reformers alike, this realism became the means through which Bonner "respond[ed] to the need for an examination of the lives of characters who must cope with economic hardships, racial and gender discrimination, deterioration of family relationships, illnesses that are particular to urban life, new religious communities, and urban multi-ethnic neighborhoods."[77] As Chicago school sociologists "went searching for principles of association," so Bonner parses the ways in which the aforementioned social realities constitute and challenge Frye Street's existence, and, as Addams "develop[ed] an understanding of interdependent community that necessitate[d] multiplicity," so Bonner explores an understanding of African American lives in a context in which community in many ways depends upon difference—interethnic, interracial, and intraracial—rather than denying it.[78] If Alain Locke envisions Harlem as a nascent race capital, then Marita Bonner imagines Chicago as a veritable laboratory of urban modernity.

On Frye Street, where foreign and native, rural and urban, self and other, collide, the paradoxes that are sublimated in "On the Altar" and "Hate Is Nothing" take center stage. Instead of leaving Frye Street free from the strained or strategic solidarity used to demarcate the world of the black middle class, Bonner depicts a working-class community invested in preserving and imposing its own facades. Critic Carol Allen notes that in the Frye Street narratives the purpose of "public urban language, written and verbal," is to "forc[e] citizens to behave acceptably."[79] Thus, although the material resources that announce middle-class respectability are in scarce supply on Frye Street, many of its residents are no less invested in the spectacles of propriety used to buttress the black bourgeoisie. One might even argue that respectability plays a greater role in this less privileged environment because it is policed through physical proximity as well as public surveillance; those not safely covered by the mantle of morality are left to an otherwise precarious existence, one exposed to the scrutiny of neighborhood critics perched on front stoops or stationed by open windows. By tracing this instability through a series of outsider figures, Bonner plumbs the modernist alienation that drifts beneath Frye Street's surface fluidity.

Lucille, the single-parent protagonist of "There Were Three" (1933), disturbs the neighborhood's surface calm by exuding transgression.[80] She threatens racial boundaries by being visibly "white" and distinctively "black": "something in the curve of her bosom, in the swell of her hips, in the red fullness of her lips, made you know that underneath this creamy flesh and golden waviness, there lay a black man—a black woman" (102–3). It is not Lucille's racial indeterminacy alone that upsets her neighbors; unlike the Parisian white bourgeoisie in *Claire-Solange,* the residents of Frye Street are accustomed to "Negroes [who] manage to look like all men of every other race." Instead, concern arises because of the manner in which Lucille capitalizes upon her visual ambiguity: she lives as a black woman in her private life but as a white prostitute in her professional one. Her choice is at once a rejection of essentialized notions of race and a reversal, albeit temporarily, of the commodification of black women's sexuality by external forces. Lucille's neighbors may know her as a "sexually degenerate" black woman, a point to which I will return later, but the product that customers buy from the "violet-eyed dazzling blonde" is white feminine beauty (102).[81] This commodity enables Lucille to support her household, financing both her economic independence and her maternal pride.

Bonner escapes the limitations of casting Lucille as an exemplary anti-heroine by refraining from romanticizing either the character or her choices. In a provocative play on conjunctions and convention, Lucille is both Madonna and whore. In patriarchal deployments of the dichotomy, women's sexuality can only be measured against the extremes of sainthood and sin; measurement is an externally rather than self-determined affair, and there is no room for nuance between the two poles.[82] In "There Were Three," however, Lucille claims sole (reproductive) responsibility for her children while working as a prostitute to support them. When responding to son Robbie and daughter Little Lou's inquiries about their paternity, Lucille answers with the claim that they are "all" hers (103). Yet, whether her goal is to defy the biological facts of procreation or distract her children from their father's (or fathers') absence, the character is "far from a nurturing, selfless mother."[83] The ferocity of her love cannot reconcile the vivid contrast between her apartment's always opulent décor and its occasionally empty table: "Things were like that at number 12 Frye Street where they lived. There were silk sheets on the beds, there was silk underwear in abundance in the bureau drawers, there were toilet waters, perfumes and flashy clothes. But sometimes there was no dinner or no breakfast" (103). If they do not always include three square meals, the extremes inside number 12 Frye Street do successfully capture the multiple excesses of Lucille's persona. The character represents an all-encompassing, individually defined womanhood that, like many of Dorothy West's fictional women, counters "the idealized tradition" of nineteenth-century constructs such as the cult of true womanhood and its twentieth-century African American variation, New Negro womanhood.[84] Like the fabrics and fragrances spilling forth from the closets and corners of her apartment, like Lacascade's unidentifiable Claire-Solange, Lucille spills over the social categories designed to contain individuals and identities. She is black and white, mother and father, rich and poor.

Lucille's interstitial identities elicit a variety of reactions from her neighbors. Some find her conspicuous consumption offensive because it both highlights their more modest means and flaunts the nature of her profession:

"What kind of woman got to go to work dressed better than Sheba when she visited King Solomon and ridin' in a taxi?" Mrs. Lillie Brown who lived at number 14 often asked her husband.

The question was purely rhetorical. The women like Mrs. Brown who waddled wearily beneath a burden of too much of what was not needed in Life—and did not know how to escape it—had already settled the answer among them. (104)

With the citation of another biblical story, in this case that of the queen of Sheba's arrival in Jerusalem with a caravan of spices, gold, and gemstones, Bonner situates Mrs. Lillie Brown on the righteous side of the late-nineteenth, early-twentieth-century battle "between the morally unacceptable economies of sex for sale and [the] morally acceptable policing of black female sexuality."[85] The passage's narrative weight, however, rests less with Mrs. Brown's surveillance of Lucille's movements than with the element that escapes Mrs. Brown's purview: the possible link between her existence as a "respectable," married woman and Lucille's as a working single mother. Because, as Judith Musser argues, "Bonner's fiction presents . . . all too many examples of uneducated women who are unqualified for employment beyond the kitchens of white people or the basements of factories and office buildings," Mrs. Brown knows "what kind of woman" Lucille is because, given the limited economic opportunities afforded poor and working-class black women, it is unlikely that her neighbor's extravagant wardrobe was purchased with the wages of a domestic servant, factory worker, or cleaning woman.[86] What is more, marriage does not exempt "women like Mrs. Brown" from the disadvantageous social circumstances that Lucille's limited occupational choices bespeak; rather, these women bear such conditions as the "burden of too much of what was not needed in Life" (104). Yet, as the narration's repeated use of the prefix *Mrs.* indicates, the married women on Lucille's block, despite their awareness of poor black women's tenuous socioeconomic positions in the early-twentieth-century United States, nonetheless prefer to hide behind their presumed moral superiority. It is almost as if they can hear Elise Johnson McDougald's suggestion that "vulgarity [is] not peculiar to Negroes" but is "peculiar" to "the working-class woman."[87]

Interestingly, however, aside from Mrs. Brown's ire, Lucille's transgressive presence raises little else within Frye Street, a neighborhood that "runs from the safe solidity of honorable marriage to all of the amazing varieties of harlotry— from replicas of Old World living to the obscenities of latter decadence—from

Heaven to Hell" (102). In fact, Frye Street accommodates Lucille and her children—as a single-parent family headed by a prostitute, as an African American family with skin colors ranging from Robbie's "bronze brownness" to Lucille and Little Lou's "creamy" and "ivory tinted" complexions—whereas other contexts presumably cannot. As Mrs. Brown surveils Lucille, other, equally observant neighborhood residents eye Robbie and Little Lou "with a measuring, waiting, stalking look" (103). Threatening to turn the siblings into urban versions of Jean Toomer's Karintha, the young rural beauty "ripened too soon" by the attentions of lascivious adults, the women of Frye Street anticipate the maturation of sixteen-year-old Robbie, while neighborhood men flirt openly with fourteen-year-old Little Lou.[88] It is only outside of Frye Street that the subversion of social categories places Lucille's family in immediate danger. When Robbie unknowingly stumbles upon his mother at work, her white client kills the "little nigger" for his presumptuous familiarity with a "white" woman (107). "There Were Three" concludes with Robbie's body unclaimed at the city morgue, Lucille's excess safely contained within an exclusive asylum, and Little Lou's fate unspecified: "But—there were three you see. Sometimes I wonder which door opened for that third" (108). Rather than provide an answer for the question "which door," Bonner instead opts for another of her signature unresolved conclusions.

If the final sentence of "There Were Three" launches an implicit interrogation of "which race Little Lou will claim to be," the "Black Map" that Bonner charts across her Chicago narratives encourages one to examine the character's situation through the wider lens of cultural geography.[89] In the wake of her brother's physical death and her mother's social one, the door opening back onto Frye Street may very well be Little Lou's most promising choice. The circumstances of Robbie and Lucille's respective deaths are notable not because they transpire outside of the black community, but because they occur outside of Frye Street. The site of Robbie's fatal encounter can be reduced to a microcosm of "the white world" only if the reader forgets that Frye Street itself is not an exclusively African American space. Bonner does not represent the neighborhood as an idyllic urban haven, but she does position it as a site in which residents are able or willing, however conditionally, to disregard or dispense with rigid categories of race, gender, sexuality, and morality. They do so because their existence turns on the contestation that critics such as Hazel Carby have identified as instrumental to 1920s African American community development but which narratives such as "The New Negro" elide.[90] Frye Street may prove more accommodating for someone with Little Lou's history, then, because of its capacity to coalesce around struggle. In keeping with author Zora Neale Hurston's "brown bag" metaphor of identity, Frye Street's residents are "bag[s] of miscellany propped against a wall . . . in company with other bags," and their shared economic, social, and geographic marginalization enables the members of these otherwise disparate groups to congregate around neighbors or events as easily as they separate over more divisive issues.[91]

In the story "Nothing New" (1926), Bonner introduces another disorderly figure in the form of Denny Jackson. The son of African American migrants to Chicago, Denny is Lucille's fictional precursor and figurative brother. As a child he upsets his father by troubling gender norms:

> Reuben [Denny's father] watched him once sitting in his sun shaft. Watched him drape his slender little body along the floor and lift his eyes toward the sunlight. Even then they were eyes that drew deep and told deeper. With his oval clear brown face and his crinkled shining hair, Denny looked too—well as Reuben thought no boy should look. He spoke:
>
> "Why don't you run and wrestle and race with the other boys? You must be a girl. Boys play rough and fight!" (70)

The episode is a significant narrative touchstone because it introduces many of the themes—among them sexuality, gender, and violence—that assume greater importance as the story progresses. If Reuben's contempt for his son's delicate appearance and contemplative behavior is disturbing, Denny's sadistic reaction to this disapproval is even more so: in order to assuage his father's masculinist fears, he attacks the family cat. The response silences Reuben's complaints but also establishes an unsettling precedent for the limited outlets Denny will have for addressing future conflicts.

Race inflects the already thorny question of gender and comportment when integrated "Young Frye Street," on a picnic in a city park, encounters the segregation of greater Chicago. In an episode reminiscent of the 1919 death of Eugene Williams and the subsequent Chicago race riots, Denny's appearance in an unfamiliar section of the park angers a strange white boy.[92] Both Denny's goal and the stranger's response reveal "Nothing New" as a realist trial of symbols and themes that would later recur in the expressionist *Purple Flower*. Denny has promised to pick a "lovely, dusky, purple" flower for his playmate Margaret

(72), and the hostile stranger's admonition that Denny "stay off the white kids' side" foreshadows the White Devils' song to the Us's.[93] Because integration is a natural, easy part of Young Frye Street, the outsider's discriminatory impulse puzzles Denny, whose initial reaction is again a contemplative one. He is, however, also pushed to prove his masculinity once again, this time to answer the insult that he is a "sissy nigger" for "picking flowers" (71), and his desire to perform the role of the chivalrous male and grant his playmate's wish devolves into violence: "The boy caught up to [Denny] as he had almost reached the flower. They fell again.—He was going to get that flower. He was going to. Tear the white kid off. Tear the white hands off his throat. Tear the white kid off his arms. Tear the white kid's weight off his chest. He'd move him—" (72). After building interracial tension by repeatedly using the modifier *white*, Bonner defuses the intensity of the episode by following it with a display of buoyant, youthful unity. More concerned with neighborhood allegiances than racial ones, Young Frye Street celebrates Denny's triumph as a collective victory. Like the Us's in *The Purple Flower*, Denny and his neighbors "construct ... a sense of solidarity" against a common target and in pursuit of a common goal.[94] And, as Bonner indicates earlier with Denny's first assertion of masculinity and later with the Us's revolution, this emergent identity is born not out of essence but out of necessity and force.

Unlike its offspring, "Old Frye Street" unites in its disapproval of Denny. A variation on the judgmental neighborhood voices of "There Were Three," Old Frye Street openly admonishes boundary crossing. Forming an urban chorus, Old Frye Street reinforces Reuben's beliefs about what manhood, nascent or fully developed, should entail. When the now teenaged Denny expresses his desire to study art at the postsecondary level, his elders complain: "'Ain't no man got no business spendin' his life learnin' to paint' ... 'He should earn money!'... 'Let him marry a wife'" (73). Although critics have read this disapproval as an indication of immigrant Frye Street's "preconceptions of appropriate African American aspirations," I would argue that this skepticism depends more on the interplay of class and gender expectations.[95] Denny has already been presented as a figure whose behavior fails to conform to heteronormative ideals, and his artistic inclinations do little to dispel such impressions. As with the Old Blood's narrow understanding of religion, Old Frye Street has inflexible conceptions of masculinity and femininity, and it considers work, money, and marriage, not art, "acceptable" concerns for a young working-class man.

It is when Denny is convicted of murdering a white man that Old Frye Street's reactions hinge principally on race. Caught in an adult replay of his childhood confrontation in the park, Denny battles the white Allen Carter for the right to court another art school classmate, the "poised," "slenderly molded," and white Pauline Hammond (75). Bonner extends the metaphor from Denny and Pauline's first encounter, when he spills purple paint on her, to his murder trial, when the press describes Pauline as a "hypnotized frail flower" (76). Similarly, Denny finally "tear[s] the white kid off" by fatally choking Carter. The subsequent trial and execution grant the now unqualified "Frye Street" a brief moment of accord before it separates into dissenting camps:

> Frye Street agreed on one thing only. Bessie and Reuben had tried to raise Denny right.
> After that point, Frye Street unmixed itself. Flowed apart.
> Frye Street—black—was loud in its utterances. "Served Denny right for loving a white woman! Many white niggers as there is! . . ."
> White Frye Street held it was the school that had ruined Denny. Had not Frye Street—black and white—played together, worked together, shot crap together, fought together without killing? When a nigger got in school he got crazy. (76)

Although "Frye Street—black" and "White Frye Street" interpret Denny's fate differently, the tenor and rhetoric of their assessments are strikingly similar. Both groups castigate Denny for upsetting the balance of life on Frye Street, for reaching too high in his pursuit of things—the purple flower, higher education, a white woman's love—traditionally the province of middle-class, non-immigrant whiteness. As a result, when Young Frye Street's song of triumph is reprised by Old Frye Street, it is not the radical cry one might expect from the forerunner of *The Purple Flower;* it is, on the contrary, an intracommunity protest whose respective verses, each echoing the other's use of the epithet *nigger,* reflect the precariousness of Frye Street's collective identity.

While the Frye Street of "Nothing New" does not achieve the revolutionary unity articulated at the end of *The Purple Flower,* in her later stories Bonner shifts her focus to the ties that, though often unrecognized, bind the residents of Frye Street to one another more profoundly. Nowhere are these bonds more apparent than in the two stories featuring Frye Street's most retiring and, ironically, most prominent non–African American resident: German Jewish immigrant Esther Steinberg/Weinstein. In "Corner Store" (1933) the narrative introduces Esther and her husband, Anton, with the surname Steinberg and describes them as the proprietors of "Steinberg's Grocery-Market on Frye Street"; when the characters reappear in "A Sealed Pod" (1936), they have been renamed "Weinstein" and their business retitled "the Corner Store Grocery Market" (141).[96] From introduction to reprise Esther's voice performs a key role in the Frye Street chorus. Although marked by the character's Yiddish- and German-inflected English, it is a voice that, unbeknownst to Esther, transcends her particular immigrant experience to speak to the lives of her neighbors as well.

In "Corner Store," Esther resides on Frye Street but is not of it. Her physical existence is circumscribed by her family's grocery, where she moves between the counter in the front and the living space in the rear, and she longs for the ethnic enclave that the persona of "On Being Young—a Woman—and Colored" rejects. The formation of the Black Ghetto denounced by Bonner mirrors that of the shtetl, or Eastern European Jewish community, remembered by Esther in that both resulted from "the enforced [settlement] of a people unwelcome in their natal land."[97] Yet Esther remembers her Old World ghetto as a place with "a nice Schule and . . . nice Jewish neighbors," an area that, if no more expansive than Frye Street, was at least culturally familiar (115). Her New World neighborhood seems to promise only estrangement and, rather than being a land of opportunity, instead becomes a menacing site where Esther is relegated to "working from dawn until midnight," "made an old woman . . . at thirty-nine," and forced to witness the disintegration of her family through Anton's infidelity and her daughter Meta's insubordination (114). Although the teenager's rebellion is partly behavioral (she dresses provocatively, talks back to her mother, and stays out late), Bonner suggests that this filial revolt is also emotional and cultural. Meta recalls their former neighborhood as "a place where dirty German kids wait around to throw mud on you when you go out" and revels in the freedom from constant harassment afforded by her family's move to the United States (115). She feels no attachment to the traditions and landscapes of European Jewry that her mother laments. Through these competing mother-daughter perspectives Bonner complicates the opposition of tradition and modernity, European nostalgia and American dream.

Somewhat paradoxically, it is this very alienation that links Esther to her new community. Her despair and subsequent internal retreat resonate with the plight of Frye Street's other immigrant and migrant women. Just as the promises of New World relocation elude Esther, so many of the promises of

New Negrohood elude her African American neighbors, including Mollie, the southern migrant in the story "Reap It as You Sow It" (1940–41). For Mollie the harsh realities of urban life soon cloud the idealized vision of the transformed America that Locke imagines for his New Negro. Marked as an outsider by her "clean country nice" looks (269), Mollie watches in disbelief as, under Frye Street's ever-observant eyes, the "tawny, easy-limbed" girl next door seduces her husband (268). Thought to be her last hope, pregnancy does not stabilize her marriage so much as further confine Mollie to her apartment at number 14 Frye Street, where, in her husband's absence, she dies in childbirth. In much the same way that Esther's kitchen becomes a prison "with its barren huddled air . . . closing her in" (118), so Mollie's domestic space becomes an inhospitable ward of distress, desertion, and eventually death.

In "A Sealed Pod," the story in which Esther briefly reappears, Bonner reinforces the ties between the character and her neighbors. If the title refers to the explicit divisions—ethnicity, race, and religion—that separate residents despite their close quarters, the plot unveils the implicit connections that hold Frye Street together. When the "blonde," "fair," and African American Viollette Davis is murdered, the circumstances of her death speak to the plight of children, mothers, and wives across the community. Like Robbie and Little Lou in "There Were Three," eighteen-year-old Viollette is left to her own devices because her mother works at night. Unlike Robbie and Little Lou, Viollette is no longer an innocent and passes her evenings with "a varied assortment of men of every race" (142). Until her daughter's death, Ma Davis is as oblivious to Viollette's actions as Esther is to Meta's extradomestic activities. Even when she learns the truth, Ma accuses the wrong paramour, and the African American Dave Jones is arrested, convicted, and executed for the murder instead of Joe Tamona, Viollette's Italian American favorite and the actual killer. This tragic chain of events leads to the disappearance of Dave's wife and children, and Frye Street comes together in the wake of the multiple tragedies.

This unity initially seems no more substantial than that joining the "blind, blind mice" of Bonner's black bourgeoisie. Indeed, Viollette's funeral is a sight to behold in league with Beth's spectacular wedding in "On the Altar": "No matter what Frye Street might think of all the incidents that led up to it, the funeral itself—with curly plumes saluting the winds from the four corners of the white automobile hearse, two rusty black open carriages entirely buried under flowers, two perspiring doctors fanning Ma, applying smelling salts to Ma's nose—a long line of automobiles filled with crepe-hung Negroes—the funeral itself, stirred the mind, uprooted the feelings, shook the soul." What the ostentatious display obscures, however, the narration exposes. From the "perspiring doctors" to the presiding minister, the men at the funeral share Ma's grief because "they had [all] known Viollette's sweetness and tenderness" (140). Bonner turns her attention to the wives of these men, and back to Esther, when rumors circulate that Susie Jones has drowned her children and herself in the river: "'Maybe she did once!' sighed Esther Weinstein, wife of Anton, who kept the Corner Store Grocery Market. She drew a breath that sobbed and touched her breast. 'Maybe she did, that Susie, throw herself in the river! So much trouble! Such a heaviness! Such a stone here!' and she smote her breast many times" (141–42). To readers who recall Esther from "Corner Store" as well as for those encountering her for the first time, these exclamations resound as more than the idle observations of a curious neighbor. Esther's words are weighted with the pain caused by her own husband's infidelity, for once again Bonner has cast Anton as an adulterer, in this case identifying him as one of Viollette's many lovers. There may be "no sense of communal responsibility" on Frye Street, as Judith Musser contends, but there is a palpable, almost painful sense of communal suffering.[98]

Although Bonner leaves any actual meeting between Esther and Susie or Esther and Mollie unrealized, the collective, contested space of Frye Street renders such literal encounters unnecessary. These stories circulate in the public forum that is Frye Street and, as demonstrated by Esther's grief at Susie's fate, resonate with the lives of other residents. As with the multiple perspectives heard in "Nothing New," the voices of these women speak, if not to each other, then to a larger, intertextual conversation carried on across Bonner's fiction. Through these interrelated narratives Bonner revisits the designation "Your People," initially interrogated in "On Being Young—a Woman—and Colored." In that remarkable first essay Bonner asks the reader to consider the limitations of facile assumptions of identity and community. She launches the difficult yet important discussion of how the "education and refinement deemed requisite for . . . New Negro[es]" may "alienate them from the masses whose lot they are supposed to improve."[99] This engagement continues in Bonner's fiction, in which her reach expands to examine how the difficulty and injustice faced by the socially marginal(ized) may connect them in spite of apparent differences in race, gender, class, generation, ethnicity, geography, religion, and nationality. By exploring the limits of exemplarity alongside the potential of diversity, Bonner joins predecessor Suzanne Lacascade and contemporaries Suzanne

Césaire and Dorothy West in challenging readers to contemplate the possibilities of communities formed and dissolved through the multiple boundaries with which societies structure and segregate themselves.

In her 1928 essay "How It Feels to Be Colored Me," Zora Neale Hurston declares her intention to represent herself as she wishes: "At certain times, I have no race. I am me. When I set my hat at a certain angle and saunter down Seventh Avenue, Harlem City, feeling as snooty as the lions in front of the Forty-Second Street Library, for instance. So far as my feelings are concerned, Peggy Hopkins Joyce on the Boule Mich with her gorgeous raiment, stately carriage, knees knocking together in a most aristocratic manner, has nothing on me. The cosmic Zora emerges. I belong to no race nor time. I am the eternal feminine with its string of beads."[100] With style, humor, and confidence, Hurston's speaker, presumably the author herself, contests the primacy of racial community as an essential or reliable means of identification. Her personal declaration of independence leads her to uncover a new, unconstrained identity, one that transcends the limits of race, class, and, with its reference to "the eternal feminine" (155), time itself. Hurston presents this individualism not as a fixed point of reference but, rather, as a mobile, shifting construct through which she expands her conception of self and community locally, on Harlem's Seventh Avenue; globally, on Paris's famed Boulevard St. Michel; and universally, through "the cosmic Zora" (154–55). Critical, like Bonner, of the models of African American identity prominent during the Harlem Renaissance, Hurston refutes, confirms, and confounds prevailing perceptions of African Americans within the space of a few pages. A night at a cabaret finds Hurston responding to an inner, primal chord: "I dance wildly inside myself; I yell within, I whoop; I shake my assegai above my head . . . I am in the jungle and living in the jungle way" (154). A mere page before this exuberant declaration, Hurston deploys the rhetoric of genteel literature with the assertion that she is "not tragically colored" but more circumstantially so (153). Ultimately, Hurston deems the body, the physical manifestation of "race," "merely the container that holds a multiplicity of elements out of which an individual identity is constituted."[101]

Given the predominance of masculinist perspectives in past and contemporary readings of African diasporic modernisms, one may be tempted to read the figure depicted here as Locke's New Negro or Gilroy's traveling subject, albeit recast with Hurston's characteristic iconoclasm and insouciance. But the more fruitful comparison results from reading Hurston's "colored me" as a whimsical counterpart to the speaker of Bonner's landmark first essay, "On Being Young—a Woman—and Colored." Foreshadowing Hurston, Bonner draws on similarly complicated conceptions of identity to uncover the many variables that shape her life as well as the lives of her characters. "On Being Young" concludes with the persona contemplating an escape from the confined social, physical, and intellectual spaces that often accompany the representation of community. Although Bonner emphasizes the importance of patience in planning this escape, she does not advocate passivity. As in most of Bonner's work, it is contestation that proves more productive and more rewarding than compliance. Thus, Bonner portrays the persona as poised to move from spectator to participant, from New Negro woman to modern citizen: "And then you can, when Time is ripe, swoop to your feet—at your full height—at a single gesture" (8). Propelled by personal initiative, this ascent gives the speaker the power and independence needed to realize her full potential. Although Marita Bonner eventually receded from public life for reasons similar to Suzanne Césaire's own retreat, it is telling that she did so only after producing a body of work that interrogates the construction, assumption, and imposition of social boundaries through an extended critique of the politics of archetypal blackness. It is fitting, too, that the definitive collection of Bonner's work bears the name *Frye Street*, for it is in this imagined space, this alternative modernist landscape, that Bonner most vividly evokes the contours and conflicts through which individuals and communities emerge, coalesce, and evolve.

Suzanne Césaire
Courtesy Bibliothèque Doucet

3 Surrealist Dreams, Martinican Realities

The Negritude of Suzanne Césaire

La poésie martiniquaise sera cannibale ou ne sera pas.

Martinican poetry shall be cannibal or shall not be.
—SUZANNE CÉSAIRE, "Misère d'une poésie" (1942)

The year after Marita Bonner receded from public life, Martinican writer Suzanne Césaire (1915–66) took up the cause of cultural revolution in the 1942 essay "Misère d'une poésie." Césaire diagnosed her island's literary health as critically anemic, and her prescription for its recovery was nothing short of "literary cannibalism," "a rewriting and magical appropriation of the literature of the other."[1] As in Bonner's evocation of the Shakespearean underpinnings of American stereotypes, Césaire's statement conjures neither the deceased Sycorax nor the cherished Miranda; it alludes, instead, to the disgruntled

Caliban, the slave whose name is an anagram of *cannibal* and whose speech rebels against the gift of (colonial) education: "You taught me language, and my profit on't / Is, I know how to curse" (1.2.361–64).[2] With Caliban as with Césaire, there is no equivocation; the challenge facing each is the strategic reception and transformation of imposed modes of expression. Unlike Suzanne Lacascade, who gradually refashions the "literature of the other" through the narrative detours of the novel, Suzanne Césaire uses the brevity of the essay to deconstruct forcefully European cultural dominance and articulate her vision of Caribbean Negritude. She imagines an alternative modernist landscape in which the open confrontation of cannibalism replaces the subversion of post-exoticism and the negotiation of race and modernity occurs not in Africa or Europe but in the Caribbean.

But who, one may ask, was this other Suzanne? Although much less well known than husband Aimé, Césaire is no longer the historical enigma that she once was and that Lacascade continues to be.[3] Suzanne Roussi Césaire was a native of Rivière Salée, Martinique, a graduate of the French university system, a teacher at Martinique's prestigious Lycée Schoelcher, an accomplished essayist, and a playwright. Césaire cofounded the journal *Tropiques* (1941–45) with her husband and their lycée colleague and fellow Martinican René Ménil, and in seven essays published during the review's four-year run she developed "un militantisme poétique" ("poetic militancy") that reads as a fitting, if more sophisticated, successor to Lacascade's acerbic fiction.[4] Imbued with the revolutionary zeal of modernism in general and surrealism in particular, Césaire charged readers to reconceptualize the Caribbean's relationship to its immediate American present as well as to its ancestral African past. After *Tropiques* Césaire wrote *Aurore de la liberté* (1952), a dramatic adaptation of Lafcadio Hearn's prose piece "Youma: The Story of a West-Indian Slave."[5] The Martinican theatrical troupe Scènes et Culture produced *Aurore* in Fort-de-France in 1952, but the play, Césaire's only known postwar work, was never published and is no longer extant. The challenge of reading Suzanne Césaire comes not from a dearth of biographical information, then, but from a scarcity of creative output.

Her relatively small (but no less instructive) body of writing is but one way in which Césaire marks a turning point in this study. In "Order, Disorder, Freedom, and the West Indian Writer," Maryse Condé identifies Césaire's declaration "la poésie martiniquaise sera cannibale" ("Martinican poetry shall be cannibal") as the lone woman's voice in the litany of commands issued to describe and dictate the state of Francophone Caribbean literature.[6] As Condé's statement reveals, Césaire's work fits squarely within canonical narratives of Negritude, although she (Césaire) did not experience the prominence or longevity of her male peers. If, as Léon-Gontran Damas asserted in his "Holy Trinity" of Francophone modernism, Senghor is Negritude's Father, Aimé Césaire its Son, and Damas its Holy Spirit, why should one not posit their contemporary and collaborator Suzanne Césaire as the movement's Madonna: its singular feminine presence, related to the Trinity but unquestionably separate?[7] Contrary to Lacascade's chronological and conceptual position outside of traditional literary historical boundaries, Césaire wrote alongside the Negritude poets, and her essays draw from the same intellectual sources (namely Frobenian anthropology and French surrealism) as Damas, Senghor, and the other Césaire. And, in a departure from the work of Lacascade, Bonner, and Dorothy West, gender does not figure as prominently in the writings of Suzanne Césaire. Caribbean women may have inspired one of the most memorable images in Césaire's final essay, to which I will return later in the chapter, but they are not the central figures there or elsewhere in Césaire's *Tropiques* contributions. Given these differences, Césaire seems atypical even among the extraordinary women with whom she is being compared.

What joins Césaire to her fellow black women modernists is the manner in which her writing ultimately privileges local specificity over diasporic representation. As in Bonner's shift from abstract nonfiction and drama to realist fiction, Césaire progresses from writing highly theoretical discussions of leading European thinkers to examining the relevance of those thinkers to the material realities of wartime Martinique. Her engagement of Negritude's intellectual roots, like Lacascade's appropriation of exoticism, is often more prescient of the Caribbean literary movements to come—including Antillanité (Caribbeanness) and Créolité (Creoleness)—than reminiscent of her own cultural and historical moment.[8] For, in using surrealism to dream of new possibilities for Martinican cultural expression, Césaire is concerned with the place of Martinique "*in* the world," rather than its ability, or that of any single element of its multiracial society, to "[stand] for the world."[9] Anthropologist and writer Ina Césaire explains the scope of her mother's work, its reach from Negritude to Créolité: "Ses écritures sont singulièrements modernes . . . contemporaines . . . un peu prophétiques" ("Her writings are singularly modern . . . contemporary . . . a bit prophetic").[10] I conclude with this observation from Suzanne Césaire's daughter in order to offer a somewhat different but not unrelated observation about the role of material realities in the lives of Césaire and her peers. According to Ina Césaire, her mother considered teaching her true vocation and writing a secondary calling; like Bonner, Césaire stopped publishing because of the demands of balancing teaching full-time with managing a family.[11] Both women not only wrote about disjunctions between everyday life (local specificity) and model modernity (diasporic representation); they also, because of their experiences as mothers, lived them.

Ironically, *Tropiques* as physical artifact threatens to obscure the nuances of Suzanne Césaire's career as much as reveal them. While her essays position Césaire as a thought-provoking and vocal intellectual, two other *Tropiques* texts, one an essay, the other a photograph, effectively perform the conceptual move to which I alluded earlier: the positing of Césaire as Negritude icon. The essay in question is André Breton's "Un grand poète noir" (1944), written when the French surrealist visited Martinique in 1941.[12] Forced into exile by World War II, Breton stopped in Martinique on his way to the United States and met both Suzanne and Aimé Césaire while on the island. Remembering his first encounters with the couple, Breton tempers his exoticization of Aimé Césaire with an appreciation of the Martinican poet's intellect:

Je retrouve ma première réaction tout élémentaire à le découvrir d'un noir si pur, d'autant plus masqué à première vue qu'il sourit. Par lui, je le sais déjà, je le vois et tout va me le confirmer par la suite, c'est la cuve humaine portée à son point de plus grand bouillonnement, où les connaissances, ici encore de l'ordre le plus élevé, interfèrent avec les dons magiques.

I can recall my quite basic initial reaction at finding him such a pure black in colour, masked all the more at first sight by his smile. In him (I already know, and see what everything will subsequently confirm) is mankind's crucible at its greatest point of fermentation, where knowledge, here moreover of the highest order, interferes with magical powers. (121/192–93)

Breton strikes no such balance in his depiction of Suzanne Césaire, whom he remembers as "belle comme la flamme du punch" ("lovely as the fire of a rum punch"; 121).[13] Whereas Aimé Césaire is Breton's Caribbean double, Suzanne Césaire is the Frenchman's "tropical Nadja," another womanly embodiment of surrealism.[14] The contrast is all the more striking for its placement just prior to Breton's meditation on the poetry of Martinique's botanic profusion. Blurring the lines between nonfiction and fiction, the almost seamless movement from "Suzanne Césaire, belle comme la flamme du punch" to "les remous d'une végétation forcenée" ("the tide of frantic vegetation"; 121/193) recalls the island-identified *doudou* of the exoticist literature with which Suzanne Lacascade contended some twenty years earlier. In Breton's juxtaposition Suzanne Césaire becomes, to paraphrase critic Nicole Aas-Rouxparis, presence and absence: she is present as exotic object yet absent as intellectual figure.[15]

This paradoxical simultaneity is both mitigated and reinforced by the other *Tropiques* text that positions Césaire as icon: the frontispiece of the 1978 Jean-Michel Place reprint of the journal. Appearing in both volumes of the two-volume set, the enigmatic photograph depicts an eighteen-year-old Césaire just before her departure for university study in France.[16] The reprint also includes, of course, the essays Césaire contributed to the journal, but, as Anne Stavney observes of the iconographic representation of African American women in the early twentieth century, the placement of Césaire's portrait in front of the text suggests a break between her image and the words that follow.[17] Césaire is not the sole *Tropiques* contributor to be represented visually, yet her male colleagues are all featured in photographs that follow the text. In the first volume individual pictures of Aimé Césaire and René Ménil appear inside the back cover; in the second a shot of André Breton with Cuban artist Wifredo Lam appears at the rear of the volume. However slight or unintended, this distinction means that, while readers always encounter the pictures of Suzanne Césaire's male collaborators with knowledge of their intellectual work, no such connection is encouraged between the image of the young Césaire and the work that would prompt A. James Arnold to deem her "a full partner in the definition of negritude."[18] Thus, although Césaire's portrait is literally appended to the contents of *Tropiques,* in the absence of contextualization the photograph is as enigmatic as Breton's narrative image.

In addition to confronting the suggestion of Césaire as Negritude-surrealist muse, critics have also had to contend with the same gendering of archetypal modernism that has resulted in the relative obscurity of Suzanne Lacascade and Marita Bonner. As one of the three ideological pillars of Francophone Caribbean literature, Negritude has had a "sharply gendered identity" that "is not only masculine but masculinist" and which has "pushe[d] literature written by women into the background."[19] This privileging of male authors establishes the very literary order criticized by Condé and manifested in the work of otherwise astute critics such as Richard Burton, who attributes his use of exclusively masculine pronouns in an analysis of Martinican intellectual culture to geography: that is, the predominance of Guadeloupean women writers in Francophone Caribbean literature precludes the inclusion of women in the essay's discussion of Martinican writers.[20] Perhaps because of the shared intellectual well from which Suzanne Césaire and the Negritude poets drew, early revisions of Negritude that sought to correct such misperceptions often privilege the work of women writers who preceded or succeeded the movement's apex.[21] In her essay "Negritude in the Feminine Mode," for example, Clarisse Zimra redefines the movement by extending its boundaries to include women's writing published during and after the 1950s.[22] While undoubtedly instructive, in particular to my own efforts to extend the consideration of Negritude back to Lacascade's 1924 novel, Zimra's model cannot chronologically accommodate Césaire's work in *Tropiques* during the early 1940s. Nor can that work, given Césaire's limited discussion of the impact of racial identification and valorization on Caribbean women, necessarily be categorized as Negritude in the "feminine" mode.

The late twentieth and early twenty-first centuries have brought several approaches to the critical conundrum posed by the work and legacy of Suzanne Césaire.[23] Within Francophone studies Condé has incorporated Césaire into her ongoing project of giving voice to lesser-known women writers, and T. Denean Sharpley-Whiting features Césaire prominently in her 2002 book *Negritude Women,* in which she focuses on Césaire's use of surrealism to articulate a distinctly Martinican poetics.[24] Surrealist studies, confronting that movement's own imbalance between participation and representation, has likewise seen growing interest in Césaire's work. Renée Riese Hubert notes that "the woman artist" of male-female surrealist collaborations "was rarely in the limelight and sometimes had to play the part of silent partner."[25] Volumes such as Michael Richardson's *Refusal of the Shadow: Surrealism and the Caribbean* (1996), Penelope Rosemont's *Surrealist Women: An International Anthology* (1998), and Georgina Colvile's *Scandaleusement d'elles: trente-quatre femmes surréalistes* (1999) have attempted to broaden the study of surrealism by reconsidering the contributions of Césaire and other women.[26] Finally, in a stimulating convergence of diasporic and surrealist studies, Robin D. G. Kelley praises Césaire as "one of surrealism's most original theorists" in his cultural history *Freedom Dreams: The Black Radical Imagination* (2002).[27] Despite their diverse disciplinary and linguistic origins, these studies share in the critical undertaking of exposing the sizable gulf between Césaire's iconic identity as the face of Negritude and her intellectual work as writer and critic.

Here I will use these and other readings to examine Suzanne Césaire's use of Negritude's primary sources, her explanation of surrealism's particular relevance to World War II–era Martinique, and her contribution to the larger intellectual project to which this study is devoted: the articulation of modern African diasporic identities outside of the language of archetypal blackness. Does Césaire successfully posit either Frobenian theory or surrealism as effective tools for Caribbean cultural liberation? If so, how does she bridge the apparent gap between surrealist dreams born in Europe and Martinican realities lived in the Americas? What are the implications of Césaire's Frobenian-inspired deployment and depiction of Africa? Where does she fall between the poles suggested by Suzanne Lascascade's exuberant *âme africaine* ("African soul") and Martinican writer Jane Nardal's more measured *Afro-Latinité*, a proposed merger of "Frenchness/Latin-ness and African-ness/blackness"?[28] Finally, how did Césaire's role as one of the few (known) women intellectuals working directly with the more celebrated male writers of Negritude influence, if at all, her limited discussion of gender? Such limits notwithstanding, there are implicit intersections between the gender dynamics explicitly questioned by Lascascade, Bonner, and West and Césaire's interrogation of racial and cultural politics. Posing these questions allows one to appreciate Césaire's poetic militancy not only within a Negritude reconceived as a dynamic, polyvocal movement but also within the broader discursive field of comparative black modernism. My inquiries will begin, as does Césaire's Negritude, with the promise and problems of articulating and deploying "Africa" in the mid-twentieth-century Caribbean.

Negritude: From Africa to Martinique by Way of Europe

Making the case for situating Suzanne Lacascade amid the black modernist currents that produced Negritude requires a reconsideration of the movement's periodization as well as its genealogy, whereas the task of distinguishing Suzanne Césaire from canonical narratives of Negritude in particular and Francophone Caribbean literary history in general is more a matter of nuanced than expansive interpretive gestures.[29] As in African American literary studies, one important conceptual block is the perception that women writers have been reluctant to produce theoretical texts.[30] A. James Arnold's observation that the masculinist implications of Caribbean literary theory have produced a marked "aversion to theorizing their project" among women writers is an insightful one, but it implicitly elides figures such as Césaire, whose work not only performs the intellectual tasks commonly associated with "high" theory (such as citing recognized European thinkers) but also suggests the alternative theoretical endeavors (such as addressing work to a nonacademic audience) cited by U.S.-based black feminist critics.[31] Another potential obstacle is the aforementioned prevalence of masculinist imagery in canonical Negritude. Arguing that Negritude poetry depicts "the return to Africa [as] one which is effected through an imagined relationship with a variously exoticized and eroticized black woman-mother-lover," Sam Haigh charges such representations with rendering Negritude alienating and inaccessible to women.[32] After all, what would women find "revitalizing" in a process of cultural discovery (in Africa) and restoration (in the Caribbean) that depicts them largely as passive objects, noble but vacant receptacles, or absent or antagonistic figures?[33] A text such as Jean-Paul Sartre's "Orphée noir" (1948) more than proves Haigh's point. Sartre claims that blackness is "à tour la femelle de la Nature et son mâle" ("both Nature's female and its male"), but this gender-inclusive gesture is overshadowed by moments such as his comparison of the white and black peasantry:

> Les techniques ont contaminé le paysan blanc, mais le noir reste le grand mâle de la terre, le sperme du monde. Son existence c'est la grande patience végétale; son travail, c'est la répétition d'année en année du coït sacré . . . Labourer, planter, manger, c'est faire l'amour avec la nature.

> Techniques have contaminated the white peasant, but the black peasant remains the great male of the earth, the world's sperm. His existence is great vegetal patience; his work is the yearly repetition of holy coïtus . . . To till, to plant, to eat, is to make love with nature.[34]

Although Sartre's aim is to explore the respective roots of folk poetry, his result is the reinscription of Negritude as a masculine project. Thus, as the New Negro archetype proved less than representative of the range of African American identities in the modernist era, so the images and experiences of heroic Negritude, with its privileging of male identity and sexuality, seemed similarly unable to uphold their claims to communal or diasporic representation.

As the work of Suzanne Lacascade and Marita Bonner demonstrates, however, androcentric articulations of blackness did not prevent women writers from entering into modernist discussions of racial identity. In his epic poem *Cahier d'un retour au pays natal (Notebook of a Return to My Native Land)*, Aimé Césaire famously poses the question "Qui et quels sommes nous?" ("Who and what are we?") as a referendum on the cultural makeup of diasporic subjects, and here I would like to posit his inquiry as an equal opportunity to interrogate the role of gender in the constitution of diasporic identities.[35] Lacascade's novel *Claire-Solange* proposes that the "nous" of early-twentieth-century reclamations of blackness can include an outspoken *mulâtresse* who embraces Africa as the site of proud, identifiable maternal ancestors. Can Caribbean racial identities not also be examined by a woman theorist who deploys notions of a primeval African past without idealizing it as fundamentally feminine or gendering it as overwhelmingly masculine? Such is the proposition that Césaire's essays present as she draws upon both European theory and African culture in analyzing life in early-twentieth-century Martinique.

Like the Negritude poets, Césaire's evocations of Africa were profoundly influenced by *Kulturgeschichte Afrikas (Histoire de la civilisation africaine;* 1933/ 1936), the landmark study by German ethnographer Leo Frobenius.[36] The interwar Francophone journal *La Revue du Monde Noir/Review of the Black World* reprinted the Frobenius essay "Le spiritisme dans l'intérieur de l'Afrique" ("Spiritualism in Central Africa"), and in prefatory remarks writer Pierre Desroches-Laroche credited Frobenius's work with "fai[re] surgir l'Afrique de la nuit des temps, avec ses traditions et sa culture passées" ("conjur[ing] up Africa from the night of ages, with its past traditions and culture").[37] The intellectual impact of Frobenius was far-reaching, also including white writers such as "Ezra Pound, W. B. Yeats, and André Malraux."[38] Although much of the art produced by European and Anglo-American modernists posited Africa and Africans as objects rather than subjects, the scholarship that inspired them challenged such representations. In a manner reminiscent of late-twentieth-century work by Édouard Glissant, Hortense Spillers, and Michel-Rolph Trouillot, Frobenius placed historiography under the same critical scrutiny previously applied to African diasporic cultures and questioned the categories through which historical narratives were structured. He asserted that, as with the notion of progress, the concept of "African barbarism" was a product of the European imagination: "L'idée du 'Nègre barbare' est une invention européenne qui a, par contre-coup, dominé l'Europe jusqu'au début de ce siècle" ("the notion of the 'barbarian Black' is a European invention which has, as a consequence, dominated Europe up to the beginning of this century").[39] The problem of defining "civilization" was not one of African lack but one of European excess in perpetuating exclusionary, overdetermined models of recording and evaluating cultural development.

Critics have adopted Suzanne Césaire's writing as a blueprint for Negritude's rehabilitation of Africa through a Frobenian lens, with Georges Ngal going so far as to declare, "On ne saurait trouver meilleur commentaire de Frobenius" ("One could not find a better commentary on Frobenius").[40] The principal task of Césaire's essay "Léo Frobénius et le problème des civilisations" ("Leo Frobenius and the Problem of Civilizations"; 1941), which appeared in the inaugural issue of *Tropiques,* is the elucidation of Frobenius's concept of the Paideuma.[41] A generative force described as "[la] créatrice des civilisations" ("[the] creator of civilizations"; 28/82), the Paideuma manifests itself in two opposing forms: "la civilisation éthiopienne" ("the Ethiopian civilization"), inhabited by the mystical "homme-plante" ("plant-man"), and "la civilisation hamitique" ("the Hamitic civilization"), dominated by the aggressive "homme-animal" ("animal-man"; 30–31/84). In Césaire's reading of Frobenius these civilizations have been preserved in their entirety on the African continent, whereas only traces of them linger in Asia, America, and Europe. This preservation has alternately been interpreted as a unity of civilizations and, in a less commonly held view, as evidence of "balanced proportions."[42] The latter is the position of Janheinz Jahn, who offers the aforementioned phrase as a more precise translation of the German phrase *Ebenmässigkeit der Bildung* and contends that Frobenius praised Africans for cultural balance, not a unified civilization. In any case both interpretations transform Africa from a site denigrated for its civilizational poverty into one celebrated for its wealth of civilizations.

As indicated by Frobenius's assertion of the fallacy of the "Nègre barbare" stereotype, the theory of the Paideuma also reverses Eurocentric models of history. Césaire explains that the Ethiopian and Hamitic civilizations coexist in Africa and that the introverted contemplation of the former's "plant-man" is neither inferior nor superior to the extroverted initiative of the latter's "animal-man" (30/84). Nor does one civilization precede the other chronologically. Césaire attributes this nonhierarchical formulation to Frobenius's synchronic view of cultural development:

> Frobénius a découvert en effet, que l'idée du progrès continu, chère au 19ᵉ siècle, qui montrait la civilisation progressant sur une ligne unique depuis la barbarie primitive jusqu'à la haute culture moderne, était une idée fausse. L'humanité ne possède pas une volonté de perfectionnement. Encore une fois, elle ne se crée pas une civilisation, qu'elle veut de plus en plus haute. Elle va, au contraire, mue par la Païdeuma interne, dans des directions multiples, de "saisissements" en "saisissements."

> In fact Frobenius has discovered that the idea of continual progress, dear to the nineteenth century, which showed civilization as progressing in a single line from primitive barbarism to the highest modern culture, is a false idea. Humanity does not possess a will to perfection. To emphasize this, it does not create civilization and then try to take it even higher. On the contrary, it develops in multiple directions transformed by the inner Paideuma, from one sudden "shock" to another. (32–33/85)

This reappraisal of the African continent encouraged Negritude poets to replace negative discursive constructs with ones that were positive, heroic, and, as previously argued, predominantly masculinist. Consequently, the multiple versions of Negritude in the "founding fathers" mode tend to offer visions of blackness that are more exclusive than expansive, a situation that some critics argue reinforces rather than reverses Eurocentric models. In one such reading J. Michael Dash faults Negritude for proposing a false universality that in fact elides "specific historical, social, and economic factors."[43]

While Suzanne Césaire uses "the masculinist language of the time" (she does not, for example, distinguish a plant- or animal-woman from the plant- and animal-man), the conclusion of "Léo Frobénius et les problèmes des civilisations" exhibits the historical specificity that Dash finds lacking in other Negritude texts.[44] Césaire moves to the concrete realm in evaluating the importance of Frobenian theory to modern thought. No longer a purely abstract concept, Frobenius's assertion of the multidirectional nature of human development becomes a means to address the social upheavals of Césaire's time. Her tone is initially speculative, pondering whether the early twentieth century is not witnessing a new civilizational "saisissement" ("shock"), but certainty replaces speculation as the essay comes to a close: "Cette véritable folie de puissance et de domination qui bouleverse l'humanité dans des catastrophes aussi terribles que les guerres de 1914 et de 1939 est le symptôme d'un nouveau jaillissement de la Païdeuma" ("This veritable mania for power and domination, which has brought humanity to catastrophes as terrible as the wars of 1914 and 1939, is symptomatic of a fresh surging of the Paideuma"; 35/87). Césaire concludes by challenging readers to use "la fécondité" ("the fertility") of Frobenian philosophy and the experiences of world war "oser se connaitre [sic] soi-même, ... oser s'avouer ce qu'on est, ... oser se demander ce qu'on veut être" ("to dare to know ourselves, to dare to admit our nature, to dare to consider what we want to be"; 87/36).

In the 1942 essay "Malaise d'une civilisation" ("A Civilization's Discontent"), Césaire's discussion of humanity and global citizenship is replaced by a conversation about Martinicans and Martinican identity.[45] Whereas "Léo Frobénius" serves as a primer of Frobenian thought, "Malaise" emphasizes application over explication, the Caribbean present over the African past. This "return" from continent to island avoids the trap of false universality because the appeal that Africa holds for Césaire is not mythic, as is the case with much of Negritude poetry, but ethnographic. In spite of its potential for encouraging essentialism, a topic to which I will return shortly, Césaire deploys the Frobenian revision of Africa in order to assess the particular malaise afflicting twentieth-century Martinique. Early in the essay the distinction between the Ethiopian *homme-plante* and the Hamitic *homme-animal* provides the framework through which Césaire will examine cultural differences between Martinicans, who are explicitly identified with the plant-man, and Europeans, implicitly identified with the animal-man (45/97). As Kara Rabbitt observes, Césaire soon "moves beyond this ethnographic description ... to analyze the ways in which repression and exclusion by colonizers have created in the colonized a desire to assimilate to the Western model."[46] Césaire traces the perceived social value of assimilation back to the French colonial legislation of difference, including laws such as those prohibiting blacks and people of color from practicing medicine (30 April 1764), working as notaries (9 May 1765), wearing the same clothes as whites (9 February 1779), and working outside of agriculture without a permit (3 January 1788). Césaire asserts that, although such decrees made whiteness—and the privileges associated with it—desirable, this desire is fundamentally impossible because of the opposing "natures" of the Martinican and the European (46–47/98). To return to the Caliban-Prospero dialectic momentarily, the malaise of Martinican civilization renders the Martinican-as-Caliban monstrous not because he is Other but because he rejects his identity in seizing upon the unrealistic goal of becoming Prospero.

The subsequent development of Césaire's argument reflects the work of both atypical women and archetypal men. Césaire advances from the colonial era to the present by contending that assimilation, from its use by enslaved and emancipated Martinicans to declare their humanity to its embrace by their descendants to improve their socioeconomic prospects, has become culturally oppressive. Rather than nurture Martinican literature, *"l'assimilation du nègre au blanc"* (*"the assimilation of the black to the white";* 46/98) only stifles creative growth. One hears in these words echoes of Suzanne Lacascade's protagonist Claire-Solange, who refuses to assimilate or fold herself into models of identity (such as whiteness or Spanishness) deemed more acceptable by her metropolitan French family. The character's critique of artificiality through phrases such as *pseudo-cousin,* her initial designation for Jacques Danzel, foreshadows Césaire's conclusion that "l'effort d'adaptation à un style étranger exigé du Martiniquais [a créé] un état de pseudo-civilisation que l'on peut qualifier *d'anormal, de tératique"* ("the effort of adaptation to an alien way of life that is required of the Martiniquan [has created] a state of pseudo-civilization that can be described as *abnormal* and *teratical* [monstrous]"; 48/99).[47] Césaire's antiassimilationist rhetoric also recalls the writing of pre-Negritude intellectual Étienne Léro, who used images of deformity and abnormality to cast Martinique's bourgeoisie of color as "une mulâtraille parasite vendue à des blancs dégénérés" ("a parasitic hybrid caste in the pocket of degenerate whites").[48] The almost effortless reach of Césaire's work from Lacascade to Léro, from subversive popular fiction to highly politicized nonfiction, underscores the importance of rethinking women writers' relationships vis-à-vis "theory" as well as Negritude.

It is equally important to acknowledge that, however critically productive, Césaire's mapping of Frobenian theory onto the Martinican sociocultural landscape encounters the same discursive problems as other articulations of Negritude: the essence that binds the Negritude hero to his African motherland seems to reappear in "Malaise d'une civilisation" as the apparently unbroken link between the Ethiopian plant-man and his Martinican descendant. The Césairean contention that the Martinican "pousse, qu'il vit en plante" ("grows, that he lives like a plant"; 45/97) is not only evocative of the "grande patience végétale" ("great vegetal patience") celebrated in Sartre's "Orphée noir" but also reminiscent of the essentialist elements of Senghor's work: "Senghor has consistently maintained the position that negritude is biologically grounded and that the specifically negroid characteristics, as he sees them, of emotion and intuitive reason, art and poetry, image and myth . . . , are both essential to black cultures and predetermined."[49] Much like Condé's critique of novelist Lacascade's engagement of exoticist tropes, Marie-Agnès Sourieau reads Césaire's adaptation of Frobenius as a rehearsal of colonial stereotypes: "Il est troublant de constater que cette conception [du Martiniquais comme l'homme-plante], que Suzanne Césaire adopte sans réserve, reprend ici l'idée stéréotypée de la passivité du colonisé nécessairement conquis par l'Occidental/Hamite" ("It is troubling to discover that this concept [of the Martinican as plant-man], which Suzanne Césaire wholly adopts, revives the stereotype of the passive colonial duly conquered by the Western/Hamite").[50] Furthermore, Césaire apparently continues to slip between cultural validation (the recognition and celebration of one's heritage) and cultural essentialism (the reduction of that heritage to innate, immutable qualities) by using terms such as *nature* and *essence* to characterize the African sources of Martinican culture. In her analysis, the Martinican is unable to avoid the pitfalls of assimilation because he is alienated from "sa véritable nature" ("his true nature"; 48/99), not because he is unaware of African influences on Caribbean cultural forms.

Césaire's writing escapes this essentialism and emerges as "modern" and "prophetic" when it acknowledges the multiple cultural sources that complicate reducing the Martinican to the Frobenian *homme-plante*. Through this acknowledgment Césaire no longer echoes colonial stereotypes and instead anticipates the post-Negritude, postcolonial work of theorist Édouard Glissant. Like Césaire before him, Glissant attributes Martinique's stunted cultural development to the colonial period, when "la pulsion mimétique" ("the mimetic impulse") encouraged the privileging of metropolitan French culture at the expense of local Martinican culture.[51] He asserts that the most effective means of combating this impulse is not to propose a new cultural essence to replace its European predecessor but, rather, to explore "les processus multipliés [et] les vecteurs enchevêtrés" ("the multiple processes [and] the confusion of indicators"; 14/1) that constitute Caribbean identity. Consequently, whereas Negritude articulates identity as a state of being, Glissant's *Antillanité* theorizes identity as an ongoing process, a continual becoming. Similarly, although Césaire idealizes the Martinican embrace of "l'attitude éthiopienne" ("the Ethiopian attitude"; 48/99), she also posits rethinking Africa-in-the-Caribbean as but one step in mobilizing the collective cultural forces of 1940s Martinique:

> Il ne s'agit point d'un retour en arrière, de la résurrection d'un passé africain que nous avons appris à connaître et à respecter. Il s'agit, au contraire, d'une mobilisation de toutes les forces vives mêlées sur cette terre où la race est le résultat du brassage le plus continu; il s'agit de prendre conscience du formidable amas d'énergies diverses que avons jusqu'ici enfermées en nous-mêmes.

> It is not at all a matter of a return to the past, of the resurrection of an African past that we have learned to understand and respect. It is a matter, on the contrary, of the mobilization of all the combined vital forces on this land where race is the result of a continual mingling. It is a matter of becoming conscious of the formidable mass of different energies that until now have been trapped within us. (48/100)

Césaire grounds her appreciation of Martinique's "continual mingling" in specific references to the island's history; there can be no return to a pure African past because the sociohistorical forces at play in Martinique render cultural purity as unattainable as seamless assimilation. Moving beyond Léro's caustic denigration of cultural mixing, Aimé Césaire's epic celebration of Africa, and Lacascade's simultaneous underplay of *métissage* and elevation of Africa, Suzanne Césaire ultimately proposes a Caribbean identity that, like the *Antillanité* to come, is shaped by dynamic, composite cultures ("[le] formidable amas d'énergies") rather than fixed to static, essential states of being.

I have purposefully truncated this last quote from "Malaise d'une civilisation" in order to highlight the resonances between Césaire and Glissant and to conclude this reading, and this section, with another, atypical connection that spans languages as well as decades. First, the conclusion to Césaire's essay bears citing in its entirety:

> Nous devons maintenant les [nos énergies diverses] employer dans leur plénitude, sans déviation et sans falsification. Tant pis pour ceux qui nous croient des rêveurs.

La plus troublante réalité est nôtre.
Nous agirons.
Cette terre, la nôtre, ne peut être que ce que nous voulons qu'elle soit.

We must now use them [our different energies] in their plenitude, without deviation or falsification. Too bad for those who consider us dreamers.

The most disturbing reality is ours.
We will act.
This earth, our earth, can only be what we want it to be.

(49/100)

Echoing Marita Bonner's play *The Purple Flower*, Césaire declares that consciousness alone, though instrumental, will not ensure the successful embrace and expression of self-determined Caribbean identities. Just as Bonner does not end her play with the consolidation of the Us's resources in Old Man's iron pot, so Césaire does not close her essay with the recognition of "the formidable mass" of cultures within Martinican society. Instead, offering a surrealist answer to Bonner's expressionist query ("Is it time?"), Césaire issues her readers yet another call to action and implies that their success is only as limited as their imaginations.[52] Those observers careless enough to mistake Martinicans for mere dreamers do so at their own peril, for they (the observers) fail to grasp the scope of surrealism, a poetics in which imagination leads to empowerment and the dream is but a step on the path to revolution.

"Un Militantisme Poétique"

Césaire and other Negritude writers used Frobenian theory to diagnose diasporic struggles with identity and alienation; they turned to surrealism, however, to conceive the social changes need to fight such struggles. Michael Richardson states that Césaire viewed the avant-garde, early-twentieth-century movement as more than mere artistic expression and found in it "a means of reflection," "a critical foundation from which to explore [her] own cultural context."[53] And, hypothetically, surrealism does reject the same limits of the Western intellectual tradition targeted by Negritude writers. In *Manifeste du surréalisme* (*Manifesto of Surrealism*; 1924), André Breton maintains that one possibility of *la surréalité* ("surreality") is "la résolution future de ces deux états, en apparence si contradictoires, que sont le rêve et la réalité" ("the future resolution of these two states, dream and reality, which are seemingly so contradictory"). It would seem to follow that this intellectual revolution could also engender the reconciliation of those elements of Caribbean culture—African, European, and indigenous—posited as mutually exclusive by colonial discourse.[54] Boundaries originally thought to be fixed would be reconceived as fluid, and this fluidity, in turn, would facilitate the renegotiation of relationships between formerly opposed states and identities.

Yet, as was the case with Frobenian ethnography, questions of essentialism and (self-) exoticization also underlie modernist Caribbean intellectuals' affiliation with surrealism. To adopt surrealism is seemingly to adopt, uncritically, its ideas regarding art as a means of reliving childhood and recapturing one's "fundamental" relationship with nature.[55] Given surrealism's development amid Europe's primitivist vogue, such ideas always already conjure images of the simple primitive who enjoys a "natural" existence from which the "civilized" (or industrialized) European subject has been estranged.[56] J. Michael Dash attributes the exoticizing tendencies of surrealism to the "romance of otherness" through which European intellectuals courted, cultivated, and portrayed New World contacts.[57] He argues further that "surrealism could not always conceal its roots as an essentially European disaffection" and that attempts to manage this alienation often resulted in representations of the Americas "in terms of nature and [an] entrancing otherness" such as that found in André Breton's depiction of Suzanne Césaire.[58] Thus, although surrealism functions as a critique of hegemony, it "(as a socially determined form) cannot remain exempt" from hegemonic influences.[59]

One year before the publication of "Malaise d'une civilisation," Césaire formally took up the surrealist challenge in the October 1941 essay "André Breton, poète . . . ."[60] Like Césaire's study of Léo Frobénius, "André Breton" functions as a simultaneous celebration of its subject and explication of his work. In an immediate sense the essay is literally a companion piece to three Breton poems that follow in the same issue of *Tropiques:* "La mort rose" and "Vigilance," both from Breton's 1932 collection *Le revolver à cheveux blancs,* and "Pour Madame," a brief prose poem dedicated to Césaire.[61] In a more far-reaching sense "André Breton" illustrates that Césaire is as much independent intellectual as she is devoted disciple. With its fond remembrance of "les petites chabines rieuses" ("little laughing *chabines*") and "les essences natives" ("the native essences"), "Pour Madame" evokes Breton's "Un grand poète noir" and the problematic undercurrents of surrealism just discussed.[62] In her essay, however, Césaire chooses to focus on surrealism's revolutionary potential. Locating the movement's viability in its embrace of artistic and intellectual disorder, she describes surrealism as "la plus extraordinaire révolution qui soit, puisqu'aussi bien elle engage plus que l'art, notre vie tout entière" ("the most extraordinary revolution that there is, seeing that it engages, more than art, our life in its entirety"; 36). Accordingly, Césaire celebrates Breton's emphasis on the uncertain, the unstable, and the unknown: surrealism provides access to the world "au delà de la conscience" ("beyond consciousness"; 31), to the "liberté de faire et de défaire" ("freedom to make and unmake"; 34), and to the "abîmes de l'inconscient . . . du merveilleux" ("depths of the unconscious . . . of the marvelous"; 35).

It is out of this liberating disorder that Césaire begins to formulate her *militantisme poétique* (poetic militancy), the deployment of surrealism as a tool for Caribbean cultural revitalization. Prior to his fascination with local Martinican color, Breton, like Frobenius, challenged historical narratives and Eurocentric rationality and called for surrealism to break with temporal and logical conventions. This rupture opened up the free expression of thought, a belief Breton elaborated in the *Second manifeste du surréalisme* (*Second Manifesto of Surrealism;* 1930):

Si nous ne trouvons pas assez de mots pour flétrir la bassesse de la pensée occidentale, si nous ne craignons pas d'entrer en insurrection contre la logique, si nous ne jurerions pas qu'un acte qu'on accomplit en rêve a moins de sens qu'un acte qu'on accomplit éveillé, si nous ne sommes même pas sûrs qu'on n'en finira pas *avec le temps,* vieille farce sinistre, train perpétuellement déraillant, pulsation folle, inextricable amas de bêtes crevantes et crevées, comment veut-on que nous manifestions quelque tendresse, que même nous usions de tolérance à l'égard d'un appareil de conservation sociale, quel qu'il soit?

If we cannot find words enough to stigmatize the baseness of Western thought, if we are not afraid to take up arms against logic, if we refuse to swear that something we do in dreams is less meaningful than something we do in a state of waking, if we are not even sure that we will not do *away with time,* that sinister old farce, that train constantly jumping off the track, mad pulsation, inextricable conglomeration of breaking and broken beasts, how do you expect us to show any tenderness, even to be tolerant, toward an apparatus of social conservation, of whatever sort it may be?[63]

When Césaire describes the relevance of surrealism to her Caribbean audience, she seizes upon the conceptual reversals advocated by Breton: "Qui doutera la réalité de ces visions? Déjà s'opèrent en nous, hors de nous les métamorphoses les plus inattendues, les plus bouleversantes. Les objets et les êtres n'ont plus de forme limitée, le temps n'existe plus" ("Who will doubt the reality of these visions? Already there is taking place within us, outside of us, the most unexpected, most staggering metamorphoses. Objects and beings no longer have a circumscribed form, time no longer exists"; 32). In the absence of "time," surrealists argue, concepts such as "history" or "progress" can no be longer used to deem colonized peoples inferior. Furthermore, if discursive forms are subject to change and dissolution, one can replace the false construct of the "Nègre barbare" with a more accurate representation of Caribbean identity. Finally, "culture" itself becomes open to interpretation when traditional qualitative boundaries have been rejected, and Caribbean individuals are no longer objects to be defined by others but subjects free to define themselves.

The radical social change at the center of Césaire's poetic militancy begins, but does not end, with language. In "Misère d'une poésie" (1942) Césaire joins her contemporaries in identifying poetry as the ideal genre for linguistic and intellectual revolution. "True poetry," however, is not to be confused with the exoticist lyric:

Allons, la vraie poésie est ailleurs. Loin des rimes, des complaintes, des alizés, des perroquets. Bambous, nous décrétons la mort de la littérature doudou. Et zut à l'hibiscus, à la frangipane, aux bougainvilliers.
La poésie martiniquaise sera cannibale ou ne sera pas.

Surely, true poetry is elsewhere. Far from the rhymes, the laments, the trade winds, the parrots. Sunstruck, we decree the death of *doudou* literature. And the hibiscus, the jasmine tree, the bougainvillea be damned.
Martinican poetry will be cannibal or will not be.[64]

Paving the way for Aimé Césaire's 1945 assertion that poetic knowledge frees the individual to explore himself and his world, Suzanne Césaire's decree exhorts Martinicans to use poetry to challenge rather than reproduce misconceptions about the Caribbean.[65] Césaire's demand for the revolution of linguistic and social paradigms also yields another convergence with and divergence from Sartre's "Orphée noir." When discussing the transformative potential of Negritude, the French philosopher observes that "le but profond de la poésie française me paraît avoir été [l']auto-destruction du langage" ("the final goal of French poetry seems to me to have been [the] auto-destruction of language"; xx/25). Yet for Césaire it is not the destruction of language that revitalizes literature but, rather, the ingestion of language, its conversion into an idiom figuratively and literally internal to the Caribbean poet. Whereas Shakespeare's Caliban speaks his adopted language to "curse" his captivity, Césaire's cannibal poet, seemingly picking up where Lacascade's Claire-Solange reached the limits of the novel form, uses French to contest exoticist reductions of the Caribbean.

One may venture to identify the rebellious poet with Césaire herself because she practices "literary cannibalism" as she promotes it.[66] As the passage quoted here, and others, illustrates, her writing manages the difficult process of incorporating and modifying French cultural influences in language that is both eloquent and incisive. In keeping with the tenets of surrealism, Césaire here reconciles two elements—poetry and cannibalism—traditionally viewed as polar opposites, the former as a pinnacle of civilization and the latter as a nadir of savagery, and a formerly derogatory term *(cannibal)* becomes an affirmation, a sign of integrity and survival. Sourieau evaluates this accomplishment as follows: "Suzanne Césaire reprend la terminologie européenne—forgée à partir d'un nom non-européen—qui lie peuple et pratique, et peut ainsi affirmer que toute production littéraire authentiquement martiniquaise est 'caraïbe' ou, de façon synonyme, 'cannibale'" ("Suzanne Césaire takes up European terminology—coined from a non-European name—that links people and practice, and can thus affirm that all authentically Martinican literary production is 'Carib,' or, synonymously, 'cannibal'").[67] While Africa was associated with cannibalism and other forms of "savagery" just as readily as the Caribbean, I am particularly drawn to Sourieau's reading because it highlights Césaire's growing interest in negotiating Martinican identities through an American lens. Her linguistic anthropophagism and its attendant opposition of industrialized Europe and the pre-Columbian Caribbean is relevant not simply to Martinique but to the entire Americas, where the disruption and decimation of indigenous cultures has been experienced region-wide. It evinces, to return to the work of J. Michael Dash, how surrealism's "radical interrogation of narrative discursive positions . . . arguably created a new hemispheric subjectivity in the imaginary of [Caribbean] writers."[68]

Surrealism also proved instrumental to Césaire and her peers because of its capacity to reach beyond the literary realm. In the politically charged "1943: Le Surréalisme et nous" ("1943: Surrealism and Us"), published in October of that year, Césaire argues that not only is surrealism alive and well; it has assumed even greater vitality and relevance in the face of world war: "Lorsque Breton créa le surréalisme la tâche la plus urgente était de libérer l'esprit des entraves de l'absurde logique et de la prétendue raison. Mais, lorsqu'en 1943 la liberté elle-même se trouve menacée dans le monde entier, le surréalisme qui n'a pas cessé un seul instant de se tenir au service de la plus grande emancipation de l'homme, se veut résumé tout entier en ce seul mot magique: liberté" ("When Breton created surrealism, the most urgent task was to liberate the mind from the shackles of absurd logic and so-called reason. But in 1943, when liberty itself is threatened throughout the world, surrealism (which has not ceased for a moment to remain resolutely in the service of the greatest emancipation of mankind) can be summed up with a single magic word: liberty").[69] The sociopolitical changes brought about by World War II provide a catalyst for the assertion of Caribbean autonomy in a manner reminiscent of World War I's impact on the relationship between Lacascade's fictional characters. Whereas the 1914–18 war enables Claire-Solange to exercise agency as an equal partner to Jacques Danzel, Lilyan Kesteloot notes that during World War II surrealist language allowed the *Tropiques* collaborators to articulate "[leur] révolte et [leur] espoir sans trop craindre les représailles" ("their revolt and hopes without too much fear of reprisal").[70] When the Vichy regime did register the extent of the journal's subversion, its May 1943 order to cease publication only fanned the flames of revolt.[71] *Tropiques'* editorial team published a defiant rebuttal of the government's charges, and, when the journal resumed publication later that year, this defiance carried through to Césaire's "1943: Le Surréalisme et nous":

Pas un moment au cours de ces dures années de la domination de Vichy, l'image de la liberté ne s'est ternie totalement ici et c'est au surréalisme que nous le devons. Nous sommes heureux d'avoir maintenu cette image aux yeux mêmes de ceux qui croyaient l'avoir rayée à tout jamais.

Not for a moment during the hard years of Vichy domination did the image of freedom completely fade here, and surrealism was responsible for that. We are glad to have maintained this image of freedom under the noses of those who believed they had erased it forever. (18/126)

No longer merely a concern of the classroom or the salon, surrealism had become a viable tool for political protest.

Césaire devotes the remainder of the essay to detailing why surrealism need not also become a vehicle for self-exoticization. In her view "surrealism is," as Kara Rabbitt observes, "neither a doctrine nor a gift, but a weapon and a choice—to be actively selected and taken up by . . . Caribbean writers."[72] Césaire's admiration depends on the movement's adaptability, its continual evolution, as much as it does on the durability of its call for liberty, and she does not consider the two elements mutually exclusive. The *Tropiques* editorial team's insistence on its right to free expression is not unlike Césaire's charge to her fellow Martinicans to alter surrealism as they see fit: "Et maintenant, un retour sur nous-mêmes. On sait où nous en sommes ici, à la Martinique" ("And now a return to ourselves. We know our situation here in Martinique"; 17/126). With the aid of a surrealism chosen because it "currently offers . . . the best chance of success" ("offre actuellement les chances les plus sûres de succès" (126/17), self-knowledge and self-empowerment will lead Martinicans to dismantle colonial discourse and the social divisions it upholds. Ideally, these changes will, in turn, result in a society in which black mulattas (à la Claire-Solange) and cannibal poetry are no longer oxymoronic because "[notre surréalisme] s'agira de transcender les sordides antinomies actuelles: blancs-noirs, européens-africains, civilisés-sauvages" ("those sordid contemporary antinomies of black/white, European/African, civilized/savage will be transcended"; 126/18). The essay concludes with the figurative yet unequivocal declaration of Martinicans as subjects in the modern, industrial world: "Purifiées à la flamme bleue des soudures autogènes les niaiseries coloniales. Retrouvée notre valeur de métal, notre tranchant d'acier, nos communions insolites" ("Colonial stupidity will be purified in the blue welding flame. Our value as metal, our cutting edge of steel, our amazing communions will be rediscovered"; 18/126). Militantly poetic and unapologetically surrealist, Césaire's vision is one not of a Martinique rooted in a distant African past but of an island anchored in and energized by the composite cultures of the modern Caribbean.

Césaire's project of reclaiming Martinican voices and identities culminates in the 1945 essay "Le grand camouflage" ("The Great Camouflage"), a text endowed with particular importance because of its position within the careers of both its journal and author. It is the final article in the final issue of *Tropiques* and Césaire's last published work. After the pointed critique of exoticist literature in her earlier essays, the lyricism of "Le grand camouflage" is stunning.[73] Césaire opens with an extended vignette tracing a hurricane's path across the Caribbean. Along the storm's route the reader encounters signs of the archipelago's visual beauty: water moves against the shore in "belles lames vertes" ("beautiful green blades"), and clouds form a "frais collier" ("fresh garland") in the sky.[74] Césaire even recounts her first epiphanic experience of the Caribbean's natural splendor: "De [Mont Pelée], je sus, très jeune, que la Martinique était sensuelle, lovée, étendue, détendue dans la Caraïbe, et je pensai aux autres îles si belles" ("From [Mount Pelée] I realized, as a very young girl, that, as it lay in the Caribbean Sea, Martinique was sensual, coiled, spread out and relaxed, and I thought of the other islands, equally beautiful"; 268/157). What begins as a seemingly uncritical meditation on nature soon becomes a prelude to a sociopolitical examination of contemporary Martinique. Césaire contrasts her idyllic childhood memory with a more critical adult perspective, one characterized by a clarity through which she is able to grasp "sur le très beau visage antillais, ses tourments intérieurs" ("the torment within the Caribbean's most beautiful face"; 269/157). It is this older, more discerning perspective that "[dismisses] Breton's primitivist fantasies" in favor of an extended discussion of the realities of Martinican life.[75]

As the essay shifts from perceptions of Martinique as apolitical exotic paradise to those of the island as politicized Caribbean site, the reader is again moved to appreciate the manner in which Césaire's Negritude both corresponds to and departs from the work of her male contemporaries. Through her opening metaphor Césaire revives the pan-American vision of "Misère d'une poésie"; the hurricane sweeping through the archipelago is felt from Puerto Rico to Haiti and on to Florida. With the exception of Puerto Rico, the itinerary evokes that traced by Aimé Césaire in *Cahier d'un retour au pays natal*:

> Et mon île non-clôture, sa claire audace debout à l'arrière de cette polynésie, devant elle, la Guadeloupe fendue en deux de sa raie dorsale et de même misère que nous, Haïti où la négritude se mit debout pour la première fois et dit qu'elle croyait à son humanité et la petite comique queue de la Floride où un nègre s'achève la strangulation, et l'Afrique gigantesquement chenillant jusqu'au pied hispanique de l'Europe, sa nudité où la mort fauche à larges andains.

> And my nonfence island, its brave audacity standing at the stern of this Polynesia, before it, Guadeloupe, split in two down its dorsal line and equal in poverty to us, Haiti where negritude rose for the first time and stated that it believed in its humanity and the funny little tail of Florida where the strangulation of a nigger is being completed, and Africa gigantically caterpillaring up to the Hispanic foot of Europe its nakedness where Death scythes widely. (46/47)

Yet, whereas Aimé Césaire's *Cahier* situates the Caribbean within a global geography, Suzanne Césaire's "Le grand camouflage" maintains its focus on the Caribbean as it pushes readers to comprehend the primarily regional context within which Martinicans relate to themselves as individuals and to each other as fellow islanders. Later in the essay Césaire's storm appears in an explicitly political guise as "la colonisation, houleuse, dévoreuse de blancs" ("the stormy, devouring colonization by the whites"; 272/160), a deployment that prefigures the organizing metaphor of novelist-critic Antonio Benítez-Rojo's *Repeating Island*. Benítez-Rojo uses chaos theory to locate in the Caribbean "processes, dynamics, and rhythms that show themselves within the marginal, the regional, the incoherent, the heterogeneous, or, if you like, the unpredictable."[76] In the words of Maryse Condé, Suzanne Césaire's goal is to demonstrate how this chaos and complexity are lost on "an outsider [when] he is overwhelmed and blinded by [the] beauty" of Martinique.[77]

What Césaire proceeds to do is offer a narrative guide to understanding the "processes, dynamics, and rhythms"—among them racial distinctions—at play in 1940s Martinique. Her approach differs from those of her peers in its studied celebration of "the notion of diversity."[78] Where Suzanne Lacascade, Aimé Césaire, and Léon-Gontran Damas prioritize the Caribbean's African heritage, Suzanne Césaire recognizes its other cultural sources as politically charged but no less constitutive of the region's identities. Indeed, her "femmes aux quatre races et aux douzaines de sang" ("women of four races and dozens of blood ties"; 268/157) read as literary predecessors of the multiracial, multiethnic *Créolistes* who proclaim themselves "ni Européens, ni Africains, ni Asiatiques" ("neither Europeans, nor Africans, nor Asians"), but Creole.[79] Césaire casts this ethno-racial mixing as a potential source of what I would call "cultural cannibalism," or the incorporation and adaptation of the various elements from the Caribbean's multifaceted heritage:

Voici un antillais, arrière petit-fils d'un colon et d'une négresse esclave. Le voici déployant pour "tourner en rond" dans son île, toutes les énergies jadis nécessaires aux colons avides pour qui le sang des autres était le prix naturel de l'or, tout le courage nécessaire aux guerriers africains qui gagnaient perpétuellement leur vie sur la mort.

Here's a West Indian, the great-grandson of a colonist and a black slave woman. Here he is in his island, ensuring its "smooth running" by his deployment of all the energies once needed by avaricious colonists for whom the blood of others was the natural price of gold and all that courage needed by African warriors in their perpetual struggle to wrest life from death. (271/159)

Rather than equate Negritude, or blackness, with Caribbeanness, Césaire posits the former as an instrumental part of the latter, more encompassing designation. Through this continual expansion of identities and categories, Negritude—or perhaps more appropriately, African diasporic modernity—in the Suzanne Césairean mode includes "la réalité créole des Antilles" ("the Caribbean's Creole reality") as well as its African legacy.[80]

One of the most remarkable ways in which Césaire addresses the difficulties of this heterogeneous Caribbean present is through a gloss of the economic dynamics of "Creole reality." If a cultural review of the island indicates an environment marked by coexistence and intermixture, an economic review reveals the social fissures that prevent the transformation of these elements into collective identification and action. Again foreshadowing Glissant's *Le discours antillais,* Césaire outlines Martinican social strata through three figures: at the summit the indirectly identified *béké,* or white Creole; beneath him the openly designated "bourgeois de couleur" ("colored bourgeois"; 271); and at the very bottom of the social and economic pyramid the "serf antillais" ("Caribbean serf"; 271/159).[81] While Césaire locates *le bourgeois de couleur* in the administrative and civil service ranks, she characterizes *le béké* as a member of Martinique's "sous-industriels et d'épiciers, [sa] caste de faux colons" ("sub-industrialists and grocers, [its] caste of false colonists"; 270/158). *Le serf antillais* suffers at the hands of both: "En attendant, le serf antillais vit misérablement, abjectement sur les terres de 'l'usine' et la médiocrité de nos villes-bourgs est un spectacle à nausée" ("Meanwhile, the Caribbean serf lives miserably and abjectly on the 'factory' lands, and the mediocrity of the market towns is a sickening sight"; 270/159). Assigning socioeconomic roles and responsibility in a similar fashion, Glissant suggests that these groups cannot think collectively because the subsistence of each involves negotiating its particular relationship to the metropole, be it through corporate subsidies *(le béké)*, bureaucratic credentials and benefits *(le bourgeois de couleur)*, or public assistance *(le serf antillais)*.[82] Glissant formulates an answer to this intracommunal division and the accompanying social stagnation through a call for localized economic and cultural production. Césaire, however, posits a different socioeconomic model, one that privileges the relationship between the Caribbean worker and his island over that between the worker and his fellow islanders. She does so in order to forgo the matter of production and return to the question with which, one might contend, the pursuit of Negritude began: the relationship between the African diasporic individual and "nature."

While traces of Frobenian essentialism linger, Césaire's final negotiations of nature and identity reflect a scope and sophistication lacking in her earlier work. "Le grand camouflage" posits nature as a means through which to read the alienation of Caribbean factory workers, among whom "une invisible végétation de désirs" ("an invisible vegetation of desires"; 271/160) fuels a revolutionary impulse. The depiction of nature as critical lens also serves to illuminate the plight of the disenfranchised peasant, whose "liberation" rests in his association with, rather than ownership of, the land. Here Césaire picks up the metaphorical thread with which the essay opens: the peasant's engagement of the land through natural (planting cycles) and musical (drumbeats) rhythms contrasts sharply with the destructive manner in which the hurricane-as-colonization "interacts" with the Caribbean islands. Likewise, Césaire opposes the peasant's behavior with that of the colonists' white descendants: "[l'] appel de tambours" ("[the] call of the drums") that inspires laborers to dance provokes panic among white proprietors (272). The challenge inherent in "Le grand camouflage" is reading these examples for their metaphorical richness rather than their literal essentialism. In neither case does Césaire use nature to present either the peasant or the worker as primitive figures who exist on the fringes, or completely outside, of modernity. Instead, Césaire conceives of Negritude and Caribbeanness as plural identities that are negotiated through, rather than fixed by, nature as well as history (as alluded to through the references to colonialism and slavery).

Although "Le grand camouflage" appears to conclude with an idealized return to "Africa," Césaire is careful to present the continent as a part of the Caribbean landscape, in this case depicted as the integrated entity "Antilles-Afrique" ("Caribbean-Africa"; 272/160). Within this hybrid space *la présence africaine* (the African presence) endures not because it exists as an unmediated essence but because it is developed through cultural forms and collective memories. Accordingly, the site that Césaire mourns in the closing lines of "Le grand camouflage" is not "mon Afrique qu'ils ont cambriolée" ("the Africa they robbed me of") but the Caribbean:

Si les fleurs ont su trouver juste les couleurs qui donnent le coup de foudre, si les fougères arborescentes ont sécrété pour leurs crosses des sucs dorés, enroulés comme un sexe, si mes Antilles sont si belles, c'est qu'alors le grand jeu de cache-cache a réussi, c'est qu'il fait certes trop beau, ce jour-là, pour y voir.

If the flowers have known how to find just the right colours to make you fall in love, if the arborescent ferns have secreted golden essences for their croziers, coiled up like a sex, if my West Indies are so beautiful, it shows that the great game of hide and seek has succeeded and certainly that day would be too lovely for us to see it. (273/161)[83]

Having addressed the particular socioeconomic dynamics of Martinique, Césaire again widens her perspective to include the entire Caribbean. She has transformed the Negritude-specific inquiry of what has become of Africa in the Caribbean into the prophetic question of what will become of the islands in the Caribbean, of the Caribbean in the world. It is this question that the poets of Negritude, initially as dazzled by African antiquity as the exoticist poets were by Caribbean beauty, fail to engage in their early work but which Suzanne Césaire, the theorist of Negritude, poses incisively in evocative, haunting language.

Reconceiving Negritude, Recreating Césaire

When asked about the challenges of pursuing a literary career while raising a family, Dominican writer Ángela Hernández Núñez responded, "All that is apparent is what I have already done, but what cannot be seen is my potential, which in literature is much greater than I have been able to display."[84] For her Martinican predecessor Suzanne Césaire, who also balanced career and family, all that is immediately apparent is the brilliant yet abbreviated body of work she produced for *Tropiques*. Those seven essays, perhaps because they constitute such a small number of pages, have inspired critics and creative writers alike to imagine Césaire's unseen potential, to recreate the Negritude theorist in a fictional guise.[85] Although African American novelist Dorothy West, the subject of the next chapter, appears in Wallace Thurman's *Infants of the Spring* (1932) as "Doris Westmore," she is neither a major character nor a narrative catalyst in Thurman's autobiographical novel.[86] In contrast, Césaire is protagonist and catalyst, respectively, in two late-twentieth-century texts: literary scholar Ronnie Scharfman's "De grands poètes noirs: Breton rencontre les Césaire" (1995) and novelist Daniel Maximin's *L'Isolé soleil* (*Lone Sun*; 1981). These works are testaments to the lasting impact of Césaire's *militantisme poétique*.

In the "fiction historico-littéraire" ("historical-literary fiction") "De grands poètes noirs," Ronnie Scharfman sets out to share "avec ceux qui ne connaissent pas [les] contributions vitales [de Suzanne Césaire] à la revue de *Tropiques* le désir de la lire, et de combler les silences" ("with those who do not know [Césaire's] essential contributions to the journal *Tropiques* the desire to read her and fill in the silences").[87] From the outset Scharfman strikes an oppositional stance to canonical accounts of Negritude with her choice of title. "De grands poètes noirs" both echoes and revises André Breton's "Un grand poète noir"; whereas Breton's title and essay privilege Aimé Césaire and elide Suzanne Césaire's intellectual work, Scharfman insists that the poetry of both Césaires figured prominently in Breton's brief Martinican sojourn. "Signed" by "Suzanne Césaire," the body of Scharfman's essay finds Césaire responding to how Breton and other critics have represented her and her work. Early in "Un grand poète noir," for example, the French surrealist describes René Ménil as "avec Césaire le principal animateur de *Tropiques*" ("the principal animator of *Tropiques* with Césaire").[88] It is in response to such elisions (with Breton's unspecified "Césaire" suggesting Aimé rather than Suzanne) that Scharfman's character asserts her contribution to the journal as part of "un véritable triumvirat qui travaillait à pied d'égalité" ("a veritable triumvirate who worked on equal footing"; 234). Curiously, however, despite the promise suggested by this assertion as well as by Scharfman's title, this creative meditation on Suzanne Césaire's career ultimately devotes more time to excusing rather than engaging the problematic aspects of Breton's work. The character "Suzanne Césaire" not only defends Breton's exoticist-tinged representations of Martinique and Martinican women but also remembers her relationship with the metropolitan

French poet in nostalgic, almost romantic terms: "J'ai joué le rôle de muse, de médiatrice surréaliste entre son ancien monde et le nouveau. Moi, à mon tour, j'écrivais sur lui, de lui, par lui, pour lui" ("I played the role of muse, of surrealist mediatrix between his old world and the new. I, in turn, wrote about him, of him, through him, for him"; 235). With these sentences the essay seems to trade the remembrance of Césaire as Negritude intellectual for that of her as surrealist muse. Scharfman steps back from this critical precipice with a conclusion in which "Césaire" envisions the appropriate restoration of her legacy:

> Mais je me rends compte, lorsque j'imagine les blancs dans les pages de l'histoire littéraire, que si je veux être lue, il faudra que je m'y déplie et que je me déploie, que j'implique moi-même ma propre histoire, afin de produire ce que mon compatriote Edouard Glissant appelle "une lecture prophétique du passé." (239)

> But I realize, when I imagine the gaps in the pages of literary history, that if I want to be read, I will have to place and display myself there, to impose my story myself, in order to produce what my compatriot Édouard Glissant calls "a prophetic reading of the past."

Here the words of Scharfman's character nicely dovetail with those of her historical counterpart; just as the essayist inserts Martinicans into early-twentieth-century discussions of modernity, so the character inscribes herself and her work into the annals of Caribbean literature.

In his novel *L'Isolé soleil* Guadeloupean author Daniel Maximin engages Suzanne Césaire "écrivain à écrivain" ("writer to writer").[89] Described by Maximin as "the dialogue [he has] wanted to have with [Suzanne Césaire]" from the moment he discovered her writing, *L'Isolé soleil* challenges the masculinist discourses generated in metropolitan literature and reproduced in Caribbean literary movements under the guise of "revolution."[90] The text features nonlinear narratives as well as atypical women as it rewrites Caribbean history through the personal correspondence, writing notebooks, and family documents of protagonist Marie-Gabriel. Through these intertextual and intergenerational exchanges Maximin navigates the personal stories linking the 1802 Guadeloupean insurrection against Napoleon's reinstitution of slavery to twentieth-century modernist revolts against artistic and social repression. Marie-Gabriel, read by scholars such as John Erickson as Maximin's double, functions as both conduit and critic in that her narrative facilitates the collection of the "unheard voices" of the past.[91] Rather than unconditionally celebrating Francophone Caribbean counternarratives, however, Marie-Gabriel seeks to understand how such alternatives have contributed to the silencing of other perspectives, particularly those of women.

Marie-Gabriel also serves as a means of recuperating and recreating Suzanne Césaire. The initial reference to Césaire appears in *L'Isolé soleil*'s first chapter, during which Marie-Gabriel declares her intention to write. This professional epiphany resonates with Marie-Gabriel's personal narrative, which reveals that the character's biological birth coincided with what might be read as Césaire's artistic death: "Tu as appris que ce n'est pas la crainte de la folie qui nous forcera à mettre en berne le drapeau de l'imagination: car tu as découvert dans le dernier numéro de *Tropiques*, . . . ce poème écrit par Suzanne Césaire, le mois même de ta naissance" ("You learned that it is not the fear of going mad that will force us to drop the banner of imagination; you learned it from a poem by Suzanne Césaire in the last issue of *Tropiques* that came out the very month of your birth").[92] Recalling Maximin's description of Césaire as "a major mythical figure," Marie-Gabriel's invocation initially suggests that Césaire's presence in *L'Isolé soleil* will be as ephemeral as it is in Breton's "Un grand poète noir"; instead, the observation leads to a critical exploration of the role Césaire's writing plays in Marie-Gabriel's intellectual development as well as in that of her mother, Siméa.[93] This line from woman author (Césaire) to mother (Siméa) to daughter (Marie-Gabriel) yields, as H. Adlai Murdoch writes, "a perceptibly feminine perspective which simultaneously dismantles the authoritarian discursive and historical precepts that are the corollary of colonialism."[94] It replaces, in other words, the model modernities of European Enlightenment and heroic Negritude with atypical, polyvocal modernities that reflect the diversity of the Caribbean.[95]

Maximin's project of dismantling rather than reinscribing hegemony involves presenting Suzanne Césaire as a writer to be interrogated as well as a figure to be admired. The potential for interpreting her *Tropiques* articles as a "mother('s) text"—or "other" text, one that eludes Francophone Caribbean literary categorization—does not exempt her work from the hermeneutic acumen of Maximin's characters.[96] In a move indicative of the novel's temporal and narrative play Marie-Gabriel finds her mother's comments on Césaire in a scene that narratively precedes but chronologically follows her father's encounter with Siméa's annotations on another Césaire piece. During this "second" encounter Louis-Gabriel discovers Siméa's impressions of Césaire's "Malaise d'une civilisation."[97] The Guadeloupean Siméa questions not only the essay's adaptation of European theories to a Caribbean context but also its apparent limiting of that context to Martinique:

> "Suzanne, tu cherches au plus profond notre essence noire, et c'est chez un ethnologue blanc! . . . Aurons-nous donc toujours besoin d'eux et de leurs raisons? À quoi sert de rejeter leur raison si c'est pour adopter leur science? . . .
>
>   "Et puis, quelle manie de parler du Martiniquais (prétention ou modestie)? Tous les Antillais ne forment-ils pas une même civilisation? Ou sinon, n'est-ce pas le seul projet qui soit à l'échelle de notre double désir d'être libres et solidaires?"

> "Suzanne, you want to find the absolute depths of our black essence and you go looking for it in the pages of a white anthropologist! . . . Will we always need *them* and their *reasons*? What's the use of rejecting their reason only to adopt their science? . . .
>
>   "And then, what is this mania of talking about Martinicans (pretention [*sic*] or modesty)? Don't all Antilleans belong to one civilization? Isn't that the only project vast enough to satisfy our double desire for freedom and solidarity?" (193/191)

In addition to marking Siméa's psychological and intellectual "(re)construction" following her student years in Paris, these annotations-as-dialogue also facilitate the recovery of Suzanne Césaire as a literary and intellectual figure.[98] Siméa strategically inserts Césaire into the narrative of French and Francophone literary history and deems her worthy of the same critical attention given to her other favorite writers, notably modernist giants Rimbaud and Breton and Negritude luminaries Damas and Aimé Césaire. Whereas canonization has failed in offering a comprehensive literary survey, Maximin, through his characters, succeeds.

L'Isolé soleil addresses the exclusionary gendering of metropolitan and Caribbean literature directly as well. When an unplanned pregnancy threatens to disrupt Siméa's studies in Paris, a subsequent abortion leaves the character feeling alienated from personal and intellectual sources of comfort. Her bourgeois mother has orchestrated the abortion from Guadeloupe, her white lover appears unprepared to lobby for her acceptance into his family, and her male literary idols seem to have no place for women in their writing: "Toi, mon poète d'avenir, et toi mon amant de demain, et toi mon ami des révoltes futures, qu'as-tu fait de nous femmes dans tes gestes et tes paroles d'aujourd'hui?" ("You, my poet of the future, and you, my lover of tomorrow, and you my friend of future revolts, what have you done with us women in your words and gestures today?"; 137/134). Siméa's circumstances illustrate the very real social ramifications of topics—pregnancy, family, and marriage—traditionally identified with women and with sentimental literature, and yet the revolutionary poets she so admires have little time for women as modern agents and subjects. This exclusion both angers and disappoints Siméa, who ultimately answers her own question: "Vous nous faites inspiratrices au départ de vos actes et consolatrices à l'arrivée, mais nous sommes absentes des chemins de votre mâle héroïsme" ("You turn us into inspiration for your acts in their beginnings and consolation at the end, but we are not on the routes of your male heroism"; 137/135).

Through the antiphonal structure of Maximin's writing Marie-Gabriel responds to her mother's inquiry and revisits the problem of gender and cultural (re)production in a letter to her writing partner, Adrien: "Si on écoute nos poètes, nos révolutionnaires, nos romanciers et leurs historiens, la seule fonction des femmes noires serait d'enfanter nos héros. . . . Cela me donne, par moments, l'envie de concevoir une histoire où seules des femmes apparaîtraient" ("If we listen to our poets and revolutionaries, our novelists and their historians, the only function of black women is to give birth to our heroes. . . . Sometimes I would like to conceive of a history where only women would appear"; 108/105). Despite this wish, *L'Isolé soleil* concludes with Marie-Gabriel achieving her original goal of writing a text that is at once novel and history, personal narrative and revolutionary saga. It is a tale peopled with women as well as with men, one that embodies Glissant's observation that the domination of history ends with the collection and validation of formerly marginalized voices. By building his novel around women as mothers and intellectuals, daughters and writers, spouses and subjects, Maximin "inscribe[s] the necessity of a nonlogocentric, nonpatriarchal discourse to this novel project of communal self-definition."[99] It is through such recreations of Caribbean identity as a series of paths rather than a singular path that both writers and critics can constructively revisit the important contributions of black women such as Césaire to Francophone Caribbean literature in the modernist period and beyond.

Although Suzanne Césaire was not a Negritude outsider in the manner of her Guadeloupean predecessor Suzanne Lacascade, her writing nonetheless troubles the orderly recounting of literary genealogies. For, as much as Césaire's *Tropiques* essays confirm the familiar contours of Negritude by falling squarely within traditional literary historical boundaries, her texts also complicate the canon by their nuanced but incontestable nonconformity. The sequence of twentieth-century Francophone Caribbean literary development is often given as Negritude, Antillanité, and Créolité, yet Césaire's work evokes all three. Colonial antinomies provided the very basis against which much of Negritude literature formed its oppositional stance, with Aimé Césaire celebrating madness over civilization, Léon-Gontran Damas choosing Africa over the Caribbean, and Léopold Sédar Senghor claiming emotion over reason, yet Suzanne Césaire theorized Caribbeanness while rejecting the binaries of "black/white, European/African, civilized/savage" outright.[100] She then concluded her writing career with a text—"Le grand camouflage"—that in a startling tour-de-force resurrects the Caribbean's floral splendor from the ashes of exoticism in order to communicate the depths of the region's suffering.

Within the broader field of comparative black modernism, Suzanne Césaire's writing is equally prescient in destabilizing expectations surrounding literary periods, cultural assimilation, and revolutionary expression. In taking a long view of history and culture, Césaire exposes the many connections and contradictions that impact Caribbean modernities; the result is a social portrait capacious enough to incorporate figures as promising and as frustrating as Suzanne Lacascade's category-defying protagonist. As Césaire's deft handling of surrealism and exoticism improves upon Lacascade's deployment of postexoticism in *Claire-Solange,* so it also echoes Marita Bonner's successful use of expressionism in *The Purple Flower.* The Martinican essayist's poetic militancy likewise paves the way for the women's voices that will succeed her: not only Daniel Maximin's Siméa and Marie-Gabriel, who insist on inserting themselves into narratives of resistance, but also Dorothy West's Cleo, Maryse Condé's Veronica, and Toni Morrison's Jadine, who, as we will see in the next two chapters, resist by insisting on their right to remove themselves from such conversations. Ultimately, the "militancy" of Suzanne Césaire is not a fixed or forced poetics meant to dictate individual behavior or literary output but, rather, a critical stance formed at the intersection of multiple intellectual currents. This simultaneity reveals the inadequacy of identifying Césaire's work solely with canonical Negritude and, as a result, speaks to the critical insufficiency of limiting one's understanding of modernity and modernism to certain archetypes and authors. The relative paucity of Césaire's publication record may be all that is apparent to a reader at first glance, but upon closer inspection one discovers an unyielding, original voice whose reach extends far beyond the space of seven essays. And, as the next chapter will disclose, all that may be apparent upon a cursory reading of Dorothy West's novel *The Living Is Easy* may be a tale of domestic discontent (and not modern engagement), but, as Césaire cautions in "Le grand camouflage," one should always consider that which is hidden behind "le grand jeu de cache-cache" ("the great game of hide-and-seek").

4 Black Modernism in Retrospect

Dorothy West's New (Negro) Women

We who were the New Negroes challenge ["the newer Negroes"] to better our achievements. For we did not altogether live up to our fine promise.
—DOROTHY WEST, "Dear Reader" (1934)

The Living Is Easy (1948), the first novel by African American writer Dorothy West (1907–98), seems an unlikely successor to the militant, controlled prose of Suzanne Césaire's essays, given its middle-class context and narrative sprawl. Cleo Jericho Judson, West's imperious protagonist, is more reminiscent of Suzanne Lacascade's headstrong Claire-Solange than Césaire's pensive speakers. Caught in the disparity between New Negro ideals and New Negro woman realities, a southern past and a northern present, Cleo navigates World War I–era Boston with a disdain not unlike that Claire-Solange initially holds for prewar Paris: "Cleo, walking carefully over the cobblestones that tortured her toes in her stylish shoes, was jealous of all the free-striding life around her. She had nothing with which to match it but her wits. Her despotic nature found Mr. Judson a rival. He ruled a store and all the people in it. Her sphere was one untroublesome child, who gave insufficient scope for her tremendous vitality."[1] The source of Cleo's contempt is the social order that opens the opportunities of the marketplace to her husband but relegates her to the domestic sphere. Although her body marks Cleo as alien to the rough-and-tumble world of the public market (her "stylish shoes" are fundamentally incompatible with the cobblestones covering area streets), her mind yearns to prove its agility beyond the circumscribed roles of wife and mother. Whereas Claire-Solange confronts the colonial antinomies prevalent in Parisian society, Cleo must face the gender antinomies deployed within her social milieu for the similar purpose of regulating individual and collective identities. Consequently, as Ann duCille notes, the desire for a life beyond sartorial and maternal correctness casts West's character as an aberration rather than an adventurer: "Pride, strength, willfulness, subterfuge, authoritativeness, manipulation, craftiness, even deceit are the stuff of which tycoons are made—the tactics by which corporations prosper. Such men society calls successful, savvy; such women it labels grotesques, bitches, Sapphires, jezebels."[2]

A skillful combination of domestic fiction and biting satire, *The Living Is Easy* chronicles Cleo's efforts to transform her home from the idyllic living space prescribed by her gender and class into the site of power demanded by her "tremendous vitality." Married to successful businessman and fellow southern migrant Bart Judson, Cleo finds that her middle-class existence leaves her few pressing concerns beyond maintaining her household, raising her only child, and planning her ascent into black society. As a result, a bored and restless Cleo capitalizes on her husband's wealth and docility to lure her sisters and their children—but not their husbands—to live with her in Boston. Her goal in gathering the family together is twofold: Cleo wants to reconstitute her beloved Carolina childhood in her adopted northern hometown and, in the process, exercise the power she is largely denied outside of the home. The scheme succeeds but not without undermining her sisters' sense of self-worth and depleting the family's financial resources, which become increasingly tenuous as the twin threats of war and modernization drain Bart's business. At novel's close Bart is forced to sell his holdings, search for work in New York, and leave a stunned Cleo in control of the family and its fortunes. Surprisingly, instead of prompting a triumphant celebration, Bart's departure spurs the once proud Cleo to ask: "Who is there now to love me best? Who?" (347). Beneath this articulated cry rests the unasked yet no less urgent question of where the character will fit best after the collapse of her domestic empire. Because although the diminution of patriarchal authority (as represented by Bart) and social oppositions (such as male/female, public/private, and North/South) has been integral to her plans, Cleo is ultimately unable to envision a life for herself outside of these familiar boundaries. Her pitiful question echoes the mournful conclusion of Césaire's "Le grand camouflage" as West simultaneously exposes and indicts the "insufficient scope" that archetypal blackness provides for the "tremendous vitality" of early-twentieth-century African American women.

Celebrated until her death as the "last surviving member of the Harlem Renaissance," essayist, fiction writer, and journalist West enjoyed a breadth and depth of experience that rendered her an astute observer of African American modernism as well as its most enduring participant.[3] She was born into and reared among Boston's black middle class as the only child of Rachel Pease Benson, a "light-skinned" beauty from South Carolina, and Isaac Christopher West, a Virginia migrant who rose from slave status to become a prosperous produce merchant known as Boston's "Black Banana King" (if these details sound familiar, it is because they inspired both the setting and characters of *The Living Is Easy*).[4] A precocious student and writer, West graduated from Boston's esteemed Girl's Latin School and attended both Boston University and the Columbia University School of Journalism. Her formal education essentially ended when her writing began to garner national attention, a turning point that came in 1926: West not only won second place in that year's *Opportunity* fiction contest for her story "The Typewriter" but, in doing so, tied with the older, more well established Zora Neale Hurston. Her trip to the awards dinner was soon followed by a move to New York City, where West became friends with Hurston, a de facto younger sibling to writers such as Countee Cullen, Langston Hughes, and Claude McKay, and a fixture of the African American literati. Friend Wallace Thurman even included West and her cousin, poet Helene Johnson, among the Harlem notables featured in his 1932 satirical novel *Infants of the Spring*.

If this remarkable biography recalls that of Marita Bonner, so, too, do the vicissitudes of West's writing career. Despite publishing more than forty short stories from 1926 through the early 1940s, from the late 1940s onward West spent the better part of three decades in relative obscurity. With the 1934 launch of *Challenge*, the literary journal she founded, edited, and published in order to "bring out the prose and poetry of the newer Negroes," West seemed on course to remain at the forefront of African American cultural production.[5] Her initial contributors included cousin Johnson and friends Hughes and Cullen, and elder statesman James Weldon Johnson provided the foreword. Yet, when the publication folded in early 1937 and was briefly revived that fall as *New Challenge,* its new incarnation hinted at the eventual parting between West and prevailing literary tides. Richard Wright joined the editorial team as associate editor, and *New Challenge* declared its purpose to be "to indicate, through examples in our pages, the great fertility of folk material."[6] However much West's career "link[ed] the Harlem Renaissance with the social realism of the thirties and forties," her subject matter did not correspond to the latter era's focus on "the life of the Negro masses."[7] The planned follow-up to *The Living Is Easy* also featured the lives of the African American middle class, and West's inability to find a publisher for the manuscript marked the beginning of her retreat from public life. Having permanently relocated to Martha's Vineyard in 1945, West did not return to national prominence until 1982, when The Feminist Press reprinted the critically acclaimed *The Living Is Easy.* This resurgence culminated in the final books of West's career: the novel *The Wedding* (1995) and the short story and essay collection *The Richer, the Poorer: Stories, Sketches, and Reminiscences* (1995). Two edited volumes have appeared since West's death in 1998: *The Dorothy West Martha's Vineyard: Stories, Essays, and Reminiscences by Dorothy West Writing in the "Vineyard Gazette"* (2001); and *Where the Wild Grape Grows: Selected Writings, 1930–1950* (2005).[8]

As with the juxtaposition of Césaire's spare nonfiction and West's expansive fiction, the connection between *The Living Is Easy* and the literary period alternately known as the Harlem Renaissance and the New Negro movement is a deliberate construction on my part, one intended to produce new ways of thinking about African diasporic modernisms. David Levering Lewis dates the period's birth to the 1919 return of "the Fifteenth Regiment of New York's National Guard," and the swan song of the Renaissance has been attributed to numerous events, chief among them the 1929 stock market crash and the 1941 arrival of world war on U.S. shores.[9] Regardless of one's preference, both dates clearly precede the 1948 publication of *The Living Is Easy.* If Lacascade's *Claire-Solange* gestures toward the Negritude that follows it, however, so West's novel offers an important opportunity to consider model African American modernity in retrospect. West herself expresses a commitment to ongoing, dialogic relationships between literary periods in "Dear Reader": "We who were the New Negroes challenge ['the newer Negroes'] to better our achievements. For we did not altogether live up to our fine promise" (39). Although West eventually deemed her *Challenge* assessment too severe, her observation nonetheless provides a means of considering how works published after the traditional periodization of the Harlem Renaissance revisit the promises and problems of New Negrohood.[10] For *The Living Is Easy* attributes the circumscription of Cleo, Althea, and Lenore's lives not only to the legacies of slavery but also to the limitations of modernity. As if resuming an intertextual conversation begun by Marita Bonner, West interrogates the frustrating gap between African American women's social progress and that of their male peers. In addition to engaging the gender divide between the New Negro and the New Negro Woman, West uses Cleo's trials to question Renaissance-era assertions that one can clearly and definitively distinguish between Old and New Negroes or "primitive" and "genteel" sympathies. Cleo's loyalty is torn between the folk South of her youth and the bourgeois North of her adulthood because each locale appeals to a different side of her personality and, more important, because neither context is entirely amenable to the character's desire to refashion herself as a modern, independent woman. In other words *The Living Is Easy*'s plot details accomplish that which its publication date alone cannot: they bolster the case for reading the novel as part of African American literary modernism.

The Charge of (New) Negro Womanhood

The cynical, independent woman that West creates in Cleo marks a significant break with the masculinist archetypes prevalent in African American modernist texts; the character's ill fit with her pre–World War I Boston context raises the question of how late-nineteenth- and early-twentieth-century ideals of racial citizenship and womanhood colluded to circumscribe women's identities even as the dawn of New Negrohood promised African Americans greater self-determination and social mobility. Although Cleo is the novel's narrative focus, West complements her protagonist's characterization with the depiction of two very different counterparts. Althea Binney is the impoverished daughter of the Black Brahmin Binneys; her family epitomizes the black elite's parallel and imitative relationship to its white peers, who were known as the Brahmin cult.[11] Lenore Evans, on the other hand, is the beautiful, wealthy gaming house proprietor known as "The Duchess"; her affluence and the manner in which it was acquired represent the modern era's disruption of nineteenth-century socioeconomic structures. Before Cleo's intervention, the link between Althea's genteel existence and the Duchess's "sporting" life appears to be purely financial; the declining economic fates of Althea's caste benefit the Duchess's business, which becomes an alternative source of revenue for Althea's male peers. Cleo's movement between and eventual union of the two worlds, however, reveals both the hidden familial connections between Althea and the Duchess and the social ties that bind all three women in their respective efforts to regain or exercise control over their lives. The extent to which they succeed or fail turns largely on their ability to mold and maintain their respective domestic spaces. As carefully as Lacascade stages Claire-Solange's various confrontations with exoticism, so West deliberately stages her characters' encounters—and clashes—with New Negro ideals. The resonance between *The Living Is Easy* and West's biography produces much more than a literary indictment of the "colorphobi[c]" Black Brahmins and her negligent fair-skinned mother.[12] Through Cleo's interactions with her peers and family, West weaves, amid the principal story of a woman's quest for power gone wrong, the subplot of a society's regulation of gender roles gone terribly right.

Not surprisingly, neither terror nor repression figure prominently in Alain Locke's vision of the New Negro. Instead, the archetype appears to be not only decidedly male but also exceedingly optimistic. Locke describes Harlem as a "laboratory of a great race-welding," a site where the gathering of black migrants from around the country and the globe has produced "race sympathy and unity."[13] The New Negro is likewise a model of balance and exceptionalism; he undergoes the following transformation as he embraces the "new mentality" of the day: "the lapse of sentimental appeal, then the development of a more positive self-respect and self-reliance; the repudiation of social dependence, and then the gradual recovery from hyper-sensitiveness and 'touchy' nerves, the repudiation of the double standard of judgment with its special philanthropic allowances and the sturdier desire for objective and scientific appraisal; and finally the rise from social disillusionment to race pride."[14] From the "migrating peasant" to the "professional man" to the "clergyman" the time has come, Locke asserts, for African Americans to be utterly confident in both their own abilities and American democratic ideals. They can exchange the hypersensitivity and self-interest that personal experiences with racism may have fostered for the self-assurance and group identity embodied in the New Negro. Should this collective social and economic ascent be fulfilled, Locke contends, "Harlem's quixotic radicalisms" (that is, oppositional stances on any matters other than race) will certainly become a thing of the past.[15]

The rhetorical and political bind in which this masculinist optimism places women can be seen in another piece from the *New Negro* anthology edited by Locke: Elise Johnson McDougald's "The Task of Negro Womanhood" (1925). Noting both the "import" of the African American woman to her race and the dual fight she has had to wage against "sex and race subjugation," McDougald opens with a woman-centered perspective that echoes the early feminist efforts of Anna Julia Cooper.[16] If the "grosser forms" of the black woman's subjugation are less apparent in New York City, the great metropolis that surrounds Locke's race capital is nonetheless a place where "the general attitude of mind causes the Negro woman serious difficulty."[17] The "touchy" nerves dismissed by Locke's male archetype would seem to be less trivial to McDougald's female subject, whom she describes as "figuratively struck in the face daily by contempt from the world around her."[18] McDougald's essay, then, is both counterattack and celebration, a means to combat the stereotypes sullying the image of Negro womanhood and replace them with sketches of African American women's lives across the economic spectrum. While McDougald uses Cooper's Sorbonne doctorate to illustrate the heights to which women of the highest class have risen, she cites the harsh labor and domestic conditions faced by women on the lowest socioeconomic rung as signs of the work yet to be done. Near the end of the essay McDougald decisively states that the ongoing struggles of the latter group indicate that "true sex equality has not been approximated."[19]

At the same time that McDougald advocates intra-gender solidarity, however, she reinscribes the class- and gender-based vanguardism that fuels Locke's philosophy of New Negrohood. "The Task of Negro Womanhood" lauds the racial uplift efforts of black women's clubs and sororities and, in the end, promotes a very limited model of womanhood, one not unlike that repeatedly critiqued by Marita Bonner. Cherene Sherrard-Johnson writes that numerous Harlem Renaissance publications favored visual images that represented African American women as "beautiful, educated, [and] middle class," a phrase that could very well describe McDougald's narrative portrayal of upper-class African American women: "The first is a pleasing group to see. It is picked for outward beauty by Negro men with much the same feeling as other Americans of the same economic class."[20] Although McDougald stops shy of closing the hermeneutic gap between "outward beauty" and "economic class" (of explaining, in other words, what money has to do with beauty), Sherrard-Johnson observes that early-twentieth-century African American publications also tended to choose "identifiably mixed-race women to represent the positive and dignified face of the New Negro woman" and that McDougald herself was depicted as such in the Winold Reiss portrait that accompanied her essay in *The New Negro*.[21] As noted in my discussion of Bonner's nonfiction, McDougald eventually concludes that women should privilege race over gender in their fight for social justice. Her "challenge to young Negro womanhood" is to trust that, given their growing enlightenment, "younger Negro men [will] show a wholesome attitude of fellowship and freedom for their women."[22] Thus, although "The Task of Negro Womanhood" closes as it opens—by linking the fate of the black race to that of the black woman—McDougald leaves the distinct impression that the task of changing that fate rests principally with men.

A comparable slippage between protofeminist and patriarchal perspectives appears in W. E. B. Du Bois's 1920 essay "The Damnation of Women." Foreshadowing McDougald's concern for improving black women's social and educational prospects, Du Bois attributes the titular predicament to the restrictive, socially constructed opposition between women's domestic duties and their intellectual and occupational pursuits. He advocates women's self-determination and social advancement while envisioning a "future woman" who would enjoy unrestricted access to education, financial independence, and "motherhood at her own discretion."[23] This modern figure contrasts sharply with the emblematic women of Du Bois's childhood—"the widow, the wife, the maiden, and the outcast"—who, in a manner recalling Hegel's master-slave dialectic, "existed not for themselves, but for men; they were named after the men to whom they were related and not after the fashion of their own souls."[24] Shifting his focus from personal anecdotes to historical sketches, Du Bois heralds individuals such as abolitionists Harriet Tubman and Sojourner Truth as precursors of the "future woman"; for him these renowned black women embody the past challenges and future possibilities of African American womanhood.

"The Damnation of Women" culminates in an apparent vision of race- and gender-blind national citizenship: "We will pay women what they earn and insist on their working and earning it; we will allow those persons to vote who know enough to vote, whether they be black or female, white or male; and we will ward race suicide, not by further burdening the over-burdened, but by honoring motherhood, even when the sneaking father shirks his duty."[25] Despite an initial emphasis on labor and suffrage, two issues central to women's integration into the public sphere, the passage closes by highlighting the image of motherhood, effectively returning women to the private realm; by its conclusion women's citizenship has become a primarily domestic, maternal enterprise. The shift is unexpected given Du Bois's claim earlier in the essay that limiting women to the occupation of homemaker constitutes domestic imprisonment, but the contradiction in fact reflects a larger pattern in Du Bois's work and that of many of his peers. As Joy James observes, when Du Bois "portray[s] African American women in an aggregate as victims, icons, or the embodiment of a cause, [he] project[s] the notion that political change transpires without black female independence and leadership."[26] In the progressive future imagined by Du Bois, the pursuit of "women's freedom" would not come at the expense of "married motherhood" because women should be able to exercise racial and national citizenship through domestic reproduction *and* intellectual production.[27] To revise an observation from Locke's "New Negro," "the choice is not between one way for the [mother] and another way for the [woman professional], but between [mothers] frustrated on the one hand and [their potential] progressively fulfilled and realized on the other."[28] As we will see in Dorothy West's characterizations of Cleo and Lenore, forgoing motherhood altogether appears to be a less viable option. Despite the protofeminist moments within "The Damnation of Women," then, the essay as a whole replicates the contentious relationship between racial identity, national and group citizenship, and gender roles found throughout modern African American social discourse.

It is important to note that the reinforcement of gender-specific spheres of movement and influence was not an exclusively patrician matter limited to the likes of Locke, McDougald, and Du Bois. In July 1923 the *Messenger,* the journal founded by labor activists A. Philip Randolph and Chandler Owen, published a special "New Negro Woman's Number."[29] Less involved in the artistic aspects of the Harlem Renaissance than the NAACP's *Crisis* or the National Urban League's *Opportunity,* the *Messenger* focused primarily on socialism and union politics; in 1925 the journal became "the official organ of the Brotherhood of Sleeping Car Porters," the union founded by Randolph.[30] Yet these unabashedly progressive politics are only partially evident in the *Messenger* special issue dedicated to the lives of African American women. Aside from replacing the generic designation *Negro woman* with the archetypal *New Negro Woman,* the issue's content, particularly its lead editorial, all but replicates Du Bois's rhetoric.

After another promising introduction, this one celebrating the New Negro Woman's contributions to fields ranging from politics to science, the *Messenger* editorial undermines this acknowledgment by explaining—and emphasizing—the black woman's charge "to create and keep alive, in the breast of black men, a holy and consuming passion to break with the slave traditions of the past."[31] Without any additional reference to the New Negro Woman's professional accomplishments, the editorial deduces that her greatest task is to help the New Negro Man "attain . . . the stature of a *full man,* a free race and a new world."[32] Even though this collaboration signals a break with the past, the rupture does not result in the same social or symbolic trajectory for the two partners: the promise of the "new world" is opened up to the New Negro Man only when the New Negro Woman's responsibilities as domestic partner supersede her accomplishments as an autonomous individual. As suggested here and openly stated by other African American leaders such as Kelly Miller, the Negro woman's definitive role was to encourage racial advancement from the subordinate position of wife and mother.[33] This apparent sacrifice of women's independence for the greater good of New Negrohood corresponds to Susan Gillman and Alys Eve Weinbaum's analysis of Du Bois's discussion of women; in both cases "female figures are essential and expendable, wailing and silent—they clear space for the production of black revolutionary masses and agency even as they are subsumed within such masses."[34] While the New Negro Man will re-produce the (image of the) race through labor and art, the Negro Woman will, as nurturer and companion, quite literally reproduce the race. Once again, the shift from specificity to iconicization posits women as the remainders of modern blackness.

Such clashes between tradition and modernity, group conformity and women's individuality, resulted in part because the emergence of modern, twentieth-century African America was irrevocably tied to the negotiation of nineteenth-century ideals and stereotypes. In her landmark work on turn-of-the-century black women's domestic fiction, Claudia Tate describes the impulse to idealize "black domesticity," which was deployed to counter "dominant racist constructions and conventions," as a manifestation of "political desire."[35] Within this context articulating black women's identities through traditional visions of wife- and motherhood represented social reform, not complacency. Defining African American womanhood in these terms did effectively counter slave-era racial stereotypes, but this characterization also depended upon a no less constricting archetype imported from the Victorian era: the "true woman." The product of the "cult of true womanhood," which stressed "domesticity, moral and sexual purity, submissiveness to authority, and removal from public affairs," the true woman had her African American analogue in the figure whom Tate christens the "true black woman."[36] This ideal was at once "domestic nurturer, spiritual counselor, moral advocate, social activist, and academic teacher"; the public positions of "social activist" and "academic teacher" were acceptable because they replicated the mother's role in racial uplift.[37]

Because the discursive possibilities and limitations of appropriating Victorian womanhood and its African American revision have been amply and ably discussed in other venues, my interest lies in the convergence, or perhaps, collision, of these archetypes with the lives of characters in black modernist women's fiction.[38] If, as historian Paula Giddings contends, "the cult [of true womanhood] caused Black *women* to prove they were *ladies*" and "forced White *ladies* to prove that they were *women*," novels such as West's *Living Is Easy* demand an updated conception of political desire, one in which economically and socially privileged African American women wish to shed the constraints of a protected "lady-hood" for the freedom of an empowered womanhood.[39] For, whereas the nineteenth-century authors discussed by Tate revised Victorian ideals to produce the true black woman, twentieth-century successors such as McDougald essentially transformed that nineteenth-century embodiment of model African American womanhood into the twentieth-century New Negro woman. Although accessible to the middle- and upper-middle-class characters found in West and writers such as Marita Bonner, Nella Larsen, and Zora Neale Hurston, this idealized femininity was no more desirable or liberating to them than it was to their white Victorian counterparts. When West's protagonist trades on the discursive power of domesticity, her concern is not so much with elevating her fellow women or advancing the cause of the New Negro but, rather, with advancing that of the new, improved Cleo.

Reading the social relevance of New Negro–era women principally through domestic roles not only returns one to Victorian ideals of womanhood but also suggests another historical appropriation characteristic of black modernism: the revival of an "ancient past as both grounds and inspiration for a reempowered present."[40] Yet, unlike Suzanne Lacascade's *Claire-Solange, âme africaine,* in which an ancient African legacy yields an image of the black woman as an articulate subject invested and integrated in the sociopolitical concerns of the present, many of the more well-known, influential, and masculinist interpretations of this past posit woman-as-timeless-(and-silent)-bearer-of-culture.[41] In a critique of artistic representations of this ideal Anne Stavney remarks, "Iconized and idealized, [the black woman] is without agency in contemporary racial and social protests, and without ground(s) in the modern urban land-scape."[42] Whereas the independence of Du Bois's "future woman" is mediated through the prism of domestic responsibility, the images critiqued by Stavney manage the power of the primitive maternal ideal by rendering her spatially and temporally groundless: she is pure archetype, a figure that exerts influence only from within a mythical, removed space.[43] From appropriated Victorian ideal to resurrected African archetype, these various negotiations of African American womanhood share a common inclination, that of positing the black woman as an instrument of rather than agent in the modernist project of reforming the present through the appropriation or revision of the past. Like André Breton's poetic renderings of Suzanne Césaire, she is an intellectual object but not an intellectual in her own right.

Whether firmly rooted in the past or wholly associated with the future, none of these incarnations of modern African American womanhood—the true black woman, the New Negro Woman, the primitive woman—enjoy or embody the unfettered independence and self-determination associated with masculine incarnations of archetypal blackness. The empowered modern black women imagined by authors such as Dorothy West do not always possess the noble "strength of character, cleanness of soul, and unselfish devotion of purpose" lauded by Du Bois, nor are they necessarily the *Messenger*'s iconic woman, "her head erect and spirit undaunted . . . resolutely marching forward, ever conscious of her historic and noble mission of doing her bit toward the liberation of her people."[44] Nor do West's characters necessarily seek to become the strong, eternal African(ized) mother immortalized in canonical Negritude as well as New Negrohood. On the contrary, one is more likely to locate subjects such as Cleo among the "bitches, Sapphires, [and] jezebels" whose sexual and social independence threatens prevailing gender norms.[45] These atypical women are vocal, independent, and willful; transgressive, migratory, and anxiogenic; complex, contradictory, and modern. Indeed, one is more likely to locate these unconventional protagonists in the company of another, more subversive turn-of-the-century archetype: the New Woman.

My intent here is not to create a totalizing, all-representative model that one might call the New Black Woman but, rather, to explore the usefulness of temporarily exploring New Womanhood as a means of articulating black women's identities outside of language that simultaneously venerates heroic masculinity and reinscribes traditional femininity. Elizabeth Ammons describes the New Woman as "a specific group of privileged white women [who] were born between the late 1850s and 1900; they married later than former generations or not at all; they had few or no children if they did marry; they attended college and had highly developed career and professional goals."[46] In her study of the British New Woman, Ann Heilmann assesses the social impact of the figure's assertion of an unapologetic, independent womanhood: "The harbinger of cultural, social and political transformations, the New Woman epitomized the spirit of the *fin de siècle*. Her political demands reflected the crisis of the *ancien régime* beleaguered by issues of class and race, authority and ideology, while her 'sexual anarchy' exacerbated deep-seated anxieties about the shifting concepts of gender and sexuality."[47] Mapping this paradigm onto the cultural context of the 1920s United States, critic Maria Balshaw similarly identifies the New Woman as a discomfiting individual who disrupted the era's notions of "managing the body as a means of controlling the body politic."[48] The figure, Balshaw observes, produced "intense cultural anxiety" by daring to embrace an "asexual image" and assert "that the primary role of woman might be something other than childbearing."[49] One finds reflected in these analyses of New Womanhood early-twentieth-century concerns about the social, economic, and political shifts brought about by "a new world of science, war, technology, and imperialism."[50] Furthermore, if one thinks of management of the black female body—through the deployment of "safe" archetypes and icons—as an integral strategy of rehabilitating and representing early-twentieth-century African American identities, what could prove more anxiogenic than a woman who would seek to reclaim individuality, to access power, to wrest control of her body, and by extension her self(hood), from overarching ideologies of group identity? How would New Negrohood reproduce itself if women refused to bear children? What would happen, in other words, if black women refused to accept the charge—or pay the price—of New Negro womanhood? As *The Living Is Easy* demonstrates, it is when the answers to such questions, if not the questions themselves, prove unsettling that women's power, particularly when wielded outside of traditional domestic networks, comes to be perceived as pathological rather than productive.

THE NEW NEGRO WOMAN *MANQUÉE*

Among West's distaff triumvirate it is Cleo who initially appears to conform the most to archetypal representations of African American womanhood. The presence of her daughter Judy confirms Cleo's domestic status as wife and mother, and the commercial success of her husband ensures her social status as an accepted newcomer in Black Brahmin circles. According to the qualities endorsed by Elise Johnson McDougald, Cleo also "looks" the part of the New Negro woman: "Cleo swished down the spit-spattered street with her head in the air and her sailor askant her pompadour. Her French heels rapped the sidewalk smartly, and her starched skirt swayed briskly from her slender buttocks. Through the thin stuff of her shirtwaist her golden shoulders gleamed, and were tied to the rest of her torso with the immaculate straps of her camisole, chemise, and summer shirt, which were banded together with tiny gold-plated safety pins. One gloved hand gave ballast to Judy, the other gripped her pocketbook" (3). Far from disturbing or contradicting the visual ideals of the New Negro, Cleo is appropriately fair-skinned, properly attired, and neatly contained in the various accoutrements (hat, clothes, and gloves) of respectable femininity. Early in the novel Cleo's preparations to move her family from an apartment in Boston's South End to a home near the more prestigious area of Brookline only seem to confirm this impression. The move will enable the five-year-old Judy to attend a better school and, perhaps more important, allow the upwardly mobile Cleo to distance herself from reminders of her Old Negro past. Although she remembers her Carolina childhood fondly, she does not appreciate the "influx of black cotton-belters" filling the South End: "Their accents prickled her scalp. Their raucous laughter soured the sweet New England air. Their games were reminiscent of all the whooping and hollering she had indulged in before her emancipation" (5). It is almost as if West has evoked Alain Locke—and his contention that different classes of blacks should be distinguished from rather than conflated with one another—in order to reinforce Cleo's identification with model African American modernity.[51]

Yet, however much Cleo plays the New Negro woman, beneath her surface conformity she is anything but. The relocation from the South End to Brookline sets in motion a series of events that gradually reveal how Cleo manipulates her domestic and communal roles to achieve her personal goals. Her relationships with her family are refracted through another form of political desire, one that seeks to counter the hegemony of masculinist as well as racist "constructions and conventions."[52] Because propriety precludes women of her class from working outside the home, for example, Cleo uses the family's impending move to solicit more money from her husband. After signing a lease for one sum, she tells Bart their rent will be twice that amount and pockets the difference without compunction. Similarly, while Judy's education does concern her mother, Cleo also secures the Brookline house as part of her plan to lure her sisters to Boston. If confining her interests to the domestic sphere is the "proper" thing to do, then Cleo will defy the public, uncircumscribed power enjoyed by men by proving that she can "bend a household of human souls to her will" (71). Indeed, Cleo's siblings are implicated in her struggle to exercise an independent, self-defined womanhood even before their arrival in Boston: "This large patent-leather pouch held [Cleo's] secret life with her sisters. In it were their letters of obligation, acknowledging her latest distribution of money and clothing and prodigal advice. The instruments of the concrete side of her charity, which instruments never left the inviolate privacy of her purse, were her credit books, showing various aliases and unfinished payments, and her pawnshop tickets, the expiration dates of which had come and gone, constraining her to tell her husband, with no intent of irony, that another of her diamonds had gone down the drain" (3–4). In contrast to the "stylish shoes" that interfere with her mobility, Cleo's purse, functioning as both ornamental object and furtive portfolio, enables her to reconfigure gender roles to suit her purposes. It becomes the substitute for the commercial space that Cleo cannot access and the means through which Cleo assumes greater control over her life and those of others.

In a departure from Suzanne Lacascade's approach to characterization, West very rarely attempts to soften her protagonist's flaws. While Lacascade's conclusion recalls the early-twentieth-century figure of the noble, self-sacrificing woman of color, West dispenses with the archetype altogether.[53] Claire-Solange and Cleo do share a steadfast sense of racial identity; both women can use their fair skin to pass, but both identify as being black. They live that identity, however, as well as its intersection with gender and class, in very different ways. In the pre–World War I Paris of Claire-Solange the physical manifestations of womanhood facilitate rather than impede the character's goal of declaring her racial heritage: her hair and body are the principal means through which she introduces and critiques exoticist representations of the Caribbean. Similarly, instead of depicting Claire-Solange's eventual marriage to Jacques Danzel as an unfortunate restriction of women's agency, Lacascade presents the coupling as a collaborative union of colonial and metropolitan identities. Although outspoken, Claire-Solange is ultimately incorporated into the social fold through the mechanics of the marriage plot. In contrast, marriage offers no such redemption for her African American counterpart. The same prewar period in Boston finds Cleo frustrated by gender constraints that force her to pursue her ambitions through deception and manipulation. A former migrant, Cleo is also less secure in her social status—hence, her reluctance to cross socioeconomic lines, as Claire-Solange does in Paris's Caribbean enclave. The latter's transparency and altruism are luxuries that Cleo, trapped within the particular gender and class dynamics of model African American modernity, cannot afford.

Through a series of flashbacks West traces the adult Cleo's oppositional social stance back to her childhood observations of gender roles and male privilege. When cavorting with white playmate Josie Beauchamp, Cleo dismisses the perks due her friend as a budding southern lady because she wants the privileges of Josie's father, the southern gentleman: "Anybody could ride an old pony. [Cleo] wanted to ride General Beauchamp's roan stallion, who shied at any touch but his master's" (13). Years later in Massachusetts, when Bart proposes marriage in order to protect her virtue, Cleo accepts because she sees another opportunity to seize control: "She wanted to get away. She couldn't stand seeing Miss Boorum's nephew moping around like a half-sick dog if woman hankering was what ailed him. If he ever came hankering after her, she'd stab him dead with an ice-pick. And no man on earth, let alone a white man, was worth going to hell for" (34–35). In this regard Cleo's apparently picture-perfect marriage does not conform to either the ideals of true black womanhood or New Negrohood. While the former narrative might have positioned Cleo primarily as a maiden-in-distress safely restored to the world of honor and virtue, the latter might have fashioned her as a spirited woman ready to trade the stifling conditions of the Boorum household for the fulfillment of being helpmate to a successful entrepreneur. Instead, Cleo considers Bart not so much a representation of New Negro promise as a potential reincarnation of her father, whom she once viewed as an obstacle to her mother's love and continues to blame for her mother's death in childbirth. This contempt for gender privilege is rivaled only by the scorn with which Cleo views racial privilege. Thus, while Cleo's marriage may be read as the fulfillment of a childhood dream, it is a dream of resisting and usurping a man's power rather than winning his love.

Cleo's subsequent conjugal and parental duties are likewise filtered through a "business-like view of the world."[54] The morality and purity conferred by her status as New Negro mother release Cleo from her cloistered existence, but her newfound ability to circulate between shopping expeditions and social engagements still falls short of Bart's license to engage in "an exterior life, realized in his business in . . . Faneuil Market and with the bankers of Boston."[55]

Consequently, although Cleo's marital status also authorizes her to embrace her sexuality, now sanctioned for the purpose of reproducing the race, her resentment of Bart's autonomy prevents Cleo from cultivating or acknowledging any emotional attachment to her husband.[56] The result is an ongoing power struggle in the one realm in which early-twentieth-century society placed husband and wife on nearly equal footing: the home. In passages rendered with a deft tragicomic touch, the couple remains celibate the first few years of marriage as Cleo's intractability collides with Bart's paternalism: while Cleo has "no intention of renouncing her maidenhood for one man if she had married to preserve it from another," Bart is initially "soothed and satisfied by the fact of his right to cherish her." The couple eventually conceives a child when Cleo's pent-up physical desire "br[eaks] down her controlled resistance" to Bart's advances, but the experience does not yield a lasting sexual truce (35). On the contrary, West presents this lapse as a tactical slip, not an emotional one, and describes Cleo as having no intention of conceiving any more children. In depriving Judy of (biological) siblings and "the race" of future citizens, Cleo begins her descent from promising or apparent New Negro Woman to New Negro Woman *manquée*.

If I have devoted particular attention to this scene, it is because the details contained within serve to introduce not only the Judson marriage but also the nuances of West's retrospective engagement with elements of model African American modernity. The marriage chapter concludes by indicating that the steely reserve with which Cleo rebuffs men—previously an admirable quality in the interracial Boorum house—has become "perversity" in the monoracial Judson home. Writing that Cleo's "need of love was as urgent as her aliveness indicated," West links this apparently negative assessment to the self-denial involved in the character's chosen path of resistance (35–36); when she refuses to acknowledge Bart's physical desire, Cleo denies her own sexual fulfillment as well. West's choice of words, however, also speaks to the manner in which Cleo's rebellion might very well register as social deviance. By refusing to accept her social limitations and perform her wifely duties, Cleo fails to contribute to New Negro social regeneration. She ignores the call to reproductive service alluded to by West and openly expressed in Nella Larsen's *Quicksand* (1928), in which Helga Crane's rejection of motherhood elicits the following response: "Few, very few Negroes of the better class have children, and each generation has to wrestle again with the obstacles of the preceding ones, lack of money, education, and background. . . . We're the ones who must have the children if the race is to get anywhere."[57] The sad irony of *Quicksand*, of course, is that Helga's eventual acceptance of her sexuality still leads to marriage and children, with the former weakening her ability to maintain any extradomestic interests and the latter, after a series of increasingly difficult births, literally draining her health. When read in tandem with Helga's tragic end, the behavior of West's protagonist becomes less a matter of perversity and more one of self-preservation. Cleo may be denying herself as much as Bart, but in so doing she avoids "the risk of being destroyed either morally or physically by her sexuality, the literary fate of many black women."[58]

It should come as no surprise, then, that once Cleo has a child motherhood also assumes a strategic valence. As the passage from Larsen suggests, New Negro parenting promoted the subordination of individual needs for the greater good. The task of parents in general, and mothers in particular, was to train their children in the ways of racial and national citizenship. As Ann duCille artfully observes, however, "Cleo would be *king,* not mother."[59] She considers Judy an asset in her quest for power in both the domestic and social realms. Within the Judson home Judy operates as a familial go-between most often used by her mother to manipulate her father. Outside the home Judy's existence legitimates Cleo's social status where the circumstances of her mother's southern, working-class birth cannot. Thanks to tutoring sessions with Black Brahmin scion Althea Binney, Judy becomes a "proper Bostonian" to whom her mother can "point with the pride of ownership" (39, 40). In one of many calculated appropriations of New Negro ideals, Cleo transforms Judy into "the site and strategy for [her] self-making."[60] If other adults cannot discern this nonmaternal possessiveness, Cleo's stratagems are not lost on the precocious Judy. West repeatedly has the little girl refer to her mother by first name, as in this observation of the inverted gender and power dynamics in the Judson household: "It was funny, but Cleo was the boss of everybody. It was like she was the boss of the house. Papa wasn't" (202).

Cleo's ambivalent parenting also becomes a lens through which West reflects upon the geography of New Negrohood. In a manner reminiscent of Marita Bonner's remapping of African American modernity, *The Living Is Easy* seizes upon Cleo's manipulative mothering to question the attribution of exemplarity to any one location. For, as much as Judy moderates Cleo's anxieties about her transformation from southern migrant to Black Brahmin, the little girl also embodies her mother's fears that this transformation might prove too successful. A chilling demonstration of New England stoicism—the free admission that emotional repression is not only necessary to family harmony but natural—suggests that, like New Negro womanhood anywhere, New Negrohood in the Bostonian mold does not come without a price. The experience leaves West's normally unflappable protagonist shaken: "Cleo felt frightened. Judy is going to grow up like that, she thought. She belongs to me. And already I can see her will to belong to herself. I want her to be a Bostonian, but I want her to be me deep down" (141). Through this split allegiance, this desire to have an independent, northern child who is also "a projection of its [southern] mother" (86), Cleo realizes, perhaps for the first time, the self- and familial alienation required by her project of social integration: "A paradox of this sort of self-willed beginning is that its 'success' depends fundamentally upon self-negation, a turning away from the 'Old Negro' and the labyrinthine memory of black enslavement and toward the register of a 'New Negro,' an irresistible, spontaneously generated black and sufficient self."[61] Despite her efforts to secure her place in Boston society by creating a new Cleo, the character cannot fully relinquish the past; her ideal home remains the "idyllic Southern paradise" of her youth.[62] She wants to inhabit North and South simultaneously, to distance herself from her "southern brothers" moving to Boston and to teach Judy about slavery through stories of the "proud," "old-time Jericho women" (5, 91). Instead, Judy threatens to become the proper Bostonian, or New Negro, that Cleo can never, and ultimately does not wish to, be.

West brings this struggle for gender and geographic simultaneity full circle through Cleo's interaction with her sisters. As Farah Griffin observes, they "allow [Cleo] access to the South as well as the power to contain it. . . . Through them the other side of the South—the communal, gentle, nurturing side— emerges."[63] While a young Cleo reluctantly admits her resemblance to her father, she sees only her mother reflected in the faces of her sisters: "Looking at her sisters, standing above the suffering boy, she saw in each some likeness of Mama—in Charity the softness and roundness, the flush just under the thin skin, the silver laughter; in Lily the doe eyes, liquid and vulnerable, the plaited hair that kept escaping in curls; in small Serena the cherry-red mouth, the dimpled cheeks. She knew that she looked like Pa. Everyone said so" (21). When the Jericho sisters arrive in Boston, their adult appearances confirm Cleo's childhood memory and reinforce the narrative's association of Cleo with her father. Whereas Pa was the center of attention in the Jericho home, Cleo positions herself as the heart of the blended Jericho-Judson household; yet, as with Cleo's desire to circulate freely in public, West indicates that Cleo has little interest in dispensing altogether with the gendered, unequal distribution of power: the character's actual goal is to replace the masculinist power structure with a gynocentric equivalent. Although she imagines herself rejecting the patriarchal domestic tableau endorsed by true womanhood and by the actions of her beloved mother, she in fact refashions her home as a site where she, rather than her father or husband, reigns over "an extended family corporation."[64]

Bart is relegated to the role of silent partner/investor when Cleo removes him from the master bedroom to "the small back room on the second floor" (199). She also extends this gendered stigma to her infant nephew Tim, whom she meets with the thought that "it really was too bad he had to be a boy" (166). West is careful to contrast the ebullient childhood scampering of Cleo's nieces with the relative immobility of Tim, whose infancy serves the dual function of restricting his movement in the house and neutralizing the threat posed by his nascent manhood. With these newly drawn zones of access and control Cleo "differentiates between the family bond and the marriage bond" by building a kinship structure around women-centered relationships.[65] The desired product is a carefully managed environment in which Cleo can reconnect with her lost mother, bask in her sisters' attention, and exercise the power that true womanhood and its twentieth-century counterpart, New Negrohood, would otherwise deny her.

Although the eventual collapse of Cleo's realm can be traced, as some critics suggest, to her tendency to replicate the masculine agency she has vowed to resist, it is also important to consider one deficiency for which Cleo's will cannot compensate: her lack of formal education.[66] Misses Peterson and Boorum, the white New England spinsters who supervise Cleo's premarital life, concentrate their respective efforts not on educating Cleo but on shielding her from unnecessary contact with men. Having brought an adolescent Cleo to Massachusetts to rescue her "sultry loveliness" from "the amoral . . . South," Miss Peterson has similar doubts about the safety of that beauty in the North (24).[67] Consequently, she reneges on her promise to educate Cleo because the route between home and school is an unsafe, unpoliced domain, a site of lurking "coachmen and butlers and porters" (25). Cleo's practical education is curtailed when her patron-employers, conscious of the link between economic autonomy and "independent action," decide not to pay her directly and instead send her wages to her mother. Wanting to keep their charge from imagining a life beyond the domestic realm, Cleo's employers "had no wish to teach her to save" (28). However much the adult Cleo envies Bart's "store and all the people in it," she cannot administer the enterprise she craves because she has been denied the proper training (70). When Cleo becomes "king" in the eyes of her indebted sisters, she is as inept at managing money as she is adept at manipulating people. Her various schemes, their effects exacerbated by the approach of World War I, deplete the family's bank accounts, and its increasingly meager resources cannot save the formerly beautiful Brookline home from becoming a dilapidated dwelling that is too expensive to heat. The parallel emotional fallout, the direct and indirect result of Cleo's actions, is no less chilling: one sister becomes morbidly obese, another divorces her husband because of colorphobic paranoia, and the third resigns herself to caring for her permanently disabled husband.

Like Larsen and Bonner before her, however, West refrains from idealizing education and its ability to radically transform either women's lives or New Negro dictates. A college degree and cultured upbringing leave the most educated woman in *The Living Is Easy* no more financially independent than Cleo or socially mobile than the characters in Bonner's *Purple Flower:* "Miss Eleanor Elliot, a Vassar graduate, was the maiden daughter of a Negro district attorney, now deceased, whose brilliance had won him high prestige and a house among the rich. . . . She was not rich now. She had been brought up with too expensive tastes to husband her modest inheritance. It was gone" (169). Her Vassar education and European sojourns have also done little to broaden Miss Elliot's sense of community and belonging. She is as blissfully unaware of how her education has reinforced dominant social paradigms as Bonner's Us's are keenly aware of the limited scope of books authored by the White Devils.[68] With her marital prospects as limited as her finances, Miss Elliot reproduces New Negro society commercially (if not biologically) by hosting a weekly dancing class in her home and maintains the belief that African Americans should discriminate as whites have before them. West completes her portrayal of this coincidence of education and narrow-mindedness when Miss Elliot describes the shifting demographics of Black Boston: "With so many of the unfortunates of our race migrating to Boston, we find ourselves becoming crusaders for our beloved city. We may soon be outnumbered by the South-Enders, or worse, diminished in the estimation of our better whites who hardly thought of us as colored before their coming" (172). For all the enlightenment one would presume would come with Miss Elliot's experiences, her behavior instead suggests another facet of the self-negation of archetypal blackness: bourgeois mimicry and internalized racism.

The encounter with the esteemed Miss Elliot provides a fitting note on which to conclude this section because, in the wake of the character's departure, West reveals Cleo's penchant for mimicry as well as mastery. Hoping to lift the mood of her embarrassed sisters, Cleo offers the following spontaneous performance: "She contorted her limber body into bosom and bustle, pitched her voice to a falsetto elegance, and launched into an imitation of Miss Eleanor Elliot that had her sisters chuckling in reminiscence all through the many dishes of their meal" (173). The family's mood is decidedly less cheery by the end of *The Living Is Easy,* and one wonders how the novel's conclusion might have differed had Cleo not been reduced to performing the "false elegance" of model modernity, whether for household entertainment or social survival. What if her life could have accommodated more of the liberties promised by the New Woman and less of the constraints associated with the New Negro? What if Cleo had been able to embrace her southern past and adapt to her northern present without suppressing her emotions or manipulating her family? What if, in other words, circumstances had allowed the character to be a successfully realized version of herself rather than a failed incarnation of someone else's archetype?

It is fitting that I bring this section to a close with a series of rhetorical questions because West leaves open the possibility that Cleo's failure is more temporary inconvenience than permanent state. As Ann duCille observes when comparing Cleo to Scarlett O'Hara: "In this text, too, tomorrow is another day whose outcome is ambiguous. The novel closes on a solitary Cleo, left alone to stew in the destruction she has wrought."[69] She does not stew for long, however, for the narration shifts from emphasizing the character's weakness—"lonely cry," "piteous heart"—to foreshadowing her resurgence: "The heart began to beat strongly. 'Make Tim love me best of all the world. Of all the world,' it commanded" (347). Cleo now views the nephew she once dismissed as an opportunity to access masculinity vicariously, to shape the man that society will not allow her to be. Although the prospect may fall short of the ideals of New Negro womanhood, it places Cleo in the company of Harlem Renaissance protagonists, men as well as women, whose transgressive behavior produces astute social commentary. Cleo's desire to play both sides of the geographic divide between migrant and native, southerner and northerner, recalls the readiness with which Max Disher, the hero of George Samuel Schuyler's novel *Black No More* (1931), decides to cross the racial line in order to become white. The sharp tongue with which Cleo criticizes Black Boston society echoes the derisive observations of Raymond Taylor, the central figure in Wallace Thurman's *Infants of the Spring*. And, finally, Cleo's insistence on setting her own course through life—a choice considered one of the hallmarks of New Negro manhood—resonates with the resolute independence of Janie Crawford, who reclaims her identity by traveling to "de horizon and back" in Zora Neale Hurston's *Their Eyes Were Watching God* (1937).[70] That *The Living Is Easy* ends with Cleo setting her sights on Tim indicates that she may be down but, like Max, Raymond, and Janie before her, no less determined to achieve a social and spatial liberation that exceeds the limits of racial exemplarity.

ENTER THE TRUE NEGRO WOMAN

If Cleo would be king, the two other members of West's principal trio are less openly antagonistic to the representative expectations of modern African American identities. Lenore Evans, called the Duchess by her exclusively male clientele, and Althea Binney, nicknamed Thea by family and friends, are both Bostonians by birth and thus free from the regional inflection of Cleo's outsider status. In a further departure from their counterpart's personal history, Lenore and Thea have also both known wealth since childhood, an experience that relieves them of the class—and in Thea's case caste as well—anxiety behind Cleo's machinations. West's characterization of the two women diverges, however, in their respective positions vis-à-vis New Negrohood. While Lenore holds the potential to modernize early-twentieth-century Black Boston society, Thea is the character who most reflects, and thus is most rewarded by, its nineteenth-century foundations.

Cleo builds her domain by subverting New Negro ideals of domesticity and womanhood, whereas the Duchess inherits her realm through the utter contravention of these principles. She is "ash-blond" and "patrician," the personification of the hue, wealth, and grace that would otherwise delight Black Boston, but the morally questionable circumstances of her birth bar entry to that world: her Black Brahmin mother was seduced by a Beacon Hill (read: white) bachelor rebellious enough to keep a black woman as his mistress but not bold enough to take her as his wife (101). The two communities' reactions to this arrangement reveal how racial and social fluidity operate quite differently in West's African American context than in the Francophone world of Suzanne Lacascade's *Claire-Solange, âme africaine*. If Lacascade distinguishes between *békés* (white Creoles) and *métropolitains* (whites from metropolitan France) in order to position the former as conservative and the latter as progressive, West differentiates between southern and northern whites primarily to indict the racism of white New Englanders as simply a more covert, more hypocritical form of the racial discrimination practiced below the Mason-Dixon Line. She does not refashion the Duchess's father through a whiteness that is fundamentally honorable in the manner that Lacascade rehabilitates Étienne and, to a lesser extent, Jacques Danzel. On the contrary, the Duchess's mother teaches her to remember "that a wealthy white protector was [not] worth a colored woman's loss of caste" (109). When her cloistered convent education is brought to an end by her parents' successive deaths, the Duchess enters adulthood as both a social outcast and an independent woman: her inheritance includes a sizable fortune, the well-appointed "family" home in Boston's West End, and a successful in-house gambling establishment. As Cleo lives suspended between North and South, so the Duchess operates her empire on the periphery of Boston's white and black elite.

Unlike Cleo, however, the Duchess enters the narrative already in possession of "the authority for the self both in the home and in the world" that Claudia Tate associates with "political desire in . . . black female texts."[71] The latter character's self-assurance, financial independence, and social marginality afford her an unprecedented freedom and power that also set her apart from previous generations of women. Wishing to die with her honor restored, the Duchess's mother turns to Carter Binney, the dean of black society and the novel's embodiment of quintessential New Negrohood, to marry her daughter to Cole Hartnett, scion of an equally if not more esteemed black family. It is to Binney's assets that the Duchess turns after the Black Brahmin leader precipitates her mother's death by engineering Cole's engagement to his own daughter, Althea. Using the gaming enterprise begun by her father to "while away the night[s]," the Duchess gradually replaces her father's white clients with Black Boston's finest men (109). The promise of easy winnings draws an unsuspecting Binney, who returns to the elegant West End home to gamble, to win, and, at the proprietor's directive, to lose. His run ends with the Duchess in control of his property and "every penny of the money from his cashed-in insurance and his wife's jewels" (115); the Duchess's plan culminates in her offering to return the assets to Binney's children in exchange for his hand in marriage. The ultimatum underscores the inverse relationship between the Duchess's exercise of agency and the efforts of her mother and Cleo to do likewise; marriage is the end at which the Duchess arrives in her quest for Black Boston approbation rather than the means with which she begins. For, after repeated visits to the gaming tables, the heavily mortgaged Carter is as financially powerless before the Duchess as her mother and other women are socially powerless before him.

Through this achievement West captures two of the signal anxieties of early-twentieth-century modernity. Like Cleo, the Duchess destabilizes gender roles; in upsetting the power base from which Carter Binney dispenses social (dis) approbation, she operates outside the acceptable paradigms of black womanhood. She is a powerful businesswoman with no apparent interest in embracing a nurturing true black or New Negro womanhood. This reversal of fortunes fittingly coincides with another key anxiety of the era: the restructuring of the pre–World War I economy and, for the characters in *The Living Is Easy*, its subsequent impact on the African American elite. By hastening her opponent's ruin, the Duchess completes the work begun by mechanization: "[Carter Binney] had been the awe-inspiring owner of a tailoring establishment in a downtown shopping center. His rent had been several thousand dollars a year, and his income had been triple that figure. His daughter and his son at Harvard had had the best of everything. Then the readymade suit grew in favor, and a well-dressed man was not ashamed of his appearance when he wore one. Where Mr. Binney's store had once stood, a great department store soared seven stories and sold readymades at a price that would have sent Mr. Binney spinning into bankruptcy sooner than he did" (93). Similar fates greet the Hartnetts, who refuse to accept the automobile as a serious threat to their livery stable, and Cleo's husband Bart, who ignores her advice to consider how emerging chain stores will impact the produce business.

A lack of foresight only compounds the problems created by the inflexibility of these entrepreneurs, none of whom groom their children to manage their businesses. "Gentlemen without higher education," Carter and his peers insist on raising degreed professionals despite residing "in a city where the majority of Negroes were too poor and ignorant to seek professional services" and whites "were confidently expecting them to attend their own, thereby effecting a painless segregation" (129). Against this backdrop the economically savvy Duchess appears to be the anti–New Negro woman. She consolidates her power by assuming responsibility for a male-centered enterprise, adapting its operations to suit her own ends, and successfully cultivating the client base necessary to implement her new master, or, perhaps more accurately, mistress plan.

If Cleo apparently fails in challenging New Negrohood, the Duchess appears to succeed as an anxiogenic figure who exposes rather than conceals the fraying seams at the limit between tradition and modernity.

In this light the resolution of the Duchess's feud with the Binney family reads as the crowning accomplishment of her atypical womanhood. Shaped by negotiating tactics of which any corporate baron would be proud, her original plan to marry Carter Binney is revised, and in his place the Duchess takes the matrimonial hand of Simeon, Carter's only son. While the framing of marriage as a socioeconomic transaction does not revolutionize patriarchal marital conventions, the manner in which this transaction occurs does. In a deal that prompts another invocation of Tate's concept of political desire, the Duchess's marriage to Simeon is brokered through a gynocentric circuit of influence that begins with Althea, to whom Carter confesses his predicament; continues on to Cleo, whom Althea enlists to confront her father's creditor; and eventually ends at the Duchess, to whom Cleo suggests Simeon as a more valuable acquisition than the elder Binney. Neither Simeon nor Carter, driven to his deathbed by the Duchess's ultimatum, plays a prominent role in this drawing room deal. As a woman who dares to use her management skills not only to run a business but also to bring men to their ruin, the Duchess promises to be no more of a New Negro helpmate to Simeon than Cleo is to Bart.[72]

The Duchess as Lenore, however, reads as an ideal candidate for New Negro womanhood. At the end of their first meeting the Duchess asks Cleo to call her "Lenore," the name with which she was christened as a tribute to her mother's childhood friend, Carter Binney's deceased wife (118). It is the sign of her private, nonprofessional persona and the means through which West distinguishes between the Duchess as empowered modern woman and Lenore as a more traditional, less subversive representation of African American womanhood. Even before her social rebirth, Lenore engages in racial uplift by favoring the students who frequent her establishment: "[she] paused, then said proudly, 'And the young men have never lost, the young men putting themselves through college'" (115). With this statement West begins to shift the balance of power between Cleo and Lenore. As Lenore ceases to be a proprietor whose existence threatens the integrity of Black Boston and becomes instead a patron, if not foster mother, whose efforts uplift young black men, her altruism as filtered through Cleo's eyes becomes a sign of weakness. No longer a contestatory, controversial figure, Lenore exercises power in order to advance the very New Negro success that often undermines women's agency. She transforms what had been explicitly marked a site of commerce, commodification, and control—particularly when one thinks of her mother's refusal and/or inability to leave the house after being seduced by her father—into a site of nurturing and (upward) mobility. Both touched and baffled by this selflessness, Cleo frames her proposition of Simeon as Lenore's opportunity to "help [him] save *The Clarion*," his progressive yet unprofitable newspaper (116). The suggestion completes the character's conversion from "the West End Duchess" into Lenore Evans Binney of Cambridge in that her marriage, now presented as an act of charity, fulfills her mother's dying wish for social restoration rather than personal revenge.

Despite the characters' markedly divergent paths, West uses Lenore's narrative to continue the critique of archetypal blackness begun with the depiction of Cleo's social and geographic mobility. According to the nineteenth-century standards of true black womanhood and their twentieth-century reincarnation through New Negro womanhood, Lenore's ascent promises to be more felicitous than that of her rebellious counterpart. As a wealthy, independent outcast, the Duchess possesses an uncontested power that is unusual among women of her time; as a Black Brahmin wife, Mrs. Simeon Binney dutifully relinquishes her power, name, and fortune to her husband and newly established racial and caste identity. West has seemingly endowed the character with every quality attributed to postbellum "black female virtue": "Christian piety, moral rectitude, intellectual talent, and personal commitment; gentility, skin color, and class status."[73] In keeping with her critical view of patriarchal social constructions, however, West forgoes a celebration of traditional gender roles in favor of continuing her interrogation of "the damnation of women." Even as Cleo relishes her triumph in trading Simeon as a marital commodity, the narration mourns the loss of Lenore's independence and self-determination: "Simeon had great intelligence. Lenore had depth and loveliness. Their children would inherit this richness. The race would be strengthened. Lenore belonged to her unborn daughters. Her soul was not hers to give or keep while the life strain was in her loins" (119). Cleo regrets that which Lenore either misses or, given her altruistic character, willingly accepts: that racial citizenship demands nothing less than the depletion of a woman's individual vitality for the reproduction and sustenance of future New Negroes. Like many of Marita Bonner's characters, including Beth from "On the Altar," Lenore will be sacrificed for the sake of group social advancement. Whatever authority and identity she has before her marriage, the institution holds for the character prospects very similar to those found in masculinist deployments of modern black womanhood: her re-definition through and subsumption to the roles of wife and mother.

Ultimately, Lenore's capacity for self-denial, particularly when coupled with her religious beliefs, is both the making and unmaking of her aspirations to New Negro womanhood. Lenore has inherited her Irish grandmother's Roman Catholic faith as well as her coloring, and she is as devoted to its tenets as her mother was before her. As a result, she seeks to maintain that which her mother has lost—good standing in the eyes of the church—by refusing to consum-mate her civil marriage to the Protestant Simeon. Yet West, once again using a mother-daughter pairing to explore the gender dynamics of African Ameri-can modernity, suggests that Lenore's position is no more socially tenable or personally rewarding than her mother's. Her decision forecloses her claims to the Du Boisian vision of "honorable" wife and motherhood by preventing her from fulfilling the responsibilities of the marital bed. However principled the motivation behind it, celibacy interferes with the project of racial uplift through sexual reproduction. Although a source of personal strength during her social isolation, Lenore's piety also produces the same outcome as Cleo's conjugal recalcitrance: sexual frustration. Her spiritual resistance cannot di-minish her physical attraction to her husband: "She could not let it happen this way, however her body yearned. Now was the time to let her body suffer for her sins. Now was the time for atonement. She freed herself from Simeon's arms, and the wrench was as terrible as tearing flesh apart. Agony was engraved on her face" (197). As West brings Lenore's narrative arc to a close, the character's penitence tragically devolves from an oppositional stance into a submissive one culminating in the stoic acceptance of Simeon's extramarital affairs. Devoid of the independence, self-determination, and agency of the Duchess, a heart-broken Lenore dies prematurely, leaving the reader to wonder, as Bonner's speaker does in "On Being Young—a Woman—and Colored," what good racial uplift and self-sacrifice serve if they result in the circumscription and, in this case, destruction of women's lives.

It is to Althea, the least assertive, least engaging member of West's triumvi-rate, that one must turn to find the character who embodies and embraces New Negro womanhood in its entirety. Indeed, so complete is Thea's deployment of femininity, gentility, and passivity that the character suggests another, more ac-curate name for the correspondence of nineteenth-century gender conventions with archetypal representations of early-twentieth-century black women: True Negro Womanhood. Far from being an insignificant play on words, replacing the modifier *new* with *true* bespeaks the extent to which model African American modernity—as the Du Bois and McDougald essays and *Messenger* editorial demonstrate—reverts to traditional ("true") depictions of women more often than it reconceives gender roles. Accordingly, newlywed Thea borrows enough of Cleo's assertiveness to demand a higher standard of living from her husband Cole, but not so much that she would "take any unladylike interest" in the means that enable him to furnish this lifestyle (318). She likewise benefits from her sister-in-law's entrepreneurial spirit and religious fervor without being touched by the stigma of either: Lenore's money helps restore the Binney name to its former splendor, and her premature death conveniently opens the position of mistress of Simeon's home, just as scandal forces Thea to end her marriage. Cleo and Lenore's respective revisions of traditional domestic roles consistently place them outside the norms of archetypal blackness, but Thea's fortunes and misfortunes always seem to find her restored to the New Negro fold. If typical womanhood cannot encompass Cleo's "tremendous vitality" or Lenore's financial and spiritual autonomy, it can provide ample scope for Thea's comfortable, conventional gentility.

As in Cleo and Lenore's narratives, West primarily examines Thea's relationship to iconic black womanhood through the themes of money and matrimony. Unlike her counterparts, who profess an interest in (Cleo) or demonstrate a facility for (Lenore) financial management, Thea reinforces her position as True Negro Woman by being noticeably disinterested in economic capital. She can afford this "removal from [the] public affairs" that money, with its suggestion of commerce and the world outside the home, represents because she possesses the equally important resource of social capital.[74] Along with the Binney name, her "very fair skin and chestnut hair" make her position in the color-conscious social firmament virtually unassailable (125). Given these credentials, material goods neither reflect nor determine her status: "She had worn the best when there was money. When there wasn't, she had been too sure of herself ever to wonder if clothes made the woman" (258). West places the distinction between tradition and modernity, representation and transgression, into sharper relief when she momentarily gives the black elite the narrative floor: "The young matrons like dear shabby Thea assured the succession of colored society. And the outlanders like handsome Mrs. Judson were bringing their money where it was badly needed" (246). This collective assessment casts Thea in the woman-identified role of reproducing "colored society" and assigns Cleo and Lenore the male-identified function of financing it. However much the two "outlanders" have the physical and fiscal wherewithal to integrate Black Brahmin society, they lack Thea's unimpeachable pedigree. Cleo and Lenore may be more captivating personalities and their stories more compelling, but only Thea can claim the nonthreatening timelessness of True Negro Womanhood.

In a self-perpetuating cycle the integrity of Thea's exalted status is reflected in and renewed by the tendency of others to presume that worldly matters are beneath her. She is often spared from making any unladylike display of power or initiative because friends and family intervene on her behalf. When the Duchess seizes the Binney assets and thus threatens Thea's marriage to penniless medical student Cole, Thea appears to be Du Bois's hapless maiden personified, an individual utterly at the mercy of social forces.[75] Like Lenore's mother before her, Thea enlists a more resourceful ally to resolve her family's dilemma: "[Cleo] looked at Thea and felt pity and impatience that Thea looked so confoundedly helpless. It would be like sending a lamb to slaughter to expect her to hold her own with a vulgar creature in a gambling dive" (96). This recruitment indeed spurs the resolution of the crisis, but it is the subsequent encounter and negotiation between Cleo and the Duchess, not Thea's turn to Cleo, that West privileges as a more exceptional display of women's authority. That Cleo's thoughts are echoed by Simeon, who laments his sister's "helplessness" when considering the Duchess's ultimatum, only affirms this impression (140). In Thea's favor West does indicate that the character has been no better served by education than Cleo. Her "natural airs and graces," refined by years as "a boarding student at a select academy," equip Thea for little more than holding and attending tea parties (92). The only thing that Thea genuinely knows how to do before her marriage, then, is to follow in the footsteps of Miss Eleanor Elliot and trade on her social capital. By tutoring the progeny of Black Boston, Thea not only finds "a genteel way to keep herself in gloves and shoes" but also prepares for her eventual role as an exemplary black mother (94).

The most significant challenge to Thea's True Negro Womanhood comes during Cleo's Christmas party, which gathers the cream of Black Boston in all its holiday splendor and hypocritical glory. According to Lawrence Rodgers, the event "functions—like that most famous of twentieth-century literary parties held in Mrs. Dalloway's Bloomsbury home—as a creative act of domesticity designed to exhibit the social artistry of the hostess."[76] The advertised purpose of the gathering is the reception of Dean Galloway, an administrator from a black college in the South, but the actual occasion is the consolidation of Cleo's social power. Performing the role of her lifetime, she displays an easy familiarity with Black Boston old (as represented by Thea Binney Hartnett) and new (as embodied by Lenore Evans Binney). When Galloway's speech threatens to disrupt this performance, Cleo interrupts his call to racial uplift and solidarity with a plea of her own:

> "I am no different from other colored women. And colored men will never understand us. They feel mean and low at every slight, at every setback, and want to weep on the world's shoulder. But colored women can't afford self-pity. They're the ones that raise the children. What kind of children would they raise if they let them see their grief and despair? They'd raise humble dogs or mad dogs. They wouldn't raise human beings.
>
> "Simeon, you know how Boston mothers feel about *The Clarion*. We keep it out of our children's way. If you print the story of a—colored killer, I will never again permit it in my house." (264)

In a show of discursive mastery that blends the feminism of Anna Julia Cooper with the accommodationism of Booker T. Washington, Cleo deploys the rhetoric of idealized African American wife and motherhood to disavow "the horrors of her Southern past."[77] Again recalling Marita Bonner's nonfiction personae, West's protagonist rejects the charge of racial uplift because it does not account for intraracial difference; unlike Bonner's speaker, who presents herself as a native northerner, Cleo refuses the charge because it reminds her of a community with which she is all too familiar: the "colored killer" in question is her brother-in-law (263). Rodgers argues that Cleo is able to deny this personal connection so easily because she has "already extracted what she most wanted from the South by reclaiming her sisters."[78] Similarly, Cleo invokes the sanctity of New Negro motherhood, an occupation she largely resents, in order to achieve her desired end of wresting control of her party from Simeon and his guest.

Yet, even with the success of Cleo's rhetorical maneuvers and Lenore's pale beauty, which sparks "an acute rush of color consciousness" among the women present, it is Thea who profits most from the social event of the season (250). West again attributes this fortune to the actions of others; Thea is able to muster just enough initiative to demand a new dress from her husband. It is left to Simeon to preserve his sister's social position when Black Boston seems poised to install Lenore as its female exemplar: "The Duchess had asked these women to tea. She would give other affairs. Thea's friends would flock to the house in which Thea had presided. And the Duchess would win them over. She had started her own campaign tonight. Well, he would start one of his own. He was handsome, brilliant. Women liked him, had even wanted him. They would learn that the road to his heart lay through Thea" (265).

Simeon's scorn is not without narrative justification; the friends ready to desert Thea had previously hoped that Lenore would be "a cheap blond with some betraying negroid feature" (250). Rather than critique this opportunism, however, or recognize his own investment in the society that has produced it, Simeon directs his fury at his wife. Although unacknowledged by the younger Binney, the link between his fraternal anguish and marital anger is seized upon by West to extend her critique of the masculinist perspectives of New Negrohood and black nationalism. Simeon may consider himself a progressive among intractable conservatives, but his misogyny suggests that he has not yet attained the (male) enlightenment on which Elise Johnson McDougald pins the hopes of Negro womanhood. Having agreed to marry Lenore because the arrangement "will enable Thea to feed on Cole," Simeon vows to defend his sister because his wife "had been nothing until he had given her the name that was Thea's before it was hers" (140, 265). Circular and cruel, this logic results in a string of affairs that devastate the innocent Lenore while protecting an oblivious Thea.

The Living Is Easy concludes with Lenore dead and Cleo weakened by Bart's unexpected departure. Thea, on the other hand, appears to emerge unscathed. Despite the fact that her brother has turned to infidelity to support her socially and her husband, a promising but poor doctor, has resorted to performing illegal abortions to support her financially, she maintains her "quiet assumption that being born a Binney was an immunity" to scandal, disgrace, and hardship (318). When Cole's profitable abortion practice results in the death of a young immigrant woman, Thea divorces him and resumes her life as a Binney. In a scene recalling the surreal wedding in Bonner's "On the Altar," Black Boston approves Thea's restoration and closes ranks by representing the otherwise grim circumstances in a socially palatable light: "Those less intimate and socially secure, who had wondered during Cole's trial what their attitude toward his wife should be if he were sentenced, were profoundly relieved to have it decided for them at [his mother's] funeral. . . . Thea, whom black did not suit, did look a pathetic figure, and everyone had the most generous feelings for her.

Thus their first meeting after Cole's imprisonment passed off beautifully in perfect surroundings" (317–18). The very society that cannot absorb outsiders Lenore and Cleo—for both characters desire or display power in a manner that raises the specter of New Womanhood rather than the banner of New Negrohood—can countenance the homecoming of insider Thea. Once back in the family home with her widowed brother, she will ostensibly become the True Negro companion and mother (to a child conveniently named after his uncle) that neither Lenore nor Cleo could be.

It is important to note that West juxtaposes Thea's outcome with the fates of her more transgressive peers not to celebrate the entrance of the True Negro Woman but, rather, to critique the "damnation" of all women through the imposition of intraracial gender and class norms. Thea's identity as True Negro Woman is consolidated at the expense of individuals, particularly other women, who fall outside the purview of model modernity. Cole's patients and Simeon's lovers become the expendable objects that Thea's iconic status exempts her from being, and, much to Cleo's irritation, Thea does not question these sacrifices until Simeon's affairs precipitate Lenore's death: "What did Thea have to worry about? . . . Certainly she was not distressed because the Duchess was dying, even though it could be said that Simeon was morally responsible. Thea should be accustomed to men killing women for her" (316). While West does not change course here and posit Cleo as a reliable women's advocate or narrative informant, the character's sarcasm nonetheless serves to cast doubt on the social order that accepts these deaths as tragic yet justifiable expenditures. West also suggests that Thea herself is damned, if not to death or disgrace, then to the sterility and isolation of an existence created, celebrated, and constrained by ideals of archetypal African American womanhood. Thea as icon is a mere shadow of the more vibrant women around her: whereas Cleo is "handsome," Thea is "shabby" (246); whereas Lenore's beauty is "startling," Thea's appearance is "pathetic" (318). What is more, the reward for her representation of True Negro Womanhood is domestic partnership with a man who resents women as much as, if not more than, he loves his sister. In a canny echo of Elise Johnson McDougald's argument that black women must subsume the quest for gender equality to the greater good of racial solidarity, West implies that Thea's life with Simeon will likewise result in the suppression of her individual needs.

Whereas West's 1934 challenge to the "newer Negroes" refers to artists' responsibility to their craft, *The Living Is Easy* suggests an additional reading, one that explores how New Negrohood failed to live up to its promise of sparking social change for all African Americans. In promoting the possibilities of self-definition over the boundaries of archetypal blackness, West's novel reclaims early-twentieth-century African Americanness as an experience to be articulated across genders, classes, and regions rather than fixed to any one social or geographic designation. It asserts that the real promise of modernity is the recuperation and assertion of the specific perspectives lost in masculinist and heroic visions of early-twentieth-century blackness. In weighing that which Wallace Thurman deemed "the price of becoming civilized," *The Living Is Easy* finds that the cost of exemplarity is too high if black women are relegated to prescribed, dated gender roles while black men are propelled into the modern world.[79] If New Negrohood does indeed provide "insufficient scope for [women's] tremendous vitality" (70), the burden of insufficiency rests not on West's atypical women but on the archetypes used to circumscribe them.

Likewise, perhaps the perceived deficiencies of West and her generation of African American writers do not rest solely with the artists but also with the critical models used to read their work. The literary "achievements" lamented in West's initial "Dear Reader" column are realized in the striking intertextual conversations that *The Living Is Easy* facilitates. With this novel West has joined other black women writers in proving the instability of articulating African diasporic identities through the lens of exemplarity. Her work builds upon Suzanne Lacascade's appropriation of the marriage plot by privileging ambiguity and subterfuge over the latter's narrative certainty and earnestness. Whereas *Claire-Solange, âme africaine* draws on the title character's intelligence and political awareness to elevate the *mulâtresse* to the status of racial advocate and marriageable partner, *The Living Is Easy* uses the same qualities to demonstrate why the roles of race woman and dutiful wife stifle other women of color. Within the greater narrative space offered by the novel, West's fiction also enlarges the dystopic view introduced in many of Marita Bonner's stories and essays. I would argue that, like Bonner, her narrative end is not the punishment of transgressive characters; it is, instead, the provocation of questions about the frequency with which atypical women meet with unfulfilling, if not outright tragic, fates amid the promises of modernity. Finally, to return briefly to Suzanne Césaire, West's writing reveals, rather than reinforces, the great sociopolitical camouflage masking the drawing room intrigues of the early-twentieth-century African American elite. Although West withdrew from the public eye from the late 1940s until the mid-1990s, her work not only continued the literary engagement of comparative black modernism but also fore-shadowed the atypical, postmodern women to come. For some thirty years after the publication of *The Living Is Easy* the same narrative ambiguity that signals Cleo's social downfall would be deployed to mark the personal liberation of Maryse Condé's Véronica Mercier and Toni Morrison's Jadine Childs.

Conclusion

Atypical Women Revisited

One had a past, the other a future, and each one bore the culture to save the race in his hands. Mama-spoiled black man, will you mature with me? Culture-bearing black woman, whose culture are you bearing?
—TONI MORRISON, *Tar Baby* (1981)

As I began my examination of comparative black modernism with the inclusion of atypical women Miranda, Défilée, and Anna Julia Cooper, so I will conclude with a further bit of conceptual and historical disorder. By the time Dorothy West published *The Living Is Easy* in 1948, the Harlem Renaissance had waned, and authors such as James Baldwin, Gwendolyn Brooks, Ann Petry, and Richard Wright (West's *New Challenge* coeditor) were ushering in a new era in African American literature, one whose urban realism not only underscored the limits of New Negrohood but also effectively signaled its death. In the Francophone Caribbean the 1950s likewise brought significant cultural changes:

changes: Suzanne Césaire retreated from public life, Aimé Césaire turned his attention to the political realm, and Édouard Glissant, the theorist of *Antillanité*, published his first novel.[1] Yet, even as these shifts occurred, the archetypal blackness associated with the Harlem Renaissance and Negritude lingered in the African American and Francophone Caribbean imaginations—and with it the need to address the relationship between gender and the conception of African diasporic modernity. So it is that in *Tar Baby* (1981) Toni Morrison's narrator formulates questions that could very well be asked of the characters and speakers found in Suzanne Lacascade, Marita Bonner, Suzanne Césaire, and Dorothy West. To whom do the past and future belong in articulations of modern African diasporic identities? Whose responsibility is it "to save the race," to bear its culture? If these questions are provocatively posed in modernist women's writing, they are explosively answered in the texts that emerged with African diasporic feminism and postmodernism in the 1970s and 1980s. My narrative of comparative black modernism ends, then, not with Lacascade, Bonner, Césaire, and West but with two of their late-twentieth-century successors: Guadeloupean Maryse Condé (b. 1937) and African American Toni Morrison (b. 1931).

I have selected *feminism* and *postmodernism* as this conclusion's touchstones because the terms speak not only to the historical moment in which Condé and Morrison produced their early works but also to contemporary discussions of comparative literature. As I noted in the introduction, while its disciplinary origins in Western European thought may have promoted the suppression of difference, the reduction of analysis to a "Europe and Its Others" model, comparison is more effectively practiced through attention to contestation, difference, and specificity.[2] Similar qualities inform nuanced appreciations of black feminism, which Deborah E. McDowell describes as "an internally (and productively) fragmented discourse," with some black women writers choosing to forgo the designation "feminist" altogether.[3] If one cannot speak of a uniform, seamless school of thought that developed across African American and French Caribbean women's intellectual circles in the 1970s and 1980s, however, one can locate two of the critical endeavors identified with black feminisms—the rejection of "false universalism" and "the realization that the politics of sex as well as the politics of race and class are crucially interlocking factors"—in much of the work produced by late-twentieth-century black women writers.[4] One can also find numerous intersections between such texts and postmodernism, through which writers from the mid-twentieth century onward have pursued aesthetic innovation through "the presentation of highly fragmented universes" and rebuffed social norms through the creation of protagonists who are more likely to be outcasts than heroes.[5] It is at this literary crossroads, where African diasporic feminism and postmodernism join to facilitate insightful, challenging explorations of black women's subjectivity, that latter-day atypical women have surfaced. Only, rather than subverting the expectations of the "culture-bearing black woman," as Claire-Solange, Cleo, and other modernist characters do, Condé and Morrison's protagonists reject the role altogether for the liberation and uncertainty of the solitary life. As Sula quips in Morrison's 1973 novel of the same name, they "don't want to make somebody else. [They] want to make [themselves]."[6]

These unlikely subjects are joined by a quality that Thadious M. Davis identifies with Harlem Renaissance writer Nella Larsen: the will to "[live] in the modern moment and [refuse] to be held captive to the past."[7] According to Davis, Larsen's "good reason" for rejecting tradition included the rigid racial paradigms of mainstream white society as well as the no less restrictive class and gender dictates of African American society. As a visibly mixed-race individual and an independent woman writer, Larsen proved too primitive for the former and too modern for the latter. Yet, instead of succumbing to this double bind, Larsen chose to redefine her identity as she saw fit; as a result, the woman born Nellie Walker in 1891 "fashioned herself into Nella Larsen," a figure with a historically significant birth date (1893, the year of the Chicago World Columbian Exposition) and an identifiably Scandinavian surname.[8] With this act Larsen asserted the biracial, international heritage that American notions of identity would have otherwise erased, and with her fiction she created sophisticated portraits of black womanhood that the idealism of New Negrohood sought to elide. As we shall see in the following readings of Condé's *En attendant le bonheur* and Morrison's *Tar Baby,* it is this insistence that places atypical women, modernist and postmodernist, beyond the limits of archetypal blackness and propels them toward the realm of an unfettered, truly liberatory modernity.

A NEW BREED OF TOURIST

First published in 1976 and then revised in 1988, *En attendant le bonheur (Heremakhonon)* chronicles the travels of Véronica Mercier, a Guadeloupean philosophy teacher who has recently moved from Paris to an unnamed West

African nation.[9] Endowed with a capacious knowledge that critic Vèvè Clark has called "diaspora literacy," an awareness of the breadth and depth of African diasporic cultures, Véronica initially seems well equipped to realize the ultimate achievement of Negritude: the return to the "motherland."[10] The character's speech and thoughts are peppered with wide-ranging references to Martinican authors Mayotte Capécia, Aimé Césaire, and Frantz Fanon; Ghanaian political legend Kwame Nkrumah, and the popular African American magazine *Ebony,* and from the outset—the novel's first page—she disparages traveling to Africa because it is "à la mode" ("the in thing to do"; 19/3). When questioned at immigration, Véronica even explains her visit in terms reminiscent of the traditional Negritude identity quest: "Raison du voyage? Ni commerçante. Ni missionaire. Ni touriste. Touriste peut-être. Mais d'une espèce particulière à la découverte de soi-même. Les paysages on s'en fout" ("Purpose of visit? No, I'm not a trader. Not a missionary. Not even a tourist. Well, perhaps a tourist, but one of a new breed, searching out herself, not landscapes"; 20/3). The disregard for nature aside, the Aimé Césaire–quoting Véronica reads as an inspired reconfiguration of the poet's "l'intourist [*sic*] du circuit triangulaire" ("nontourist of the triangular circuit").[11]

Much like her critical corpus, however, Condé's creative work indicts rather than endorses the veneration of blackness through grand narratives. While heroic quests and cultural myths may be comforting, Condé contends, they also reinscribe stereotypes and prove "binding, confining, and paralyzing," especially for those on society's margins.[12] Consequently, she uses her remarkable first novel to replace the idealized Africa of Negritude and the celebrated Caribbean of Créolité with locales marred by social stratification and to reimagine the noble yet popular hero of both as an apolitical, egocentric woman protagonist. As *En attendant le bonheur* progresses, Condé reveals that Véronica's journey is not so much a triumphant return as it is an ongoing escape from prescriptive social forces. Her departure from Guadeloupe is precipitated by contradictions between the continued racial hierarchization of island society and her family's assimilationist values; the black bourgeois Merciers are outraged by Véronica's affair with a mulatto, even though they continue to revere white French culture. Similar dynamics surround her decision to leave France, where self-styled Caribbean revolutionaries view her relationship with a white man as race traitorship. Through a series of flashbacks and interior monologues Véronica spends as much time revisiting these episodes as she does living in Africa, a dynamic that places her in what Clark describes as "the dialectic of cultural imagery, of memory versus actuality."[13] Whereas her critics deploy impossible (because idealized) notions of blackness to regulate women's behavior, Véronica ignores the political realities of her African present in order to negotiate the unresolved issues of her Guadeloupean and French pasts. When the deaths of her student Birame III and colleague Saliou, both victims of government repression, finally break this determination to remain indifferent, the novel concludes with one last departure, yet, instead of returning to Guadeloupe, Véronica leaves Africa for France.

With this narrative trajectory Condé creates not only "a new breed" of tourist but also a new kind of "libertarian discourse," one that thrives on "anarchy and subversion" rather than regulation and conformity.[14] If Suzanne Lacascade disrupts French Caribbean literary order by choosing an unorthodox vehicle—an independent and outspoken *mulâtresse*—for rehabilitating African culture, Condé does so by exposing the limitations of both model modernity and the revisions it has engendered. She eschews the consolidated racial identities of the early twentieth century for the "plurality, ambiguity, and instability" that H. Adlai Murdoch identifies with postcolonial French Caribbean fiction.[15] Unlike the canonical Negritude heroes, Véronica's stance toward Africa is that of a participant observer, a figure who is *in* the field but never quite *of* it. Several months into her teaching position she is still unable to speak any of the country's national languages, and she likewise refuses political engagement because it might interfere with her personal agenda: "Je ne suis pas venue me mêler de leurs querelles, trancher, prendre parti. Je suis venue pour me guérir d'un mal" ("I didn't come here to get mixed up in their quarrels and take sides. I came to find a cure"; 71/42). Marking a departure from the perspective of Lacascade's Claire-Solange, who emphatically declares, "Je suis Africaine . . . !" ("I am African . . . !"), Véronica asserts an interstitial identity and claims to be *sans papiers,* undocumented.[16] Her uncertainty extends to the ethical realm as well: lacking the royal African great-grandmother of her literary predecessor, Véronica takes an aristocratic but politically suspect lover in order to anchor her floating, New World identity to his traceable African heritage. The conscientious Claire-Solange resists falling in love with her white "pseudo-cousin," but the rebellious Véronica rejoices in finding her "nègre avec aïeux" ("nigger with ancestors"; 132/89), however problematic he may prove to be.

Yet, in keeping with Condé's critique of cultural hegemony, be it Euro- or Afrocentric, "authentic" Africanness does not cure what ails Véronica. The character's true challenge rests in understanding the multiple variables that constitute her selfhood, rather than in fixing her allegiance to any one place or cause. She must confront the inquiry that James Clifford terms the "intercultural identity question," in which the principal concern is "not so much 'where are you from?' but 'where are you between?'"[17] While the geocultural answer to this question—Guadeloupe, France, and Africa—is readily apparent, Condé also engages the notion of in-between-ness to examine how Véronica exists among the various models of womanhood available to her in the aforementioned sites. Her itinerary begins in Guadeloupe, where the lines of caste, class, gender, and race are clearly drawn if repeatedly tested. These boundaries are policed through the deployment of cultural myths and social types, and residents are expected to conform to the behavior appropriate to their station. For Véronica this expectation entails upholding the standards of black bourgeois womanhood even as the dictates of one category contradict those of another.

The familial context in which Véronica negotiates Guadeloupean social contradictions recalls both the female and male poles of model black modernity. On the former end Véronica's mother embodies the delicacy and propriety of ladyhood so well that she is rendered a virtual nonentity in her daughter's memory: "Ma mère ne m'a jamais beaucoup impressionnée. Elle n'était rien que reflet de l'astre paternel" ("My mother never impressed me very much. She was just a moon round the paternal planet"; 48/24). Véronica's words read as a filial precursor of Marie-Gabriel's disapproval in Daniel Maximin's *L'Isolé soleil:* whereas Marie-Gabriel criticizes male poets for relegating women to ancillary positions, Véronica implicitly accuses her mother for not being a more substantial presence. If Véronica spends more time remembering sisters Aïda et Jalla, it is because they are the primary barometer against which Véronica's inappropriateness is measured; in the shadow of their picture-perfect obedience she is "Véronica pleine d'anti-grâces" ("Veronica, full of anti-grace"; 24/6). Condé underscores this oppositional stance to iconic womanhood by devoting significantly more of her protagonist's thoughts to those characters who live fully outside the realm of normative bourgeois femininity: Mabo Julie, the family nursemaid whose occupational status renders her as indispensable and invisible to her black employers as her slave-era counterparts were to their white owners, and Véronica's Aunt Paula, no longer mentioned in polite conversation because "[elle] avait la cuisse légère" ("[she] was an easy lay"; 28/9).

They are the women who captivate Véronica's heart and intellect and, consequently, command the most narrative space.

At the male end of the spectrum Véronica's father occupies the role of ideal black patriarch: a noted lawyer, amateur man of letters, and, as indicated by Véronica's nickname for him, "le marabout mandingue" ("the Mandingo marabout"; 21/5), proud race man. He embraces his African ancestry, and the ostensible bedrock of Mercier family identity is its blackness. As Véronica's childhood memories unfurl, however, they reveal the consistency with which class allegiance supersedes racial pride for the Caribbean black bourgeoisie to which her family belongs. In conjunction with their talk of "Notre-Race-Notre-Race-Notre-Race" ("Our Race, our Race, our Race"; 66/37), her parents routinely evoke the class vanguardism evident in Paulette Nardal's "Eveil de la conscience de race" and attacked in Léon-Gontran Damas's "Hoquet." Véronica and her sisters are taught that bourgeois propriety must be maintained at all times, even if it means wearing shoes at the beach or, because "le rire fait le nègre" ("the laugh makes the nigger"; 119/77), stifling laughter. That which Murdoch describes as the paradox of French Caribbean postcolonialism—Guadeloupe and Martinique's continued cultural and administrative ties to the metropole after the end of colonialism—manifests itself in the Merciers' regular vacations in France, a tradition mirrored in Mr. Mercier's prized photo album turned visual pantheon of French officialdom: "Préféts, ministres des D.O.M.-T.O.M., évêques s'y bousculent. Le trophée majeur une photo d'Éboué en grand costume, dédicacée, du temps de son bref passage comme gouverneur de l'île" ("Prefects, ministers for overseas territories, bishops, and, the top prize, a dedicated photo of Eboué in full morning dress dating from his short stay as governor of the island"; 59/33).[18] When Véronica calls her father an African holy man, then, it is with the pointed sarcasm of a Marita Bonner narrator and not with the blind adoration of a dutiful daughter.

Condé draws on her protagonist's ongoing rebellion in order to conjure the less-celebrated personages of model modernity. These are the figures who represent the underside of archetypal blackness, the negatives whose existence simultaneously threatens and reinforces positive racial types. Sharing Paulette Nardal's and Alain Locke's discomfort with radical politics, Véronica's father labels her an "intellectuel de gauche" ("left-wing intellectual"; 27/9) when she turns a discerning eye to her family's admiration of white European culture. The critique of the Merciers' internalized racism, however, is a minor offense when compared to Véronica's open transgression of sociosexual boundaries. The politics of race and gender collide when the teenage Véronica falls for Jean-Marie de Roseval of the wealthy, mulatto de Rosevals; her outraged family responds by citing the tale of Marilisse, a slave woman who lived with a white man: "Marilisse! tu te fais Marilisse!" ("Marilisse! You're making yourself Marilisse!"; 39/17).[19] Both utterances, "intellectuel de gauche" as well as "Marilisse," are intended to regulate Véronica's wayward comportment, to return her to the fold of acceptable blackness. Yet Véronica, rejecting these recuperative gestures, instead uses the rhetoric of typical modernity to defend herself: "Je ne suis pas une Mayotte Capécia. Ah non! Pas mon souci, éclaircir la Race! Je le jure" ("I'm no Mayotte Capécia. No! I'm not interested in whitening the race! I swear"; 55/30). The rebuttal serves not only to represent Véronica's affection for Jean-Marie as genuine but also to confront Frantz Fanon's castigation of author Capécia in *Peau noire, masques blancs (Black Skin, White Masks)*. As Susan Andrade reminds us, "the Fanonian race/gender paradigm represents women of color without agency"; in taking on this paradigm and in identifying with her Aunt Paula rather than with more "appropriate" models of womanhood, Véronica exercises the self-determination that both her family and Fanon refuse her as a single black woman.[20]

Because of Guadeloupe's departmental status, Condé posits metropolitan France as both a departure from and extension of the social dynamics that structure Véronica's life in the Caribbean. The Merciers send Véronica to Paris in order to staunch the scandal surrounding her relationship with Jean-Marie, but the relocation frees neither the "upstanding" family nor its willful offspring from the weight of overdetermined race and gender roles. Although Véronica completes high school with honors, she dashes hopes for any return to respectability by dating Jean-Michel, a white architect. Lest the reader construe the metropole as a more cosmopolitan and thus less judgmental site, in France the ire of the assimilationist bourgeoisie (as embodied by Véronica's family) is compounded by that of Antilleans on the opposite end of the political spectrum:

Pas comme ces Antillais au festival des Caraïbes.
Qu'est-ce qui m'avait pris d'aller dans un truc pareil? Tout ce que je fuis d'habitude: la biguine et le punch! La nostalgie sans doute. On a beau dire, neuf ans, c'est long. Jean-Michel m'accompagnait avec un petit

goût d'exotisme. . . . Et il y avait ces jeunes Antillais coiffés du béret noir des Black Panthers. Tout le mépris de leur regard. C'était, comme des années auparavant, leurs regards sur moi.

Comme des années auparavant j'ouvrais la bouche pour répondre. Expliquer. Expliquer. Ils n'entendaient rien. Leurs voix étaient sifflantes.

—Marilisse! Tu te fais Marilisse!

Not like those West Indians at the Caribbean Festival.

What got me to go to such a place? Everything I usually run from: biguine and punch. Probably nostalgia. Whatever you say, nine years is a long time. He was accompanying me, a little touch of exoticism. . . . And there were these young West Indians with their Black Panther berets. All contempt. As in years before, all eyes on me.

And, as in years past, I opened my mouth to explain. Explain. They didn't hear a word. Their voices hissed:

— "Marilisse! Marilisse!" (41/19–20)

I have cited this rather lengthy passage in its entirety because it so eloquently demonstrates Condé's contention that, whether assimilationist or militant, the African diasporic ideals deployed to counter Eurocentrism often circumscribe Caribbean lives, especially those of women, as much as the discourse they (the ideals) are meant to challenge. As a result, while the extensive interior monologues such as that just noted illustrate Véronica's detachment from the world around her, they also establish the character's desire for something largely missing in her interpersonal exchanges: the opportunity to explain and represent herself. It is when France proves no more conducive to this self-expression than Guadeloupe that Véronica decides to move on to an African country "qu'on dit peu touché par l'Occident" ("supposed to be untouched by the West"; 42/20). Her goal is not "to save the race"; it is to find the agency denied women in articulations of model black identities.

What, then, to evoke the African American poet Countee Cullen, is Africa to Véronica?[21] Like the Negritude protagonists before her, Véronica seeks a site free from the identity crises that plague the diaspora. She quips: "Je suis venue chercher une terre non plus peuplée de nègres—même spirituels, ah, surtout pas spirituels—, mais de Noirs. C'est-à-dire, en clair, que je suis à la recherche de ce qui peut rester du passé. Le présent ne m'intéresse pas" ("I came to see a land inhabited by Blacks, not Negroes, even spiritual ones. In other words,

I'm looking for what remains of the past. I'm not interested in the present";
89/56). If Condé's phrasing reminds the reader of traditional Negritude quests,
the plot's subsequent twists suggest that the author's intent is to subvert rather
than celebrate such pursuits. As critic Leah Hewitt notes, one of the strengths
of Condé's fiction is its depiction of "les polémiques entre pays, entre cultures,
à travers les aventures individuelles" ("debates between countries, between cultures, through individual adventures"), and Véronica's African sojourn is certainly controversial.[22] Whereas conventional Negritude protagonists declaim
their respect for Africa, Véronica admits that her excavation of the continent's
past will come at the expense of acknowledging its present. While poems such
as Aimé Césaire's *Cahier d'un retour au pays natal* and Léopold Sédar Senghor's
"Femme noire" feminize the African landscape, *En attendant le bonheur* upsets
this dynamic through Véronica's affair with government minister Ibrahima
Sory.[23] Even once fully aware of Sory's reactionary politics, Véronica holds fast
to the objective of validating her New World identity through her lover's noble
African ancestry: "Attendez! . . . J'ai la conviction. Basée sur quoi? Je ne sais,
continuons. J'ai la conviction qu'il peut me sauver. Me réconcilier avec moi-
même, c'est-à-dire avec ma race. Nous disons plutôt avec mon peuple" ("Wait!
I'm convinced . . . I'm convinced he can save me. Reconcile me with myself, in
other words with my race or rather with my people"; 104/67). Her own past
may have been unduly complicated by the constraints of model modernity,
but Véronica believes that she can find an uncontaminated surrogate in Sory's.

But, to play on the title of Jessie Fauset's first novel, there is contamina-
tion.[24] The contradiction between the idealized cultural purity Sory embodies and the actual political repression he enacts proves the imperfection of any
reductionist conception of blackness or Africanness. In his work on the relationship between Africa and its diaspora Stuart Hall argues that "Africa is the
name of the missing term, the great aporia, which lies at the centre of [dias-
poric] cultural identity and gives it a meaning," yet he also cautions that the
"original 'Africa' is no longer there," that "it too has been transformed."[25] Although Véronica fails to appreciate this transformation when waxing poetic
over her relationship with Sory, she does come to appreciate some of the political nuances of postcolonial Africa. One of her most disturbing African encounters occurs when the interior of a friend's villa summons memories of
her bourgeois family home in Guadeloupe. The experience recalls Fanon's *Les
damnés de la terre (The Wretched of the Earth),* in which he explains the psy-
chology of the "bourgeoisie nationale," the postcolonial peer of E. Franklin

Frazier's "black bourgeoisie": "Au sein de la bourgeoisie nationale des pays coloniaux l'esprit jouisseur domine. C'est que sur le plan psychologique elle s'identifie à la bourgeoisie occidentale dont elle a sucé tous les enseignements" ("In the colonial countries, the spirit of indulgence is dominant at the core of the bourgeoisie, and this is because the national bourgeoisie identifies itself with the Western bourgeoisie, from whom it has learnt its lessons").[26] Véronica may not have read these words, but her description nonetheless reads as a virtual case study from the classic on African decolonization: "[La villa de Ramatoulaye] est meublée en style Directoire. *Directoire.* La tête me tourne! Car ce style Directoire, c'est celui qu'affectionnait le marabout mandingue, ne me demandez pas pourquoi. Notre maison était donc meublée en Directoire.... Quel coup!" ("[Ramatoulaye's villa] has Directoire furnishings. I feel dizzy! It was this style that the Mandingo marabout had a liking for, don't ask me why. Our house then was furnished in Directoire.... What a shock!"; 115/75).[27] The Directoire furniture of Véronica's childhood reappears in this adult context not because of a fundamental racial connection between the creolized Caribbean and a pure, timeless Africa but because the bourgeoisie of both places have styled their lives after those of their European peers. Despite its origins in what Homi Bhabha has called "colonial mimicry," Véronica's visceral reaction indicates that her body has registered that which her intellect has not yet accepted: that there are connections to be made between Africa and its diaspora, just not in the manner typically celebrated in Negritude.[28]

The Africa in which Véronica lands also proves reminiscent of France and the Caribbean in its circumscription of women's sexuality. Upon her arrival Véronica meets the apparent embodiment of selfless black womanhood in the form of Oumou Hawa, her colleague Saliou's wife and Ibrahima Sory's sister. Véronica describes Oumou Hawa as "la gazelle noire célébrée par le poète" ("the black gazelle extolled by the poet"; 22/5); she is beautiful, pregnant, and, according to Véronica, content to serve her husband and guest without joining them. As noted earlier, Condé reconfigures this feminized ideal as male through Sory, who becomes the racio-cultural icon through whom Véronica wishes to heal her divided diasporic self. When her politicized students learn of the affair, however, their gendered critique interrupts Véronica's African idyll and returns her to a scenario with which she is already familiar: "'Nous détruirons les Ministres.... Leurs Mercedes ... Et leurs Putains.' ... Hostilité, mépris. Encore mépris" ("WE SHALL DESTROY THE MINISTERS, THEIR MERCEDES AND THEIR WHORES.... Hostility, contempt. Contempt yet again"; 106/68). The incident gives Véronica pause, yet it does not impede what is perhaps the most constant aspect of her personality: the determination to define her sexuality as a private matter rather than a racial duty. As the stress of balancing her attachment to Saliou with her ties to Sory begins to mount, Véronica candidly identifies sex as the best antidote for her despair: "En somme ce qu'il me faut pour voir la vie presque en rose, c'est *a good fuck*. Pas qu'en cela je sois différente du reste des humains, remarquez" ("What I need to see life through rose-colored glasses is a good fuck. Not that I'm any different, mind you, from anybody else"; 177/125). This mind-set is, as Condé notes, a marked departure from that of Annaïse, the love interest in Jacques Roumain's 1944 novel *Gouverneurs de la rosée (Masters of the Dew):* whereas sex enables Annaïse to show her devotion and deference to hero Manuel, Véronica's sexuality is at times a question of racial reconciliation, at others one of self-medication, but always entirely her own.[29]

As with Dorothy West's *The Living Is Easy,* it is important to read gender and sexuality in *En attendant le bonheur* as integral parts of Véronica's struggle against model modernity without reducing the character to either variable. In other words, Véronica's string of controversial relationships is not unlike Cleo's desire to ride General Beauchamp's stallion and to build an enterprise to rival Bart's. West's protagonist wants to be a man because in her early-twentieth-century context she cannot conceive of being a woman and enjoying the freedom and agency she desires. Similarly, Véronica pursues affairs with Jean-Marie and Jean-Michel because "[ils avaient r]ien à prouver, encore moins. Ils étaient ma Liberté" ("[they had] nothing to prove. They were my freedom"; 63/36). As her relationship with Ibrahima Sory progresses, it becomes apparent that he, too, represents freedom to Condé's "voyageuse paumée" ("down and out traveller"; 131/89). By novel's end the women in Véronica's life have either been punished or confined by their respective choices; icons such as Oumou Hawa are re-incorporated into gendered family hierarchies, bourgeoises such as Ramatoulaye lost amid the absurdity of colonial mimicry, and rebels such as Aunt Paula destined to remain social outcasts. Véronica's male lovers, conversely, consistently emerge from their respective imbroglios unscathed. They are allowed to be independent, sexual beings fully in control of their identities. They are allowed, to return to Véronica's own phrasing, to be free.

Rather than resulting in Véronica's climactic fusion with African culture, *En attendant le bonheur* concludes with the character's return to Paris. It is tempting to interpret this decision as a sign of failure or lack of engagement on Véronica's part. If the question of "what is Africa" to Condé's protagonist is addressed within the novel, the answer to the question of what the Caribbean is to her seems less clear. Why, then, would Véronica, enlightened and emboldened by her nine-year absence, not choose to return to Guadeloupe? Murdoch takes the intriguing stance that Véronica's choice of France over the Caribbean can be read as a "*prise de conscience*," as an epiphany, rather than as an act of assimilation.[30] And indeed, although the novel opens with Véronica convinced that she needs an external anchor in order to find the liberty and identity she desires, it ends with the character aware of her ability to create her own autonomy, a possibility she first articulates midway through her African sojourn: "Et puis j'en suis peu à peu venue à penser que cette forme de fuite n'était pas valable, qu'elle cachait tout autre chose. Car enfin j'aurais pu fuir en sens inverse. Combler la distance qu'ils avaient créée. Me réenraciner" ("And then gradually I came to thinking that this form of escape was not valid, that it was hiding something else. I could have escaped in the other direction. Make up for the distance they had lost. Put down roots within myself"; 86/52). These self-generated roots may not be fully developed by the novel's final page, but, unlike Suzanne Lacascade's Claire-Solange, who is resigned to Paris, and Dorothy West's Cleo, who is stranded in Boston, Véronica leaves Africa free to explore not only the manner in which she wishes to define herself but also the location.

THE NOMADIC ANTIHEROINE

Toni Morrison's 1981 novel *Tar Baby* also confronts the specters of archetypal blackness through a series of arrivals and departures. In a trajectory that recalls Véronica's triangular itinerary, protagonist Jadine Childs commutes between Europe, the Caribbean, and the United States in search of a place where she can be at peace with herself. A Paris-based, French-speaking African American woman with fair skin and straight hair, Jadine projects self-confidence but harbors self-doubt. Her existential uncertainty reaches its peak in a supermarket encounter with a "vision [of black womanhood] in a yellow dress," beautiful enough to draw stares and bold enough to spit in Jadine's face.[31] The encounter leaves Jadine feeling enamored and "inauthentic," and she leaves Paris for the Caribbean Isle des Chevaliers, where residents—her patron, white candy magnate Valerian Street, his wife Margaret, and their employees, Jadine's Uncle Sydney and Aunt Ondine—will question neither her identity nor her behavior. Although divided by race, class, gender, and generation, these five individuals constitute a de facto family, the only one that Jadine has really known and the one with which she can spend a tranquil Christmas.

Instead, Morrison transforms the fractured holiday and the events that follow into an extended commentary on the role labels and archetypes play in relationships within and across racial, social, and ethnic lines. In place of Michael, Valerian and Margaret's prodigal son, the holidays bring Son, "a black man with dreadlock hair" who has jumped ship and stowed away in Margaret's closet (80). His presence exposes both the fissures between the African American Childses and their white employers and those between himself, the Childses, and the black residents of nearby Dominique. In the wake of this disruption Jadine realizes that there is no stable, apolitical, or timeless asylum in which she can weather her identity crisis. Just as L'Arbre de la Croix, the Street home, is inevitably part of the landscape in which it has been built, so Jadine's momentary doubt about her status there—"Should she? Should the—what?—social secretary buy a present for the son of her employer/patron?" (90)—is inextricably tied to her insecurity about her place in the world at large. When asked to choose sides, to ally herself with Margaret and Valerian's paternalistic racism, Son's essential blackness, or Sydney and Ondine's bourgeois respectability, Jadine follows Véronica's lead and chooses herself. The novel closes with the character en route to France, while everyone else remains on Isle des Chevaliers.

Morrison opens *Tar Baby* by problematizing the perception of Isle des Chevaliers as a neutral paradise. In a figurative parallel that foreshadows their eventual narrative meeting, both Son and Valerian envision the Caribbean as a site where they can recreate themselves away from the burdens of their pasts. Through the personification of nature, however, Morrison suggests that no reinvention occurs in a historical vacuum. When Son leaps off the ship on which he has been working and toward a new life, the warm water in which he lands becomes a seductive but deadly "water-lady" who "nudge[s] him out to sea," away from the shore (5). The setting (at sea) and the circumstance (Son's flight) recall the enslaved Africans for whom, through external force or personal volition, the Middle Passage ended in the Atlantic's watery depths. The character's allegorical name, revealed later in the novel, likewise posits him as the descendant of the slave trade's countless unnamed victims. The epitome of white male privilege, Valerian represents the opposite end of the historical spectrum. His retirement to the Caribbean is meant to remove him from the constraints of his life in Philadelphia, from the ghosts of his own past of loneliness and discontent. His privilege nonetheless follows him to his new home, where the development he spurs leaves the island's river "ill and grieving" and its ancient trees "wild-eyed and yelling" (9, 10). As Evelyn Hawthorne notes, the character's disinterest in this destruction "reflect[s] an older history of discovery and conquest"; like the European colonists before him, "Valerian's treatment of the land is exploitative and wasteful."[32] The Caribbean is no more a tabula rasa for these twentieth-century travelers than it was for their ancestral and imperial predecessors, and, in an apparent replay of colonial politics, Isle des Chevaliers becomes the battleground on which Morrison's characters wage their respective struggles for autonomy and agency.

The novel's introduction of Valerian and Son reflects both the racialization and the gendering of modernity as viewed through the prism of New World conquest; hence, my detour from Jadine to discuss the characterization of two male figures. Because white and black men represent the limits of identity, the rational subject and the radical other, in Eurocentric philosophies such as the Enlightenment and in Afrocentric revisions such as Negritude, it is within and against these conceptual parameters that Morrison's Sorbonne-educated anti-heroine initially defines herself.[33] Valerian's interactions with his wife reveal how gender and class impact claims to normative whiteness. The long-awaited male heir of wealthy Philadelphia WASPs, Valerian is married to Margaret, whose startling beauty made her the odd person out in her working-class Italian immigrant family in Maine. After their move to the Caribbean, Valerian alternates between listing Margaret as one of his prized possessions—"The rest of what he loved he brought with him: some records, garden shears, a sixty-four-bulb chandelier, a light blue tennis shirt and the Principal Beauty of Maine" (11)—and berating her perpetual discomfort with "the appropriate codes of conduct in the practices and technologies of everyday bourgeois life."[34] In neither case does he relinquish power or acknowledge Margaret as his equal; like the New Negro women examined by Marita Bonner and Dorothy West, Mrs. Valerian Street is encouraged to produce the next generation's modern subject, but she is not invited or empowered to be one. Upon realizing the disconnect between the newlywed Margaret's beauty and education, a woman in Valerian's circle "pat[s] Margaret's stomach" and advises, " 'Get to work, fast, sweetheart' " (58).

Against the backdrop of Valerian's whiteness, Son emerges as a late-twentieth-century Negritude hero, a postmodern race man bearing the new standard of blackness. This archetypal status is conferred in part by the character's name, which, as noted earlier, connotes a foundational diasporic identity. Son himself describes the appellation as "the name that called forth the true him. The him that he never lied to, the one he tucked in at night and the one he did not want to die" (139). As in *Sula* (1973), however, in which the mythic name "Ajax" is revealed to be an abbreviation of "Albert Jacks," Son's allegorical title is the result of unwavering family habit and not a monumental event; in fact, the character's given name is the much more prosaic "William Green" (146). Son's rebellious hair, like that of Lacascade's Claire-Solange, also contributes to his racial credentials. The dreadlocks that function as a basic descriptor when Son is first discovered come to serve as evidence of his fundamental, indisputable blackness: "The man chose [a shampoo] and stood before the mirror looking at his hair. It spread like layer upon layer of wings from his head, more alive than the sealskin. It made him doubt that hair was in fact dead cells. Black people's hair, in any case, was definitely alive. Left alone and untended it was like foliage and from a distance it looked like nothing less than the crown of a deciduous tree" (132). Morrison joins Lacascade and Condé in upsetting the conventional gender roles of model black modernity, and this reversal continues as Jadine and Son's relationship evolves. The African savannas of Senghor's "Femme noire" ("Black Woman") find their diasporic equivalent in the "spaces," "mountains," and "savannas" that Jadine sees in Son's face (158), and, as Judylyn Ryan observes, his arboreal qualities metaphorically link the character to the mythical "swamp women" of Sein de Veilles.[35] In order to extricate herself from the swamp's sinking ground, Jadine thinks, "Count. Just count. Don't sweat or you'll lose your partner, the tree. Cleave together like lovers" (182). Through these images Son emerges as nature and, by extension, blackness, personified.

Whether Valerian's white male superiority or Son's black male essence, neither pole allows for the emergence of Jadine as confident, independent modern subject. Although she forges personal and professional alliances exclusively with white men prior to meeting Son, like Condé's Véronica she also intuitively recognizes the troubled history that impinges upon such relationships. Jadine's interaction with Valerian paints an intimate portrait of cultural imperialism; his patronage theoretically raises the Sorbonne graduate above her aunt and uncle's occupational status, but the sycophantic gratitude it produces renders the young woman a domestic servant of another sort.[36] Just as Ondine supervises household logistics from the kitchen, so Jadine attempts to manage L'Arbre de la Croix's social interactions from her perch at the dining room table: "Jadine thought she may have imagined it, but she believed Valerian was comforted, made more secure, by her presence at the table. That she exercised some restraint on the man; that Valerian believed that in her presence the man might be kept manageable" (92). The narration's chain of equivocation ("thought," "may have imagined," "believed") suggests that Jadine senses her subordinate status even if she does not acknowledge it. By remaining at Valerian's side during his first conversation with Son, the unnamed "man" in the passage, Jadine becomes that which white Harlem Renaissance patron Charlotte Osgood Mason sought from her African American charges: a personal mascot and interpreter of all things black and exotic. This comparison is only reinforced when Morrison's protagonist passionately defends Picasso while discussing "the relative merit of European art versus traditional African art" with Valerian.[37] To the young woman's credit, in addition to disclosing Jadine's problematic identification with white hegemony, the Picasso reference also expresses the character's desire to resist racial stereotyping. Her exchanges with younger white men in particular are distinguished by a level of circumspection not found in her veneration of Valerian. Before dismissing Ondine's concerns about her new sealskin coat, a gift from her fiancé, Jadine alludes to the multiple ways in which both gift and proposal can be interpreted when she questions her fiancé's intentions: "What will happen when he finds out that I hate ear hoops, that I don't have to straighten my hair, that Mingus puts me to sleep, that sometimes I want to get out of my skin and be only the person inside—not American—not black—just me?" (48). The suspicion particularly resonates with Jadine's experience with Valerian's son Michael, who equates authentic blackness with folk art and militant politics. It is his misguided efforts that prompt the Picasso defense, for, according to Jadine, in Michael's mind the generic "black girl" should spend her time "'string[ing] cowrie beads or sell[ing] Afro combs'" (73).

Son makes different but nonetheless constricting demands on Jadine's negotiation of black womanhood, in part because his views on gender roles are as uneven as Jadine's thoughts on race. Thus, while he claims that "anybody who thought women were inferior didn't come out of north Florida" (268), his first encounter with Jadine shows that he, like Michael and Valerian, wishes to remake her in his own image: "He had thought hard during those times in order to manipulate her dreams to insert his own dreams into her so she would not wake or stir or turn over on her stomach but would lie still and dream steadily the dreams he wanted her to have about yellow houses with white doors which women opened and shouted Come on in, you honey you! and the fat black ladies in white dresses minding the pie table in the basement of the church and white wet sheets flapping on a line, and the sound of a six-string guitar plucked after supper while children scooped walnuts up off the ground and handed them to her" (119). This bucolic, masculinist fantasy no more suits the urbane Jadine than the constraints of small-town domesticity suit Zora Neale Hurston's Janie in *Their Eyes Were Watching God* (1937), and the violence implied here devolves into actual physical confrontations when the object of Son's desire insists on being a subject in her own right. Son's insistence on suppressing rather than understanding the intricacies of her personality forces Jadine to revisit a childhood memory of a female dog's humiliating public abuse, first by a circle of male dogs and later by an irate male neighbor. The traumatic episode establishes Jadine's resolve "then and there at the age of twelve in Baltimore never to be broken in the hands of any man" (124). As a result, in order to become Son's lover, Jadine follows the lead of Condé's protagonist and rationalizes her participation in an equally, if not more problematic, relationship. Jadine emphasizes the emotional and social capital that Son brings to her "orphaned," "inauthentic" experience. Only when conditions begin to disintegrate does she appreciate the cost of being "unorphaned" by "her fine frame, her stag, her man" (229, 223). In order to hold on to him she must let go of the leashes she has used not only to control her childhood demons but also to maintain her cherished independence.

Further complicating Son's representation of blackness is the opposing racial model upheld by Jadine's Uncle Sydney and Aunt Ondine, who work at L'Arbre de la Croix as Valerian's butler and housekeeper, respectively. When Valerian decides to amuse himself (and upset Margaret) by inviting Son to dine, the resulting disorder proves the fallacy of monolithic notions of race. In the safety of her kitchen Ondine seethes: "The man upstairs wasn't a Negro—meaning one of them. (She had made Sydney understand that)" (102). Sydney, buoyed by his status as head of the Childs family, is much more direct when Son apologizes for intruding into their lives: "I know you, but you don't know me. I am a Phil-a-delphia Negro mentioned in the book of the very same name. My people owned drugstores and taught school while yours were still cutting their faces open so as to be able to tell one of you from the other. And if you looking to lounge here and live off the fat of the land, and if you think I'm going to wait on you, think twice!" (163). This rhetorical tour de force differentiates Son's blackness from that of the Childs family on multiple levels. By citing the 1899 W. E. B. Du Bois study *The Philadelphia Negro,* Sydney brings the weight of history to bear on his argument. He dismisses the symbolic value of Son's allegorical identity and in its place stresses the importance of documented ancestry. Should the intruder misread the older man's position as a butler a sign of inferiority, Sydney also accentuates the social distinction of the "best class of Philadelphia Negroes," whom Du Bois identifies as the "caterers, clerks, teachers, professional men, small merchants, etc. . . . who constitute the aristocracy of the Negroes."[38] A more passionate, more openly elitist rendering of ideas presented in Alain Locke's "The New Negro," Sydney's philosophy illustrates how historical and economic differences, along with gender divides, impact and impede racial solidarity. Indeed, Sydney is so sure of the merits of his position that he later reassures Ondine that Jadine will not run off with Son because "she's worked hard to make something out of herself, and nothing will make her throw it all away on a swamp nigger" (191).

Yet, as the narration interrogates the representative capacity of Son's blackness across class and gender lines, so it also challenges the Childses' claims to racial exemplarity. Continuing the slippage between certainty and smugness Sydney, Ondine, and Jadine all consider themselves superior to the local blacks employed at L'Arbre de la Croix. In this intradiasporic relationship archetypal naming serves as a means of managing and maintaining difference. The African American Childses have no qualms about calling the handyman "Yardman" because, they reason, tending Valerian's grounds is one of his duties, and, although he seems to bring a different female helper to work each day, the Childses never trouble themselves to learn each woman's name: "They all referred to her as Mary and couldn't ever be wrong about it because all the baptized black women on the island had Mary among their names" (40). Only after Son's arrival does the reader—along with Sydney, Ondine, and Jadine—learn that Yardman's actual name is Gideon and that "the Marys" are usually the same woman, Gideon's Aunt Thérèse. This dismissive attitude is countered by Thérèse's synecdochic reduction of Ondine and Sydney to their hair and uniform, respectively: she calls the former, who wears her hair in two carefully arranged braids, "machete-hair," and the latter, ever fastidious in his butler's attire, "bow-tie" (108). Thérèse also marshals her limited English to rename Jadine, who becomes "the fast-ass" in the Caribbean woman's satirical lexicon (107). For, although Jadine speaks French and reads Aimé Césaire, she behaves like Sydney and Ondine in failing to express any interest in Gideon and Thérèse, incarnations of the Caribbean poor described in Césaire's poetry, beyond their occupational roles.[39] As Véronica discovers in *En attendant le bonheur,* the intradiasporic connection celebrated in Negritude poetry often plays out quite differently amid the petty, banal prejudices of everyday life.

Morrison's interrogation of exemplarity, particularly with regards to womanhood, reaches its zenith as Jadine's quest enters its final narrative arc. When a disastrous Christmas dinner exposes the rifts and resentments beneath the surface calm of L'Arbre de la Croix, Jadine flees to the United States with Son. Leaving is a male prerogative in Césaire's *Cahier,* in which the speaker expresses his desire "to go away ("Partir"), but it is Jadine who organizes the departure from Isle des Chevaliers.[40] While the escape is initially successful, Jadine's willful rejection of the past results in a direct confrontation with the "culture-bearing black wom[e]n" who have preceded her: the woman in yellow from Paris, the swamp women from Isle des Chevaliers, and the mothers, sisters, and aunts from Jadine and Son's pasts. Although strangers in the waking world, in the dream world the women join forces to demand a nocturnal audience with *Tar Baby*'s atypical protagonist:

> They stood around in the room, jostling each other gently, gently—there wasn't much room—revealing one breast and then two and Jadine was shocked. This was not the dream of hats for in that she was asleep, her eyes closed. Here she was wide-awake, but in total darkness looking at her own mother for God's sake and *Nana*dine!
>
> "I have breasts too," she said or thought or willed, "I have breasts too." But they didn't believe her. (258)

Upon Jadine's return to L'Arbre de la Croix her aunt suggests that this disbelief stems from a disjuncture between her niece's personal goals and her familial (or communal) responsibilities: "Jadine, a girl has got be a daughter first. She have to learn that. And if she never learns how to be a daughter, she can't never learn how to be a woman" (281).[41] What Ondine does not explain, however, is equally if not more relevant to Jadine's predicament. How does a woman "learn how to be" an individual? Must she choose between learning how to function within family bonds and discovering how to navigate the world at large? Because Jadine fears losing her autonomy as much as she misunderstands the figurative depths of Ondine's words, she answers her aunt with the defiant "I don't want to learn how to be the kind of woman you're talking about because I don't want to be that kind of woman" (282).

In these words are echoes not only of Jadine's desire, expressed earlier in the novel, to belong to herself but also of two distinct yet resonant visions of the relationship between African diasporic peoples and their pasts. Fanon argues that the colonized intellectual wishing to draw on the past should do so "dans l'intention d'ouvrir l'avenir, d'inviter à l'action, de fonder l'espoir" ("with the intention of opening the future, as an invitation to action and a basis for hope").[42] The past must become a means of continually moving forward rather than of solely looking back. If not, in the haste to construct "imaginary family trees" one risks obscuring the realities of modern life with the facade of archetypal blackness.[43] Such is the sentiment of Spéro, the protagonist and male, modern-day Défilée in Condé's 1992 novel *Les derniers rois mages (The Last of the African Kings)*. "Le passé doit être mis à mort" ("The past must be condemned to death"), Spéro warns; "sinon, c'est lui qui tue" ("otherwise, it will become the killer").[44] Finding more pain than empowerment in their respective pasts, Jadine and Véronica resolve to stay on the move, lest they be destroyed by the physical, social, and psychological manipulations of black women that abound in African American and Francophone Caribbean history. In both Morrison and Condé, the real trap (or "tar baby") is not the atypical woman or her archetypal partner; it is the cumulative deception of model modernity.

At the end of *Tar Baby*, as with the conclusion of *En attendant le bonheur*, the nomadic antiheroine emerges as the character who is the best prepared and the least inclined to negotiate the competing claims of modern identity. In her airport encounter with Alma Estée, one of the Marys, Jadine misses a prime opportunity to acknowledge the young Caribbean woman's own attempt to claim the right of self-determination. Morrison's protagonist also forgoes reaching any accord with Son, who follows her back to Isle des Chevaliers. In the novel's final scene Thérèse, deeming Jadine unworthy because "she has forgotten her ancient [feminine] properties," deposits Son on the island's uninhabited side (305). Thérèse leaves him so that he might join the legendary blind horsemen who have given the island its name, and Son stumbles ashore destined, or doomed, to attain the status of iconic manhood. In contrast, the lasting impression the novel leaves of Jadine, flaws and all, is one of mobility and agency. Morrison may have placed her representative black man on a pedestal, but she places her irrepressible black woman on a plane.

It is fitting that Jadine's journey—and that of Véronica before her—should end in flight because, as James Clifford argues, travel "offers a good reminder that all translation terms used in global comparisons—terms like culture, art, society, peasant, mode of production, man, woman, modernity, ethnography—get us some distance *and* fall apart."[45] Condé and Morrison continue the work begun by Lacascade, Bonner, Césaire, and West in reiterating how idealized models of French Caribbean and African American identities "get us some distance" before collapsing in the relegation of women to symbolic roles and the subordination of questions of gender, geography, and class to those of race. *En attendant le bonheur* and *Tar Baby* also disrupt more recent scholarly discussions of diasporic identities such as that found in Paul Gilroy's *Black Atlantic* (1993). While Gilroy's critique of "anti-essentialist essentialism" resonates with Condé's and Morrison's creative engagement of prescriptive models of identity, he tacitly imposes his own order by depicting one of his defining figures, the traveling intellectual, as predominantly male. Prior to a perceptive reading of Morrison's *Beloved* (1988), Gilroy's profiles of Martin Delany, W. E. B. Du Bois, and Richard Wright dominate his examination of diaspora through the lenses of modernity and double consciousness. Far from foreshadowing Gilroy's distinguished triumvirate, fictional travelers Véronica and Jadine navigate the shoals of modern racial identities from perspectives that are neither androcentric nor gynocentric nor Afrocentric. It is egocentrism, not exemplarity, that motivates the characters' respective quests and, more than any idealization of diasporic identity, enables the self-examination that both Condé and Morrison posit as necessary for excavating one's past, negotiating one's present, and, ultimately, determining one's future.

Like the literary historical categories with which it engages, this study is itself a construction, an attempt to test and contest canonical boundaries in order to examine the work of previously marginalized black women writers. Suzanne Lacascade, Marita Bonner, Suzanne Césaire, and Dorothy West all contributed to the articulation of African American and Francophone Caribbean modernism through the publication of their respective works, yet these contributions have gone largely underappreciated in Harlem Renaissance and Negritude studies. This disjuncture invites a final return to the seminal question of Aimé Césaire's *Cahier:* "Qui et quels sommes nous?" ("Who and what are we?"). Who, in fact, was the "nous" of Negritude, the "we" of New Negrohood? Were these entities plural in number, gender, and perspective or in number only? The work of Lacascade, Bonner, Césaire, and West demonstrates that no single political stance or cultural archetype can adequately reflect the myriad complexities of African diasporic identities, and its resonance with the late-twentieth-century fiction of Condé and Morrison likewise indicates how the maintenance of literary historical order, the restriction of a line of inquiry to preexisting analytical models, can foreclose the full appreciation of African American and Caribbean women's intellectual work across genres, languages, and periods.

I began this project with the goal of exploring how women writers used the tensions between model modernity and literary modernism to express a "will to belong to [themselves]" as artists and intellectuals.[46] Analyzing their work solely to construct a "new, improved" canon would have been to endorse a "return to the past," to replicate the exclusions of masculinist interpretations of the Harlem Renaissance and Negritude and of Eurocentric interpretations of modernism. A cosmetic alteration of previously traveled critical terrain would have also obscured the fact that readings of Lacascade, Bonner, Césaire, and West—along with Condé and Morrison—cannot be easily unified through their shared gender identity; the links between their writings are "relational," not essential.[47] Whereas Lacascade uses marriage as an allegory for racial and national integration, West depicts the institution as an instrument in the repression of women. Whereas Bonner uses the intimacy of the personal essay to launch her critique of archetypal blackness, Césaire's method of choice is the distanced perspective of the theoretical treatise. Whereas Bonner and West spurn the ideals of New Negrohood altogether, Lacascade and Césaire transform Negritude from within through their respective valorizations of the Caribbean's African heritage. And, if these modernist-era women were unable to sustain their respective careers in the manner of their male peers, their challenge lives on in the intricate, exquisite prose of successors Condé and Morrison. Daring to articulate modern blackness beyond male heroism and think literary modernism beyond white exceptionalism is not only to accommodate such incommensurability but also to appreciate it.[48] Suzanne Césaire answers the call to return to the past with the charge to "becom[e] conscious of the formidable mass of different energies that until now have been trapped within" Caribbean peoples.[49] May this work follow her lead by calling for reader and critic alike to become conscious of the formidable mass of women's voices present in the many texts, contexts, and subtexts of comparative black modernism.

Notes

Introduction

1. Maryse Condé, "Order, Disorder, Freedom, and the West Indian Writer," *Post/Colonial Conditions,* ed. Françoise Lionnet and Ronnie Scharfman, spec. issue of *Yale French Studies* 83 (1993): 130.

2. Carole Boyce Davies, *Black Women, Writing and Identity: Migrations of the Subject* (New York: Routledge, 1994) 4.

3. Rey Chow, "The Old/New Question of Comparison in Literary Studies: A Post-European Perspective," *ELH* 71 (2004): 290.

4. Haun Saussy, "Exquisite Cadavers Stitched from Fresh Nightmares: Of Memes, Hives, and Selfish Genes," *Comparative Literature in the Age of Globalization,* ed. Haun Saussy (Baltimore: Johns Hopkins UP, 2006) 10–11.

5. Chow 296, 295. For discussions of disciplinary history more developed than I have space for here, see also, among others, Charles Bernheimer, ed., *Comparative Literature in the Age of Multiculturalism* (Baltimore: Johns Hopkins UP, 1995); Margaret R. Higonnet, ed., *Borderwork: Feminist Engagements with Comparative Literature* (Ithaca, NY: Cornell UP, 1994); Natalie Melas, *All the Difference in the World: Postcoloniality and the Ends of Comparison* (Stanford: Stanford UP, 2007); Saussy, ed., *Comparative Literature in an Age of Globalization;* and Gayatri Spivak, *Death of a Discipline* (New York: Columbia UP, 2003).

6. Melas 36.

7. Susan Sniader Lanser, "Compared to What? Global Feminism, Comparison, and the Master's Tools," *Borderwork: Feminist Engagements with Comparative Literature* 297; Saussy 11.

8. Alice Conklin, "Who Speaks for Africa? The René Maran–Blaise Diagne Trial in 1920s Paris," *The Color of Liberty: Histories of Race in France,* eds. Sue Peabody and Tyler Stovall (Durham: Duke UP, 2003) 302–37.

9. Hazel V. Carby, *Race Men: The W. E. B. Du Bois Lectures* (Cambridge: Harvard UP, 1998) 13.

10. Brent Hayes Edwards, *The Practice of Diaspora: Literature, Translation, and the Rise of Black Internationalism* (Cambridge: Harvard UP, 2003): 13, 16–25.

11. Elizabeth McHenry, *Forgotten Readers: Recovering the Lost History of African American Literary Societies* (Durham, NC: Duke UP, 2002) 16. See also Deborah A. McDowell, "Introduction: Regulating Midwives," *Plum Bun: A Novel without a Moral,* by Jessie Redmon Fauset (1929; Boston: Beacon P, 1990), ix–xxxiii; Thadious M. Davis, *Nella Larsen, Novelist of the Harlem Renaissance: A Woman's Life Unveiled* (Baton Rouge: Louisiana State UP, 1994); T. Denean Sharpley-Whiting, *Negritude Women* (Minneapolis: U of Minnesota P, 2002); and Cheryl A. Wall *Women of the Harlem Renaissance* (Bloomington: Indiana UP, 1995).

12. Edwards, *Practice of Diaspora* 120–21. For excellent readings of the masculinist slant of early

critical interpretations of the Harlem Renaissance and Negritude, see also Condé, Davis, McDowell, Sharpley-Whiting, and Wall. I will discuss the work of these critics in greater detail in the chapters to come.

13. Susan Stanford Friedman, "Definitional Excursions: The Meanings of *Modern/Modernity/Modernism,*" *Modernism/Modernity* 8.3 (2001): 501. I concur with Friedman's definition right until its conclusion, which limits the aforementioned engagement to "Europe, Britain, and the United States."

14. Houston A. Baker Jr., *Modernism and the Harlem Renaissance* (Chicago: U of Chicago P, 1987) xiii; and Aimé Césaire, "Poésie et connaissance," *Tropiques* 12 (1945): 159–61. Translated as "Poetry and Knowledge," trans. Krzysztof Fijalkowski and Michael Richardson, *Refusal of the Shadow: Surrealism and the Caribbean,* ed. Michael Richardson (New York: Verso, 1996) 136–38.

15. Harry Levin, "What Was Modernism?" *Eighteen Essays in World Literature,* ed. Stanley Burnshaw (New York: New York UP, 1962) 307–29.

16. Friedman 500–501.

17. Here I am borrowing from the work of Joyce W. Warren, who calls for the destabilization of canonical literary periods by recognizing them as constructs for "a critical establishment that was male-dominated for a predominantly white male literary tradition." See Warren, "Introduction: The Challenge of Women's Periods," *Challenging Boundaries: Gender and Periodization,* ed. Joyce W. Warren and Margaret Dickie (Athens: U of Georgia P, 2000) ix.

18. Gertrude Stein, "Melanctha," *Three Lives,* ed. Linda Wagner-Martin (1909; Boston: Bedford/St. Martin's, 2000) 87–187.

19. Simon Gikandi, "Picasso, Africa, and the Schemata of Difference," *Modernism/Modernity* 10.3 (2003): 456.

20. Simon Gikandi, *Writing in Limbo: Modernism and Caribbean Literature* (Ithaca, NY: Cornell UP, 1992) 1.

21. Paul Gilroy, *The Black Atlantic: Modernity and Double Consciousness* (Cambridge: Harvard UP, 1993) 49.

22. Édouard Glissant, *Le discours antillais* (1981; Paris: Gallimard, 1997) 227. Translated as *Caribbean Discourse: Selected Essays,* trans. J. Michael Dash (Charlottesville: UP of Virginia, 1989) 64. See also Gikandi, *Writing in Limbo* 2.

23. Glissant, *Le discours antillais* 330/100.

24. Glissant, *Le discours antillais* 227/64. Emphasis in translation.

25. Abena P. A. Busia provides a useful early gloss of these readings in "But Caliban and Ariel are Still Both Male: On African Colonial Discourse and the Unvoiced Female," *Crisscrossing Boundaries in African Literatures, 1986* (Washington, DC: Three Continents P and the African Literature Association, 1991) 130.

26. Sylvia Wynter, "Afterword: Beyond Miranda's Meanings: Un/silencing the 'Demonic Ground' of Caliban's 'Woman,'" *Out of the Kumbla: Caribbean Women and Literature,* ed. Carole Boyce Davies and Elaine Savory Fido (Trenton: Africa World P, 1990) 363.

27. Joan Dayan, *Haiti, History, and the Gods* (Berkeley: U of California P, 1995) 47. Other historical figures discussed by Dayan include military leader Marie-Jeanne Lamartinière, who commanded forces in the Battle of Crête-à-Pierrot in 1802, and revolutionary priestess Cécile Fatiman, who officiated in the 1791 Bois-Caïman ceremony, which launched the slave revolts that ultimately culminated in the Haitian Revolution.

28. Dayan 45.

29. Dayan 17.

30. Elizabeth Alexander, "'We Must Be about Our Father's Business': Anna Julia Cooper and the In-Corporation of the Nineteenth-Century African-American Woman Intellectual," *Signs* 20.2 (1995): 338. Emphasis added.

31. For more on the Atlanta address and *Souls* as inaugural texts of African American modernity and modernism, see Baker, *Modernism and the Harlem Renaissance;* and Gilroy, *Black Atlantic.*

32. Anna Julia Cooper, "Our Raison d'Être," *A Voice from the South, The Voice of Anna Julia Cooper,* ed. Charles Lemert and Esme Bhan (New York: Rowman & Littlefield, 1998) 52.

33. Alexander 337.

34. Cooper, *Voice from the South* 63. For more on Cooper's life and career, see Hazel Carby, *Reconstructing Womanhood: The Emergence of the Afro-American Woman Novelist* (New York: Oxford UP, 1987); Ann duCille, *The Coupling Convention: Sex, Text, and Tradition in Black Women's Fiction* (New York: Oxford UP, 1993); Kevin K. Gaines, *Uplifting the Race: Black Leadership, Politics, and Culture in the Twentieth Century* (Chapel Hill: U of North Carolina P, 1996); Paula Giddings, *When and Where I Enter: The Impact of Black Women on Race and Sex in America* (1984; New York: William Morrow, 1996); and Claudia Tate, *Domestic Allegories of Political Desire: The Black Heroine's Text at the Turn of the Century* (New York: Oxford UP, 1992).

35. J. Michael Dash, *The Other America: Caribbean Literature in a New World Context* (Charlottesville: UP of Virginia, 1998) 42, 45.

36. Baker, *Modernism and the Harlem Renaissance* 31.

37. See C. L. R. James, *The Black Jacobins: Toussaint L'Ouverture and the San Domingo Revolution* (1938; New York: Random House, 1963); and Baker, *Modernism and the Harlem Renaissance.*

38. Michel-Rolph Trouillot, *Silencing the Past: Power and the Production of History* (Boston: Beacon P, 1995) 23.

39. Carby, *Reconstructing Womanhood* 97.

40. Césaire, "Poésie et connaissance" 157/134, 164/140.

41. Gikandi, *Writing in Limbo* 5, 6.

42. Gikandi, *Writing in Limbo* 6.

43. Gilroy 56.

44. Gikandi, "Picasso, Africa, and the Schemata of Difference" 457.

45. Fredric Jameson, "Modernism and Imperialism," *Nationalism, Colonialism, and Literature,* by Terry Eagleton, Fredric Jameson, and Edward W. Said (Minneapolis: U of Minnesota P, 1990) 50–51. It is important to note that Jameson distinguishes Joyce from the modernism of E. M. Forster and Virginia Woolf and calls the Irish writer a practitioner of "Third World" modernism. Although Forster's publication of *A Passage to India* (1924) might seem to contradict Jameson's argument, it was not written until after Forster's 1912 visit to India. My thanks to Nandini Dhar for raising this question.

46. Dash, *Other America* 32.

47. Michael North, *The Dialect of Modernism: Race, Language, and Twentieth Century Literature* (New York: Oxford UP, 1994) 10.

48. Baker, *Modernism and the Harlem Renaissance* xiii. For more on Locke's position, see Locke, "Negro Youth Speaks," *The New Negro,* ed. Alain Locke (1925; New York: Touchstone, 1997) 51.

49. Nellie Y. McKay, *Jean Toomer, Artist: A Study of His Literary Life and Work, 1894–1936*

(Chapel Hill: U of North Carolina P, 1984) 49; Jean-Paul Sartre, "Orphée noir," preface, *Anthologie de la nouvelle poésie nègre et malgache de langue française*, ed. Léopold Sédar Senghor (1948; Paris: Quadrige/PUF, 1992) xxxv. Translated as "Black Orpheus," trans. John MacCombie, *Massachusetts Review* 5 (1964): 43.

50. Claude McKay quote and incredulous remarks about Fauset's fictional milieus in David Levering Lewis, *When Harlem Was in Vogue* (1981; New York: Penguin Books, 1997) 124.

51. Baker, *Modernism and the Harlem Renaissance* 4–5.

52. Ezra Pound, *Make It New* (London: Faber and Faber, 1934).

53. Michel Fabre, "The Reception of *Cane* in France," *Jean Toomer and the Harlem Renaissance*, ed. Geneviève Fabre and Michel Feith (New Brunswick: Rutgers UP, 2001) 204.

54. Alain Locke, "The New Negro," *New Negro* 3–16. Lewis, *When Harlem Was in Vogue* 89, 115, 117. A Harvard Ph.D., Locke taught philosophy at Howard University in Washington, DC. For more on Locke's biography, see Lewis, *When Harlem Was in Vogue* 87, 149–55.

55. Locke, "New Negro" 12.

56. Locke, "New Negro" 14.

57. Henry Louis Gates Jr., "The Trope of the New Negro and the Reconstruction of the Image of the Black," *America Reconstructed, 1840–1940*, spec. issue of *Representations* 24 (1988): 129.

58. Wall, *Women of the Harlem Renaissance* 4.

59. Elise Johnson McDougald, "The Task of Negro Womanhood," *New Negro* 369–82. "New Negro Woman's Number," spec. issue of *Messenger* July 1923. However progressive relative to Locke's representation of New Negrohood, these acknowledgments of gender difference are not without their own elisions.

60. Locke, "New Negro" 9.

61. Locke, "New Negro" 5.

62. Gates, "Trope of the New Negro" 131.

63. Gates, "Trope of the New Negro" 136–37.

64. W. E. B. Du Bois, "The Talented Tenth," *The Negro Problem: A Series of Articles by Representative American Negroes of To-day*, ed. Booker T. Washington (New York: James Pott & Co., 1903) 31–75. Note the emphasis on representation in the collection's title. Joy James, *Transcending the Talented Tenth: Black Leaders and American Intellectuals* (New York: Routledge, 1997) 19.

65. Crystal J. Lucky, "Black Women Writers of the Harlem Renaissance," *Challenging Boundaries* 96. See also Gates, "Trope of the New Negro" 135, 147.

66. Philippe Dewitte, *Les mouvements nègres en France, 1919–1939* (Paris: L'Harmattan, 1985) 20.

67. Dewitte 21, 352. France's colonial presence in west and central Africa was neither as long nor as extensive as its colonial pursuits in the Americas; in the area that constitutes present-day Senegal, only residents of the *quatre communes* (four communes) were granted French citizenship at birth. Another outcome of this historical difference was a distinction in colonial administration: rather than relying on assimilationist policy throughout its time in Africa, France ultimately shifted to the policy of *association*, in which local African leaders were recruited to work in concert with French colonial authorities. For more on French colonial policy in the early twentieth century, see Gary Wilder, *The French Imperial Nation-State: Negritude and Colonial Humanism between the Two World Wars* (Chicago: U of Chicago P, 2005).

68. Shireen K. Lewis, *Race, Culture, and Identity: Francophone West African and Caribbean Literature and Theory from Négritude to Créolité* (Lanham, MD: Lexington Books, 2006) xviii.

69. Countee Cullen, "Heritage," 1925, *The Norton Anthology of African American Literature,* ed. Henry Louis Gates Jr., Nellie Y. McKay, et al. (New York: Norton, 1997) 1311. I am indebted to Meta DuEwa Jones for alerting me to the contrast between Cullen and Damas.

70. Léon-Gontran Damas, *Pigments* (1937; Paris: Guy Lévi Mano; Présence Africaine, 1962). Damas, "Blanchi," *"Pigments" suivi de "Névralgies"* (Paris: Présence Africaine, 1972) 59. Translation of the last four verses from Lilyan Kesteloot, *Black Writers in French: A Literary History of Negritude,* trans. Ellen Conroy Kennedy (Philadelphia: Temple UP, 1974) 135.

71. Translation is mine.

72. Claude McKay, *Banjo: A Novel without a Plot* (New York: Harcourt, 1928) 90–91.

73. Aimé Césaire, *Cahier d'un retour au pays natal (Notebook of a Return to My Native Land),* 1939, *Aimé Césaire: The Collected Poetry,* trans. and ed. Clayton Eshleman and Annette Smith (Berkeley: U of California P, 1983) 76/77.

74. A. James Arnold, *Modernism and Negritude: The Poetry and Poetics of Aimé Césaire* (Cambridge: Harvard UP, 1981) 36. For more on this disconnect, see Frantz Fanon, *Peau noire, masques blancs* (Paris: Seuil, 1952), translated as *Black Skin, White Masks,* trans. Charles Lam Markmann (New York: Grove P, 1967), esp. chaps. 1 and 6.

75. Kesteloot, *Black Writers in French* 195.

76. Léopold Sédar Senghor, "Nuit de Sine" and "Femme noire," *Anthologie de la nouvelle poésie nègre et malgache de langue française* 149–50, 151. Both poems were originally published in *Chants d'ombre* (Paris: Seuil, 1945). Translation of "Femme noire" from Melvin Dixon, trans., *The Collected Poetry,* by Léopold Sédar Senghor (Charlottesville: UP of Virginia, 1998) 8–9.

77. Senghor, "Congo," *Anthologie de la nouvelle poésie nègre et malgache de langue française* 168. Originally published in *Ethiopiques* (Paris: Seuil, 1956). Translation from Dixon 76.

78. Sartre, "Orphée noir" xxxiii/40, xxxii/39.

79. T. Denean Sharpley-Whiting, "Erasures and the Practice of Diaspora Feminism," *Small Axe* 17 (2005): 130. Sharpley-Whiting is referring to comments Damas made in an interview with Keith Q. Warner. See Warner, *Critical Perspectives on Léon-Gontran Damas* (Washington, DC: Three Continents P, 1988) 24.

80. Oruno Lara, *Question de couleurs (Blanches et noirs): roman de mœurs* (Paris: Nouvelle Librairie Universelle, 1923); and Suzanne Lacascade, *Claire-Solange, âme africaine* (Paris: Eugène Figuière, 1924). Neither novel has been translated into English. Even more likely candidates for recuperation, such as the 1927 editorial "Le mot 'nègre'" ("The Word *Nègre*") penned by radical labor activist Lamine Senghor, tend to drop out of Negritude creation myths. See "Le mot 'nègre,'" editorial, *La Voix des Nègres* (Paris), Jan. 1927: 1. Although he also was Senegalese, Lamine Senghor was of no relation to Léopold Sédar Senghor.

81. Arnold 37. Leo Frobenius, *Kulturgeschichte Afrikas* (Frankfurt: Phaidon Verlag, 1933). Translated as *Histoire de la civilisation africaine,* trans. H. Back and D. Ermont, 3rd ed. (1936; Paris: Gallimard, 1952). For more on the Nardals, see Edwards, *Practice of Diaspora,* esp. chap. 3; Sharpley-Whiting, *Negritude Women,* esp. chaps. 2, 3, and 4; and Lewis, *Race, Culture, and Identity,* esp. chap. 3.

82. Aimé Césaire once criticized the *Revue* as too "superficial." Georges Ngal, *Aimé Césaire: un homme à la recherche d'une patrie* (Paris: Présence Africaine, 1994) 52.

83. Zita C. Nunes, "Phantasmatic Brazil: Nella Larsen's *Passing,* American Literary Imagination, and Racial Utopianism," *Mixing Race, Mixing Culture: Inter-American Literary Dialogues,* ed. Monika Kaup and Debra J. Rosenthal (Austin: U of Texas P, 2002) 60, 61.

84. Martin Summers, *Manliness and Its Discontents: The Black Middle Class and the Transformation of Masculinity, 1900–1930* (Chapel Hill: U of North Carolina P, 2004) 113.

85. Hortense J. Spillers, "Mama's Baby, Papa's Maybe: An American Grammar Book," *diacritics* 17.2 (1987): 79.

86. My conceptualization of intellectual citizenship is indebted to legal scholar Linda Bosniak's discussion of the geopolitical parameters of citizenship. See Bosniak, "Citizenship Denationalized," *Indiana Journal of Global Legal Studies* 7.2 (2000): 447–509.

87. Langston Hughes identified Fauset as one of the people who "midwifed the so-called New Negro literature into being," and Martinican novelist Joseph Zobel memorialized Nardal as "the godmother of Negritude." See Hughes, *The Big Sea* (1940; New York: Hill and Wang, 1963) 218; and Joseph Zobel quoted in Marie-Agnès Sourieau, "La Revue du Monde Noir," *Encyclopedia of Latin American Literature*, ed. Verity Smith (Chicago: Fitzroy Dearborn, 1997) 453. Although Hughes also includes Alain Locke and Charles Johnson in his grouping of literary midwives, the gendered term has had the greatest impact on Fauset's intellectual legacy.

88. Dorothy West, "Dear Reader," *Challenge* 1.1 (1934): 39.

89. Condé, "Order, Disorder, Freedom, and the West Indian Writer" 126.

1. A Dying Exoticism

1. Jack Corzani, *La Négritude*, vol. 3 of *La littérature des Antilles-Guyane françaises* (Fort-de-France: Désormeaux, 1978) 211.

2. Suzanne Lacascade, *Claire-Solange, âme africaine* (Paris: Eugène Figuière, 1924). Subsequent references will be noted parenthetically in the text.

3. Maryse Condé, "La littérature féminine de la Guadeloupe: recherche d'identité," *Présence Africaine* 99–100 (1976): 156. This and all other unmarked translations are mine.

4. In Martinique and Guadeloupe the terms *mulâtre* (mulatto) and *mulâtresse* (mulatta) can refer to an individual who is the child of an interracial (conventionally black-white) union or to an individual who, because of his or her descent from *gens de couleur* (people of color) of a certain social standing, belongs to the social category *mulâtre*. In Aurore's case, Lacascade uses *mulâtresse* in the latter sense: Claire-Solange refers to her "grands-parents mulâtres" (36). For more on socio-racial categories in Martinique and Guadeloupe, see Michel Leiris, *Contacts de civilisations en Martinique et en Guadeloupe* (Paris: UNESCO/Gallimard, 1955), particularly the section "Les relations entre catégories fondées sur l'origine" 117–87.

5. Jean Vignaud, "La vie littéraire," *Le Petit Parisien* 10 Nov. 1924: 6; and Charles Régismanset, "Exotisme," *La Dépêche Coloniale et Maritime* [Paris] 7–8 Dec. 1924: 2. The Guadeloupean newspaper *Le Nouvelliste* announced the publication of *Claire-Solange* in a December 1924 issue and excerpted the Vignaud and Régismanset reviews in a January 1925 issue. See "Le mois littéraire," *Le Nouvelliste* [Point-à-Pitre, Guadeloupe] 6 Dec. 1924 and 10 Jan. 1925: 1–2.

6. Régismanset, "Exotisme."

7. It is important to note that racism and discrimination often tempered the acceptance of these newly created French citizens by their white metropolitan compatriots. For more on assimilation in the interwar period, see Philippe Dewitte, *Les mouvements nègres en France, 1919–1939* (Paris: L'Harmattan, 1985) 40–93; Brent Hayes Edwards, *The Practice of Diaspora: Literature, Translation,*

and the Rise of Black Internationalism (Cambridge: Harvard UP, 2003) 73; and Elizabeth Ezra, *The Colonial Unconscious: Race and Culture in Interwar France* (Ithaca, NY: Cornell UP, 2000).

8. T. Denean Sharpley-Whiting, *Negritude Women* (Minneapolis: U of Minnesota P, 2002) 52.

9. Paulette Nardal, "Éveil de la conscience de race" ("Awakening of Race Consciousness"), *La Revue du Monde Noir* 6 (1932): 29. Unless otherwise noted, all translations are from the journal. The exhibition in question was the 1931 Exposition Coloniale Internationale held in Paris's Bois de Vincennes.

10. Étienne Léro, "Misère d'une poésie," *Légitime Défense* 1 (1932): 10. Translated as "Poverty of a Poetry," *Refusal of the Shadow: Surrealism and the Caribbean,* ed. Michael Richardson, trans. Krzystof Fijalkowski and Michael Richardson (New York: Verso, 1996) 55. While the Fijalkowski/Richardson translations are, on the whole, excellent, I do wish to note a slight disjunction between *abâtardie,* which literally means "bastardized" or "mongrelized," and *corrupt,* which, though it connotes pollution, does not necessarily communicate the sense of genealogical impurity so relevant to the Caribbean context.

11. For more on Léro and *Légitime Défense,* see Shireen K. Lewis, "*Légitime Défense:* A Precursor to Modern Black Francophone Literature," *Race, Culture, and Identity: Francophone West African and Caribbean Literature and Theory from Négritude to Créolité* (Lanham, MD: Lexington Books, 2006) 1–22; and Michael Richardson, introduction, *Refusal of the Shadow* 1–33.

12. André Breton, *Manifeste du surréalisme* (1924; Paris: Gallimard, 1962) 17–19. Translated as *Manifesto of Surrealism,* trans. Richard Seaver and Helen R. Lane (Ann Arbor: U of Michigan P, 1969) 7–9.

13. Valérie Orlando, *Of Suffocated Hearts and Tortured Souls: Seeking Subjecthood through Madness in Francophone Women's Writing of Africa and the Caribbean* (Lanham, MD: Lexington Books, 2003) 37.

14. Nicole Aas Rouxparis, "Espace antillais au féminin: présence, absence," *French Review* 70 (1997): 854.

15. Frantz Fanon, *Peau noire, masques blancs* (Paris: Seuil, 1952) 33–50. Translated as *Black Skin, White Masks,* trans. Charles Lam Markmann (New York: Grove P, 1967) 41–62. In subsequent references the title will be abbreviated as *PNMB.* Mayotte Capécia, *Je suis martiniquaise* (Paris: Corrêa, 1948). In 1950 Capécia published a second novel, *La négresse blanche,* with the same publisher. Both texts have been translated into English in the volume *"I Am a Martinican Woman" and "The White Negress": Two Novelettes,* trans. Beatrice Stith Clark (Pueblo, CO: Passeggiata P, 1997). For more on Capécia, see Clark's introduction and Christiane P. Makward, *Mayotte Capécia, ou l'aliénation selon Fanon* (Paris: Editions Karthala, 1999).

16. Fanon, *PNMB* 38/47.

17. Fanon, *PNMB* 37 n 5/46 n 5.

18. Maryse Condé, *La parole des femmes: essai sur des romancières des Antilles de langue française* (1979; Paris: L'Harmattan, 1993) 75; and "La littérature féminine" 159. Corzani, *La Négritude* 211.

19. Roger Toumson, *La transgression des couleurs: littérature et langage des Antilles, XVIIIe, XIXe, XXe siècles,* 2 vols. (Paris: Éditions Caribéennes, 1989) 301, 299.

20. See Brent Hayes Edwards, "Black Globality: The International Shape of Black Intellectual Culture," diss., Columbia U, 1998, 226–28; Micheline Rice-Maximin, *Karukéra: présence littéraire de la Guadeloupe* (New York: Peter Lang, 1998) 78–79; Orlando, *Of Suffocated Hearts and Tortured*

Souls 37–50; and Sharpley-Whiting, *Negritude Women* 14–16. Edwards also discusses Lacascade in *Practice of Diaspora* 53–58.

21. Edwards, "Black Globality" 171.

22. Léon-Gontran Damas, "Hoquet," *"Pigments" suive de "Névralgies"* (Paris: Présence Africaine, 1972) 38.

23. Aimé Césaire, *Cahier d'un retour au pays natal, Aimé Césaire: The Collected Poetry*, ed. and trans. Clayton Eshleman and Annette Smith (Berkeley: U of California P, 1983) 36/37, 40/41.

24. Léopold Sédar Senghor, "Femme noire," *Anthologie de la nouvelle poésie nègre et malgache de langue française*, ed. Léopold Sédar Senghor (1948; Paris: Quadrige/PUF, 1992) 151.

25. Orlando 59.

26. Carole Boyce Davies, *Black Women, Writing and Identity: Migrations of the Subject* (New York: Routledge, 1994) 84.

27. Toumson, *La transgression des couleurs* 308–9.

28. Édouard Glissant, *Le discours antillais* (1981; Paris: Gallimard, 1997) 442. Translated as *Caribbean Discourse: Selected Essays*, trans. J. Michael Dash (Charlottesville: UP of Virginia, 1989) 149.

29. Lilyan Kesteloot, *Les écrivains noirs de langue française: naissance d'une littérature* (Brussels: Université Libre de Bruxelles, 1965) 35/26.

30. Jack Corzani, *Splendeur et misère: l'exotisme littéraire aux Antilles* (Point-à-Pitre: GURIC, Centre d'Enseignement Supérieur Littéraire, 1969) 3, 11; Toumson, *La transgression des couleurs* 308–9.

31. Régis Antoine, *La littérature franco-antillaise: Haïti, Guadeloupe et Martinique* (Paris: Karthala, 1992) 335.

32. Antoine 333, 334. See, for example, Médéric Louis Elie Moreau de Saint-Méry, *Description topographique, physique, civile, politique et historique de la partie française de l'île Saint-Domingue* (1797/98; Paris: Société de l'Histoire des Colonies Françaises et Librairie Larose, 1994); and Nicolas Germain Léonard, *Lettre sur un voyage aux Antilles* (1783) in *Oeuvres de M. Léonard recueillées et publiées par Vincent Campenon* (Paris: Didot Jeune, 1798). Note that in French *les îles Fortunées* can also connote the Canary Islands.

33. J. Michael Dash, *The Other America: Caribbean Literature in a New World Context* (Charlottesville: UP of Virginia, 1998) 32; Julia V. Douthwaite, *Exotic Women: Literary Heroines and Cultural Strategies in Ancien Régime France* (Philadelphia: U of Pennsylvania P, 1992) 8.

34. See Antoine 336, Rice-Maximin 70, and Kesteloot 29–43/19–36.

35. Toumson, *La transgression de couleurs* 280; Corzani, *Splendeur et misère* 34. Ever incisive, Léro called Thaly "un des pontifes de cette poésie de classe" ("one of the pontiffs of this class poetry"). Léro, "Misère d'une poésie" 10/56.

36. Thaly's early poetry is identified with that of the Parnassians (*Les Parnassiens*), metropolitan French poets who emerged as a group after 1860 and opposed the excesses of Romanticism with poetry that was largely "objective, impersonal, and restrained" and that "confined itself to descriptions of nature, remarkable for their static, pictorial quality . . . and often introducing an exotic element." Sir Paul Harvey and J. E. Heseltine, eds., *The Oxford Companion to French Literature* (1959; Oxford: Oxford UP, 1993) 539.

37. Daniel Thaly, "Chanson," *Le jardin des tropiques: Poèmes, 1897–1907* (Paris: Editions du Beffroi, 1911) 97. Thaly's work has not, to my knowledge, been widely translated. For more on Thaly, see Corzani, *Exotisme et régionalisme*, vol. 2 of *La littérature des Antilles-Guyane françaises*.

38. Nardal, "Eveil de la conscience de race" 28.

39. Thaly, "Le Caraïbe," *Chants de l'Atlantique suivis de Sous le Ciel des Antilles* (Paris: Garnier Editeur, 1928) 74; "Marchande martiniquaise," *Le jardin des tropiques* 19; and "Le planteur," *Le jardin des tropiques* 33.

40. René Ménil, "De l'exotisme colonial," *La Nouvelle Critique* (1959), rpt. in *Tracées: Identité, négritude, esthétique aux Antilles* (Paris: Robert Laffont, 1981) 18.

41. Dash, *Other America* 36.

42. Condé, "La littérature féminine" 157.

43. I use *women of color* here rather than *black women* not to suggest that any residents of the Caribbean are without color—that is, racial identity—but, rather, to indicate the distinction made between mixed-race and black women in colonial discourse and the primacy of the former in exoticist rhetoric. For a powerful case against using the phrase *women of color* in Caribbean literary criticism, see Vera M. Kutzinski, *Sugar's Secrets: Race and the Erotics of Cuban Nationalism* (Charlottesville: UP of Virginia, 1993) 31 n. 39.

44. Françoise Lionnet, "Reframing Baudelaire: Literary History, Biography, Postcolonial Theory, and Vernacular Languages," *diacritics* 28.3 (1998): 65. See also Dash, *Other America* 22.

45. In *Le discours antillais* Glissant writes that the *da* "[a] son équivalent dans toute la région caraïbe et dans le Sud des États-Unis" ("has her equivalent all over the Caribbean region and southern United States"). One might say that the *da* is comparable to the figure of the mammy in southern U.S. history and folklore. Glissant, *Le discours antillais* 826/264.

46. M. L. E. Moreau de Saint-Méry, *Description topographique, physique, civile, politique et historique de la partie française de l'isle Saint-Domingue,* 2 vols. (Philadelphia, 1797–98) 92, *Eighteenth-Century Collections Online,* 18 June 2007, http://galenet.galegroup.com.ezproxy.lib.utexas.edu/servlet/ECCO. Translation is mine. Translated and abridged as *A Civilization That Perished: The Last Years of White Colonial Rule in Haiti,* trans. and ed. Ivor D. Spencer (Lanham, MD: UP of America, 1985).

47. Condé, *La parole des femmes* 61.

48. Aimé Césaire, "Poésie et connaissance," *Tropiques* 12 (1945): 159. Translated as "Poetry and Knowledge," trans. A. James Arnold, *Lyric and Dramatic Poetry, 1946–82,* trans. Clayton Eshleman and Annette Smith (Charlottesville: UP of Virginia, 1990) xliv.

49. English translation of verse is from Baudelaire, "For a Creole Lady," *The Flowers of Evil,* trans. James McGowan (New York: Oxford UP, 1993) 129. All subsequent French-language citations of *Les fleurs du mal* are from Charles Baudelaire, *Les fleurs de mal,* ed. John E. Jackson (1857; Paris: Librairie Générale Française, 1999).

50. The poem was inspired by Emmeline Autard de Bragard and initially sent to her husband, Gustave-Adolphe Autard de Bragard. The Autard de Bragards were wealthy white Creoles who hosted Baudelaire during his 1841 visit to Mauritius. Lionnet, "Reframing Baudelaire" 66.

51. The work of Sharpley-Whiting offers one possible explanation of the interchangeability of the *mulâtresse* Claire-Solange with the white "dame créole." Sharpley-Whiting contends that, whereas "their colonial experiences" separated white Creole women from their metropolitan counterparts, "with the black woman the Creole share[d] culture, nationality, and geographic space." *Black Venus: Sexualized Savages, Primal Fears, and Primitive Narratives in French* (Durham: Duke UP, 1999) 45.

52. Robert Greer Cohn, "Intimate Globality: Baudelaire's *La Chevelure,*" *French Studies* 42

(1988): 296. Baudelaire did pen a series of poems about or inspired by Duval, but it is unclear to this author what exactly constitutes "Caribbean" hair.

53. Edward J. Ahearn, "Black Woman, White Poet: Exile and Exploitation in Baudelaire's Jeanne Duval Poems," *French Review* 51.2 (1977): 217.

54. Ahearn 215, 218.

55. Antoine 343.

56. Jean-Pierre Jardel, "Représentations des 'Gens de Couleur' et du métissage aux Antilles," *L'Autre et Nous: Scènes et Types*, ed. Nicolas Bancel, Pascal Blanchard et al. (Paris: ACHAC/SYROS, 1995) 115. Jardel notes that Balzac published the novel under the pseudonym Mme Aurore Cloteaux.

57. See Leiris 162.

58. Fanon, *PNMB* 93/116.

59. Leiris 161. For a discussion of similar assessments in African American history, see Noliwe Rooks, *Hair Raising: Beauty, Culture, and African American Women* (New Brunswick: Rutgers UP, 1996) 11–14.

60. Aden is a former British colony now part of the Republic of Yemen.

61. George L. Mosse, *Toward the Final Solution: A History of European Racism* (New York: Howard Fertig, 1978) 22.

62. For a useful gloss of this myth, see Claude Blanckeart, "Of Monstrous Métis? Hybridity, Fear of Miscegenation, and Patriotism from Buffon to Paul Broca," *The Color of Liberty: Histories of Race in France*, ed. Sue Peabody and Tyler Stovall (Durham: Duke UP, 2003) 42–70.

63. Antoine 344.

64. bell hooks, "The Oppositional Gaze: Black Female Spectators," *Black Looks: Race and Representation* (London: Turnaround, 1992) 115–31, rpt. in *Feminist Film Theory: A Reader*, ed. Sue Thornham (New York: New York UP, 1999) 308.

65. hooks 317.

66. Laura Mulvey, "Visual Pleasure and Narrative Cinema," *Screen* 16.3 (1975), rpt. in *Narrative, Apparatus, Ideology*, ed. Philip Rosen (New York: Columbia UP, 1986) 203.

67. Susan McClary, *Georges Bizet: Carmen*, Cambridge Opera Handbooks (New York: Cambridge UP, 1992) 30. See also Edward Said's influential *Orientalism* (New York: Vintage, 1978).

68. For a useful discussion of the difficulty of translating French racial signifiers into English, see Edwards, *Practice of Diaspora* 25–38. The socio-racial hierarchy found here comes from "Le mot 'nègre,'" editorial, *La voix des nègres* [Paris], Jan. 1927: 1.

69. "Le mot 'nègre.'" *La voix des nègres* was the official organ of the CDRN. For more information on Lamine Senghor, a World War I *tirailleur* (sharpshooter) turned radical intellectual, and the CDRN, see Edwards, *Practice of Diaspora* 28–34; and Philippe Dewitte, *Les mouvements nègres en France* 127–72.

70. Oruno Lara's 1923 novel *Question de couleurs (Blanches et noirs)*, which I will return to later in the chapter, also features a bourgeois, mixed-race character who embraces the identity *nègre*, but that character is male. Lara, *Question de couleurs (Blanches et noirs). Roman de mœurs* (Paris: Nouvelle Librairie Universelle, 1923).

71. "Le mot 'nègre.'"

72. Condé, *La parole des femmes* 28.

73. Dash offers the following schema of this recreation: "Western European thought . . . map[s]

the Americas in fictive terms, from images of alluring wildness to metaphors of violence and savagery. The New World is then invented in terms of Europe's prevailing cultural order of the time. It is within this imaginative space that the Americas are essentialized and a pattern of cultural and moral dichotomies is established." *Other America* 23.

74. Condé, "La littérature féminine" 157.

75. Glissant, *Le discours antillais* 128. Passage not included in Dash's translation.

76. Condé argues that "Lacascade se trompe en croyant détruire les stéréotypes" ("Lacascade is mistaken in believing that she is destroying stereotypes"; "La littérature féminine" 159).

77. Claudia Tate, *Domestic Allegories of Political Desire: The Black Heroine's Text at the Turn of the Century* (New York: Oxford UP, 1992) 65.

78. Edwards, "Black Globality" 228.

79. Fanon, *PNMB* 39/49.

80. Ezra, *Colonial Unconscious* 3, 2, 4. See also Sharpley-Whiting, *Black Venus* 4.

81. Condé alludes to the possibility of reading Jacques as France in observing that by novel's end Claire-Solange's desired audience is no longer Jeanne or Jacques but Europe. Condé, *La parole des femmes* 31.

82. Tate, *Domestic Allegories of Political Desire* 66.

83. After World War II the 1946 *loi de départementalisation* (law of departmentalization) resulted in the political assimilation of *les vieilles colonies* as overseas departments, administrative units equal to the departments of metropolitan France. A. James Arnold, *Modernism and Negritude: The Poetry and Poetics of Aimé Césaire* (Cambridge: Harvard UP, 1981) 169. In contrast the post–World War I shift in France's approach to its African colonies resulted in the policy of association, which dictated the "preserv[ation of] African culture and [the] use [of] local institutions and roitelets to help administer the colonies." Brett A. Berliner, *Ambivalent Desire: The Exotic Black Other in Jazz-Age France* (Amherst: U of Massachusetts P, 2002) 145.

84. See Berliner, *Ambivalent Desire* 71–106; Alice Conklin, "Who Speaks for Africa? The René Maran–Blaise Diagne Trial in 1920s Paris," *Color of Liberty* 302–37; and Edwards, *Practice of Diaspora* 69–118.

85. For a fictionalized but unromanticized portrayal of Solitude, see André Schwarz-Bart, *La mulâtresse Solitude* (Paris: Seuil, 1972). Conceived during *la pariade,* or the period "généralement un mois avant l'arrivée aux ports antillais des bateaux négriers, lorsque les femmes esclaves étaient livrées aux marins dans les mêlées reproductrices forcées" ("generally a month before the arrival of slave ships in Caribbean ports, when women slaves were delivered to the sailors in a melee of forced reproduction"; Rice-Maximin 52), Solitude has become a mythic figure in Guadeloupean history because of her participation in the 1802 rebellion.

86. Lara outlines his philosophy of race and gender in the novel's preface. He contends that, once conscientized, women of color ("les femmes de couleur") can follow the example of their metropolitan French sisters and serve as a moral example for the nation. Lara, preface, *Questions de Couleurs* n.p.

87. Edwards, *Practice of Diaspora* 161.

88. Orlando 45.

89. Renée Lacascade and André Pérye, *L'île qui meurt,* 3rd ed. (Paris: Calmann-Lévy, 1930). Renée is reputed to be the sister of Suzanne Lacascade, although my research has yielded no documented confirmation of this relationship.

90. Toumson 296.

91. Despite its groundbreaking critique of French colonialism, the Prix Goncourt winner *Batouala* exoticizes and idealizes life in the African bush. It is, however, an important precursor to Negritude literature. See René Maran, *Batouala: un véritable roman nègre* (1921; Paris: Albin Michel, 1938). Translated as *Batouala*, trans. Barbara Beck and Alexandre Nboukou (London: Heinemann, 1973). For more on Maran, see Conklin, "Who Speaks for Africa?"; Edwards, *Practice of Diaspora;* Michel Fabre, *From Harlem to Paris: Black American Writers in France, 1840–1980* (Urbana: U of Illinois P, 1991) 148–50; and Gary Wilder, *The French Imperial Nation-State: Negritude and Colonial Humanism between the Two World Wars* (Chicago: U of Chicago P, 2005).

92. Joyce W. Warren, "Introduction: The Challenge of Women's Periods," *Challenging Boundaries: Gender and Periodization,* ed. Joyce W. Warren and Margaret Dickie (Athens: U of Georgia P, 2000) ix.

93. One debate, for example, centers around whether to declare the movement's defining moment the 1932 publication of the Étienne Léro-helmed *Légitime Défense* or the 1935 publication of the journal *L'Étudiant Noir,* whose contributors included Aimé Césaire and Léopold Sédar Senghor. See Edward O. Ako, "*L'Étudiant Noir* and the Myth of the Genesis of the Negritude Movement," *Research in African Literatures* (1984): 341–53.

94. Léro, "Misère d'une poésie" 12/58.

95. Corzani, *Splendeur et misère* 24.

96. Warren xiii.

97. Condé, "La littérature féminine" 165. For an extended discussion of gendered critiques of Francophone Caribbean literature, see Condé, "Order, Disorder, Freedom and the West Indian Writer," *Yale French Studies* 83 (1993): 121–35.

98. In its entirety Nardal's remark reads: "Si l'on examine les œuvres de ces précurseurs, on y trouve évidemment la glorification des petites patries lointaines, des 'Iles de beauté' (la mode est déjà à l'exotisme), mais rien qui ressemble à la fierté de race" ("If we examine the works of these precursors, we certainly meet with the glorification of their small far-away mother-lands, the 'Isles of Beauty' (Exoticism was already the fashion), but no race pride is to be found there"). Nardal, "Eveil de la conscience de race" 28.

99. Due to the dearth of biographical information on Lacascade, I am unable to surmise whether she indeed traveled to or lived in Africa, as did Martinican colonial officer turned author Maran, or whether her relationship to the African continent was primarily an intellectual and imaginative one. For more on Caribbean Negritude's inventive impulses, see Clarisse Zimra, "Négritude in the Feminine Mode: The Case of Martinique and Guadeloupe," *Journal of Ethnic Studies* 12.1 (1984): 53–77.

100. The character exclaims, "Je suis Africaine, clamait Claire-Solange, . . . Africaine, par atavisme et malgré mon hérédité paternelle!" ("I am African, Claire-Solange cried out, . . . African out of atavism and in spite of my paternal heredity!" 66).

101. See Arnold, *Modernism and Negritude* 33–40.

102. Corzani, *La Négritude* 213.

103. Sam Haigh, *Mapping a Tradition: Francophone Women's Writing from Guadeloupe* (London: Maney Publishing, 2000) 65.

104. See Condé, *La parole des femmes* 30.

105. Glissant, *Le discours antillais* 48/20. This sentence is condensed in J. Michael Dash's abridged translation, which does not include the phrase enclosed in brackets.

106. Glissant, *Le discours antillais* 54/24. In the *Cahier* Césaire writes, "Au bout du petit matin bourgeonnant d'anses frêles, les Antilles qui ont faim, les Antilles grêlées de petite vérole, les Antilles dynamitées d'alcool, échouées dans la boue de cette baie, dans la poussière de cette ville sinistrement échouées" ("At the end of the wee hours burgeoning with frail coves, the hungry Antilles, the Antilles pitted with smallpox, the Antilles dynamited by alcohol, stranded in the mud of this bay, in the dust of this town sinisterly stranded"; 34/35).

107. In the 1989 manifesto *Éloge de la créolité (In Praise of Creoleness),* authors Jean Bernabé, Patrick Chamoiseau, and Raphaël Confiant reject the privileging of any one racial or ethnic identity. They launch their argument with a proclamation whose tone is reminiscent of that of Claire-Solange: "Ni Européens, ni Africains, ni Asiatiques, nous nous proclamons Créoles" ("Neither Europeans, nor Africans, nor Asians, we proclaim ourselves Creole"). Bernabé, Chamoiseau, and Confiant, *Éloge de la créolité/In Praise of Creoleness,* trans. M. B. Taleb-Khyar (Paris: Gallimard, 1993) 13/75.

108. Orlando 43.

109. Glissant; *Le discours antillais* 57/26.

110. Edwards, "Black Globality" 225; Dash, *Other America* 34. See also Tyler Stovall, *Paris Noir: African Americans in the City of Light* (Boston: Mariner Books/Houghton Mifflin, 1996) 31.

111. Baker arrived in Paris in September 1925 as a performer in La Revue Nègre, emerged as the show's star, and spent the rest of her life and career primarily in France. Once settled in Paris, Baker worked on stage and screen and, through sensation (walking a pet leopard through city streets) and service (working in the French Resistance during World War II), became a national icon. For more on Baker, see Sharpley-Whiting, *Black Venus* 9–10, 105–18; and Stovall, *Paris Noir* 49–56. For more on depictions of Caribbean women in French popular culture, see Berliner, *Ambivalent Desire* 148–50.

112. Condé, *La parole des femmes* 3–4.

113. The designation *âme africaine* (African soul) might be no less essentialist than those made by Lacascade's male Negritude successors, but my concern here rests in the fact that it is a designation that Claire-Solange chooses for herself rather than accepts from an outside source.

114. Aas Rouxparis 854.

115. Dash, *Other America* 41–42.

116. Gary Wilder, "Framing Greater France between the Wars," *Journal of Historical Sociology* 14 (2001): 204.

117. Gary Wilder, "Panafricanism and the Republican Political Sphere," *Color of Liberty* 245. For an extended discussion of these issues, see Wilder, *French Imperial Nation-State.*

118. Claire-Solange's remark also recalls the manner in which the line between colonial subject and caged animal was often blurred by the European penchant for exhibiting exotic humans in the late nineteenth and early twentieth centuries. See Berliner, *Ambivalent Desire* 107–22; and Ezra, *Colonial Unconscious* 21–46.

119. See Nardal, "Eveil de la conscience de race" 31; and Lacascade and Pérye, *L'île qui meurt* 5, 68, 220.

120. Corzani, *La Négritude* 211.

121. Sharpley-Whiting, *Black Venus* 83.

122. Suzanne Césaire, "Le grand camouflage," *Tropiques* 13–14 (1945): 269. Trans. as "The Great Camouflage," *Refusal of the Shadow* 157.

123. Sharpley-Whiting, *Black Venus* 121. Sharpley-Whiting's comments reflect those of Maryse Condé in "Order, Disorder, Freedom and the West Indian Writer."

2. The Limits of Exemplarity

1. Lorraine Elena Roses and Ruth Elizabeth Randolph, "Marita Bonner: In Search of Other Mothers' Gardens," *Black American Literature Forum* 21.1–2 (1987): 166–67.

2. This notable list also includes Cooper's fellow clubwoman and Oberlin alumna Mary Church Terrell (1863–1954), who taught with Cooper at the M Street School, Washington's most prestigious black high school and, in its original incarnation as Preparatory High School, the city's first public high school. M Street later became Dunbar High School, where Jessie Fauset taught French before moving to Harlem. For more on Fauset's time in Washington, DC, see David Levering Lewis, *When Harlem Was in Vogue* (1981; New York: Penguin Books, 1997) 121. For more on Bonner's teaching career, see Roses and Randolph 167–68. For a general history of the African American elite in Washington, DC, see Jacqueline M. Moore, *Leading the Race: The Transformation of the Black Elite in the Nation's Capital, 1880–1920* (Charlottesville: UP of Virginia, 1999).

3. W. E. B. Du Bois, "The Talented Tenth," *The Negro Problem: A Series of Articles by Representative American Negroes of To-Day*, ed. Booker T. Washington (New York: James Pott & Co., 1903) 45.

4. Du Bois, "Talented Tenth" 45.

5. Alain Locke, "The New Negro," *The New Negro*, ed. Alain Locke (1925; New York: Touchstone, 1997) 9.

6. Marita Bonner, "On Being Young—a Woman—and Colored," *Crisis* (June 1925): 63–65; "Tin Can," *Opportunity* (July 1934): 202–5, (Aug. 1934): 236–40; and *The Purple Flower, Crisis* (Jan. 1928): 9–11, 28, 30. The two journals often published winning pieces after prizes were announced, hence the different award and publication dates for the latter two works. For more on these prizes, see Kim Jenice Dillon, "Marita Bonner," *The Concise Oxford Companion to African American Literature*, ed. William L. Andrews, Frances Smith Foster, and Trudier Harris (New York: Oxford UP, 2001) 40–41; and Kathy A. Perkins, introduction, *Black Female Playwrights: An Anthology of Plays before 1950* (Bloomington: Indiana UP, 1989) 5.

7. See Roses and Randolph 166. Marita Bonner, *Frye Street and Environs: The Collected Works of Marita Bonner*, ed. Joyce Flynn and Joyce Occomy Stricklin (Boston: Beacon P, 1987). Unless otherwise noted, all subsequent Bonner references will be taken from *Frye Street and Environs* and noted parenthetically in the text. Through their correspondence and interviews with Bonner's children, Roses and Randolph discovered several unpublished stories recorded by Bonner in a notebook that is now housed with Bonner's papers at the Schlesinger Library at the Radcliffe Institute for Advanced Study. *Frye Street and Environs* includes these stories.

8. See Nathan Irvin Huggins, *Harlem Renaissance* (New York: Oxford UP, 1971); and Lewis, *When Harlem Was in Vogue*, esp. 121–22, 126–28.

9. Deborah McDowell, "Introduction: Regulating Midwives," *Plum Bun: A Novel without a Moral*, by Jessie Redmon Fauset (1929; Boston: Beacon P, 1990) ix–xxxiii. Playing on Langston Hughes's characterization of the work of Fauset, *Opportunity* editor Charles Johnson, and *New*

Negro editor Alain Locke as literary midwifery, McDowell argues that Fauset should be read as a full participant in, rather than simply as a midwife of, the Harlem Renaissance.

10. See Cheryl A. Wall, "On Being Young—A Woman—and Colored: When Harlem Was in Vogue," *Women of the Harlem Renaissance* (Bloomington: Indiana UP, 1995) 2–29. Scholars have also begun to include Bonner's work in a number of anthologies, among them *Black Female Playwrights: An Anthology of Plays before 1950,* ed. Kathy A. Perkins; *The Norton Anthology of African American Literature,* ed. Henry Louis Gates Jr., Nellie Y. McKay, et al. (New York: Norton, 1997); and *The Crisis Reader,* ed. Sondra K. Wilson (New York: Modern Library, 1999).

11. Wall 7.

12. Locke, "New Negro" 6.

13. Wall 6.

14. Locke, "New Negro" 9; Elise Johnson McDougald, "The Task of Negro Womanhood," *New Negro* 369.

15. McDougald 381.

16. Lewis 47, 48.

17. Locke, "New Negro" 15.

18. Lewis 97.

19. Harper's 1893 novel *Iola Leroy* explains the challenge facing post–Civil War blacks as follows: "Other men have plead his cause, but out of the race must come its own defenders. With them the pen must be mightier than the sword. It is the weapon of civilization, and they must use it in their own defense. We cannot tell what is in them until they express themselves." Frances Ellen Watkins Harper, *Iola Leroy, or Shadows Uplifted* (1893; Boston: Beacon P, 1987) 115–16.

20. Lewis 238.

21. Lewis 239.

22. Langston Hughes, "The Negro Artist and the Racial Mountain," 1926, *Norton Anthology of African American Literature* 1268; Du Bois quoted in Lewis 225.

23. Hughes, "Negro Artist and the Racial Mountain" 1271.

24. Alain Locke, "Negro Youth Speaks," *New Negro* 48.

25. Kevin Gaines, *Uplifting the Race: Black Leadership, Politics, and Culture in the Twentieth Century* (Chapel Hill: U of North Carolina P, 1996) 3. Gaines further argues that the black intelligentsia considered the assertion of an empowered black patriarchy essential to combating the distorted views of black sexuality produced and perpetuated during the slave era. His chapters on educator and clubwoman Anna Julia Cooper and writer Alice Dunbar-Nelson (1875–1935) are particularly useful in their exploration of black women's necessarily complicated engagements with uplift ideology.

26. Gaines 107.

27. W. E. B. Du Bois, *The Souls of Black Folk,* 1903, *Norton Anthology of African American Literature* 615.

28. Du Bois, "Souls of Black Folk" 615.

29. Locke, "New Negro" 7.

30. Henry Louis Gates Jr., "Harlem on Our Minds," *Critical Inquiry* 24 (1997): 10.

31. Nella Larsen, *Quicksand and Passing,* ed. Deborah E. McDowell (Rutgers: Rutgers UP, 1986) 3, 5; Zora Neale Hurston, *Their Eyes Were Watching God* (1937; New York: Harper & Row, 1990) 48–51.

32. McDougald 371.

33. Locke, "New Negro" 10; Judith Musser, "African American Women and Education: Marita Bonner's Response to the 'Talented Tenth,'" *Studies in Short Fiction* 34 (1997): 79.

34. Quasimodo is the protagonist of Victor Hugo's 1831 novel *Notre-Dame de Paris (The Hunchback of Notre Dame)*.

35. Maria Balshaw, "New Negroes, New Women: The Gender Politics of the Harlem Renaissance," *Women: A Cultural Review* 10.2 (1999): 128.

36. Locke, "New Negro" 3.

37. Du Bois, *Souls of Black Folk* 614.

38. Gilroy argues that this view does not allow for "fragmentation," or differentiation, within the African diaspora. Paul Gilroy, *The Black Atlantic: Modernity and Double Consciousness* (Cambridge: Harvard UP, 1993) 100.

39. Werner Sollors, *Neither Black nor White yet Both: Thematic Explorations of Interracial Literature* (New York: Oxford UP, 1997).

40. C. Hugh Holman and William Harmon, "Expressionism," *A Handbook to Literature*, 5th ed. (New York: Macmillan, 1986) 195.

41. Peter Bauland, "Expressionism in Modern American Drama," *Amerikanisches Drama und Theater in 20. Jahrundert*, ed. Alfred Weber and Siegfried Neuweiler (Göttingen: Vandenhoeck and Ruprecht, 1975) 32, 29.

42. Flynn, introduction, *Frye Street and Environs* xvii. Jean Toomer also experimented with expressionist drama, most notably in *Natalie Mann* (1922) and *The Sacred Factory* (1927). For more on Toomer's plays, see Nellie Y. McKay, *Jean Toomer, Artist: A Study of His Literary Life and Work, 1894–1936* (Chapel Hill: U of North Carolina P, 1984) 59–81; and Darwin T. Turner, ed., *The Wayward and the Seeking: A Collection of Writings by Jean Toomer* (Washington, DC: Howard UP, 1980) 237-41.

43. Perkins 4.

44. Bauland 18.

45. Shannon Steen, "Melancholy Bodies: Racial Subjectivity and Whiteness in O'Neill's *The Emperor Jones*," *Theatre Journal* 52 (2000): 345. For more on O'Neill and expressionism, see Bauland 18–21. For more on the racial politics of *The Emperor Jones*, see, among others, David Krasner, "Whose Role Is It Anyway? Charles Gilpin and the Harlem Renaissance," *African American Review* 29.3 (1995): 483-96; Michèle Mendelssohn, "Reconsidering Race, Language and Identity in *The Emperor Jones*," *Eugene O'Neill Review* 23.1–2 (1999): 19–30; and Gabriele Poole, "'Blarsted Niggers!' *The Emperor Jones* and Modernism's Encounter with Africa," *Eugene O'Neill Review* 18.1–2 (1994): 21–37.

46. Perkins 3. See also Nellie Y. McKay, "Black Theater and Drama in the 1920s: Years of Growing Pains," *Massachusetts Review* 28 (1987): 619–21.

47. Allison Berg and Merideth Taylor, "Enacting Difference: Marita Bonner's *Purple Flower* and the Ambiguities of Race," *African American Review* 32.3 (1998): 470.

48. C. Eric Lincoln, *The Black Muslims in America* (Boston: Beacon P, 1973) 78–81.

49. Berg and Taylor 470.

50. Booker T. Washington, "The Atlanta Exposition Address," *Up from Slavery: An Autobiography* (1901; New York: Modern Library, 1999) 144.

51. Du Bois, "Talented Tenth" 34.

52. Genesis 22, *Holy Bible: New International Version* (Grand Rapids, MI: Zondervan, 1990). It is important to note that God sends Abraham an animal, not another human being, as the alternative sacrificial object.

53. Nellie McKay, "Black Theater and Drama in the 1920s" 626.

54. For a gloss of the groundbreaking nature of Bonner's use of expressionism, see McKay, "Black Theater and Drama in the 1920s" 626. For a critical genealogy of "black revolutionary drama," see Errol Hill, "The Revolutionary Tradition in Black Drama," *Theatre Journal* 38.4 (1986): 408–26.

55. Stories followed by hyphenated dates are those from Bonner's notebook. They were unpublished prior to their appearance in *Frye Street and Environs;* hence, the years listed reflect their period of composition rather than date of publication.

56. For more on these columns and their social impact, see Henry Louis Gates Jr., "The Trope of the New Negro and the Reconstruction of the Image of the Black," *America Reconstructed, 1840–1940,* spec. issue of *Representations* 24 (1988): 129–55; Daylanne K. English, "Selecting the Harlem Renaissance," *Critical Inquiry* 25 (1999): 807–21; and Anne Stavney, "'Mothers of Tomorrow': The New Negro Renaissance and the Politics of Maternal Representation," *African American Review* 32.4 (1998): 533–61. Gates argues that these pictures were displayed to counter the horrific images of lynching and minstrelsy prevalent in the early-twentieth-century U.S. media. I would argue, however, that, in addition to serving this reconstructive purpose, the photographs, like their literary counterparts, also contributed to the representation of New Negrohood as a consolidated identity.

57. E. Franklin Frazier, *Black Bourgeoisie* (1957; New York: Free P Paperbacks, 1997) 20.

58. Frazier 26, 213.

59. Roses and Randolph 173.

60. Later in the story Gran refers to Jerry as "Jerry Jackson" (236). As "On the Altar" is one of the notebook stories first published in the *Frye Street* collection, one might assume that Bonner either neglected to standardize the character's name during the three-year period (1937–40) in which she composed the story or transcribed the name incorrectly when copying the story into her notebook.

61. Roses and Randolph 173.

62. Ann duCille, *The Coupling Convention: Sex, Text, and Tradition in Black Women's Fiction* (New York: Oxford UP, 1993) 87.

63. duCille 87.

64. Roses and Randolph 173.

65. Michel Foucault's discussion of the Panopticon, a circular prison tower constructed in order to create the impression of constant surveillance, resonates with Bonner's characterization of the self-interested vigilance of the African American bourgeoisie. Bonner depicts the two extremes of Foucault's model, that of actual surveillance, as demonstrated in Gran's network of contacts in "On the Altar"; and that of perceived and/or self-surveillance, as deployed in Lee's conflicted homecoming. See Michel Foucault, *Discipline and Punish,* trans. Alan Sheridan (New York: Vintage Books, 1979) 200–204.

66. Virginia Woolf, *A Room of One's Own* (1929; New York: Harcourt, 1957).

67. duCille 32.

68. Frazier 174.

69. Dorothea Löbbermann, "Harlem as Memory Place: Reconstructing the Harlem Renaissance in Space," *Temples for Tomorrow: Looking Back at the Harlem Renaissance,* ed. Geneviève Fabre and Michel Feith (Bloomington: Indiana UP, 2001) 210. Houston A. Baker Jr., *Modernism and the Harlem Renaissance* (Chicago: U of Chicago P, 1987) 73.

70. Bonner apparently intended to collect her Frye Street narratives in a work entitled "Black Map," which "was planned on a scale comparable to James Joyce's mapping of the Irish capital in *Dubliners.*" Joyce Flynn, introduction, *Frye Street and Environs* xx.

71. Édouard Glissant, *Le discours antillais* (1981; Paris: Gallimard, 1997) 330. Trans. as *Caribbean Discourse: Selected Essays,* trans. J. Michael Dash (Charlottesville: UP of Virginia, 1989) 100.

72. Glissant 330/100.

73. Carla Cappetti, *Writing Chicago: Modernism, Ethnography, and the Novel* (New York: Columbia UP, 1993) 10.

74. Cappetti 11.

75. Priscilla Wald, "Geographics: Writing the Shtetl into the Ghetto," *Revista Canaria de Estudios Ingleses* 39 (1999): 211. For more on the Chicago school, see Cappetti; for more on Addams's work at Hull-House, see Jane Addams, *Twenty Years at Hull-House* (1910; New York: Penguin, 1998).

76. Judith A. Musser, " 'The Blood Will Flow Back to You': The Reactionary Proletarian Fiction of Marita Bonner," *Canadian Review of American Studies/Revue Canadienne d'Études Américaines* 32.1 (2002): 55.

77. Musser, " 'Blood Will Flow Back to You' " 55.

78. Wald 211; Judy D. Whipps, "Jane Addams's Social Thought as a Model for Pragmatist-Feminist Communitarianism," *Hypatia* 19.2 (2004): 120.

79. Carol Allen, *Black Women Intellectuals: Strategies of Nation, Family, and Neighborhood in the Works of Pauline Hopkins, Jessie Fauset, and Marita Bonner* (New York: Garland Publishing, 1998) 91.

80. "There Were Three" is the first of three vignettes grouped together in "A Possible Triad on Black Notes."

81. Hazel Carby, "Policing the Black Woman's Body in an Urban Context," *Critical Inquiry* 18 (1992): 739.

82. A helpful discussion of the virgin-whore dichotomy can be found in Gloria Anzaldúa's *Borderlands/La Frontera: The New Mestiza* (San Francisco: Aunt Lute Books, 1987) 27–31. Although Anzaldúa's argument focuses on the circumscription of Chicana womanhood, her explanation is salient to this discussion of early-twentieth-century African American womanhood.

83. Nancy Chick, "Marita Bonner's Revolutionary Purple Flowers: Challenging the Symbol of White Womanhood," *Langston Hughes Review* 13.1 (1994): 29.

84. Chick 28.

85. The story of Sheba's visit to Solomon is told in 1 Kings 10. Carby 741.

86. Musser, "African American Women and Education" 80.

87. McDougald 370, 379.

88. Jean Toomer, *Cane* (1923; New York: Liveright, 1993) 2.

89. Chick 28.

90. Carby writes, "The twenties must be viewed as a period of ideological, political, and cul-

tural contestation between an emergent black bourgeoisie and an emerging black working class." Carby 754.

91. Zora Neale Hurston, "How It Feels to Be Colored Me," 1928, *I Love Myself When I Am Laughing . . . And Then Again When I Am Looking Mean and Impressive: A Zora Neale Hurston Reader,* ed. Alice Walker (Old Westbury, NY: Feminist P, 1979) 155.

92. Williams, an African American teenager, drowned when he inadvertently crossed the implicit boundary between black and white sections of Chicago beachfront and was attacked by whites angered by his apparent trespassing. For more on the Williams incident, see Balshaw, *Looking for Harlem: Urban Aesthetics in African-American Literature* (London: Pluto P, 2000) 90–91; Flynn xvi; and Musser, " 'Blood Will Flow Back to You' " 58–59.

93. The White Devils sing, "*You stay where you are! / We don't want you up here!*" (32). Also, the strange boy in "Nothing New" steps out from behind a bush to confront Denny just as the White Devil in *The Purple Flower* emerges from behind a bush to attack Sweet. See "Nothing New" 71; and *Purple Flower* 38.

94. Robin D. G. Kelley, " 'We Are Not What We Seem': The Politics and Pleasure of Community," *Race Rebels: Culture, Politics, and the Black Working Class* (New York: Free P, 1994) 51.

95. Balshaw, *Looking for Harlem* 91.

96. Given the similarities between the names, characterizations, and Bonner's intention of folding the Frye Street stories into the larger Black Map project, it is likely that Esther Steinberg and Esther Weinstein are one and the same. See Flynn, introduction, *Frye Street and Environs* xi–xxvii.

97. Wald 215.

98. Musser, " 'Blood Will Flow Back to You' " 60.

99. Balshaw, *Looking for Harlem* 84.

100. Hurston, "How It Feels to Be Colored Me" 154–55.

101. Wall 29.

3. Surrealist Dreams, Martinican Realities

1. Maryse Condé, "Unheard Voice: Suzanne Césaire and the Construct of a Caribbean Identity," *Winds of Change: The Transforming Voices of Caribbean Women Writers and Scholars,* ed. Adele S. Newson and Linda Strong-Leek (New York: Peter Lang, 1998) 62.

2. William Shakespeare, *The Tempest,* ed. Robert Langbaum (New York: Penguin, 1987).

3. Suzanne and Aimé Césaire met while they were students in Paris. They married in France in 1937, returned to Martinique in 1939, and separated in 1963. After the separation, Suzanne Césaire returned to Paris, where she taught before dying of cancer in 1966. For more on Suzanne's biography, see Georgiana Colvile, "Suzanne Césaire," *Scandaleusement d'elles: Trente-quatre femmes surréalistes* (Paris: Jean-Michel Place, 1999) 74; and Kara Rabbitt, "Suzanne Césaire," *île en île,* 23 June 2007, www.lehman.cuny.edu/ile.en.ile/paroles/cesaire_suzanne.html.

4. Ina Césaire, personal interview, 27 Mar. 2001. Ina Césaire is one of Aimé and Suzanne Césaire's six children. All translations from interview are mine.

5. Although Georgiana Colvile approximates the play's completion date as 1955, Michel Leiris states that *Aurore de la liberté* was performed in Fort-de-France in 1952. See Colvile 74; Leiris, *Contacts de civilisations en Martinique et en Guadeloupe* (Paris: UNESCO/Gallimard, 1955) 88.

6. Suzanne Césaire, "Misère d'une poésie," *Tropiques* 4 (1942): 50. Translation from Condé, "Unheard Voice" 64. Maryse Condé, "Order, Disorder, Freedom, and the West Indian Writer," *Post/Colonial Conditions,* ed. Françoise Lionnet and Ronnie Scharfman, spec. issue of *Yale French Studies* 83 (1993): 122. All subsequent Césaire citations will be noted parenthetically in the text.

7. Keith Warner, *Critical Perspectives on Léon-Gontran Damas* (Washington, DC: Three Continents P, 1988) 24.

8. In "Unheard Voice" Condé writes, "Suzanne Césaire can justly be regarded as the precursor of Glissant's Antillanité and even Créolité" (65).

9. Natalie Melas, *All the Difference in the World: Postcoloniality and the Ends of Comparison* (Stanford: Stanford UP, 2007) 36.

10. Ina Césaire, personal interview, 27 Mar. 2001.

11. Ina Césaire, personal interview, 27 Mar. 2001.

12. André Breton, "Un grand poète noir," *Tropiques* 11 (1944): 119–26. Translated as "A Great Black Poet: Aimé Césaire," trans. Krysztof Fijalkowski and Michael Richardson, *Refusal of the Shadow: Surrealism and the Caribbean,* ed. Michael Richardson (New York: Verso, 1996) 191–98. Unless otherwise indicated, all subsequent translations are from Richardson.

13. This translation of Breton's observation is from Condé, "Unheard Voice" 62.

14. J. Michael Dash, "*Le Je de l'autre:* Surrealist Ethnographers and the Francophone Caribbean," *L'Esprit Créateur* 47.1 (2007): 86. *Nadja* is the title of Breton's 1928 novel depicting his brief but passionate relationship with the beautiful and mentally unstable title character. André Breton, *Nadja* (Paris: Gallimard, 1928). For more on Breton's life and career, see Margaret M. Bolovan, "André Breton," *Dictionary of Literary Biography, Literature Resource Center,* Thomson Gale, U of Texas Libraries, Austin, 10 July 2007, http://galenet.galegroup.com.ezproxy.lib.utexas.edu.

15. Nicole Aas-Rouxparis, "Espace antillais au féminin: présence, absence," *French Review* 70 (1997): 854.

16. Roger Toumson and Simonne Henry-Valmore, *Aimé Césaire: le nègre inconsolé* (Fort-de-France: Vent des Îles, 1993). Toumson and Henry-Valmore include the same portrait, along with a caption indicating Césaire's imminent departure for France, in their volume in an unpaginated collection of photographs appended between pp. 120 and 121.

17. Anne Stavney, "'Mothers of Tomorrow': The New Negro Renaissance and the Politics of Maternal Representation," *African American Review* 32 (1998): 546.

18. A. James Arnold, *Modernism and Negritude: The Poetry and Poetics of Aimé Césaire* (Cambridge: Harvard UP, 1981) 12.

19. A. James Arnold, "The Gendering of Créolité: The Erotics of Colonialism," *Penser la créolité,* ed. Maryse Condé and Madeleine Cottenet-Hage (Paris: Karthala, 1995) 21. Arnold discusses Negritude along with the *Antillanité* and *Créolité* movements.

20. Richard Burton, "Between the Particular and the Universal: Dilemmas of the Martinican Intellectual," *Intellectuals in the Twentieth-Century Caribbean,* vol. 2: *Unity in Variety: The Hispanophone and Francophone Caribbean,* ed. Alistair Hennessy (London: Macmillan, 1992) 207.

21. For examples of scholarship interrogating the geographic-ideological split of Negritude, see, among others, Arnold, *Modernism and Negritude;* and Maryse Condé, "Négritude césairienne, négritude senghorienne," *Revue de Littérature Comparée* 3.4 (1974): 409–19, both of which offer instructive comparisons of Aimé Césaire and Léopold Senghor's respective Negritudes.

22. Clarisse Zimra, "Négritude in the Feminine Mode: The Case of Martinique and Guadeloupe," *Journal of Ethnic Studies* 12.1 (1984): 53–77.

23. See also Kara M. Rabbitt, "Suzanne Césaire's Significance for the Forging of a New Caribbean Literature," *French Review* 79.3 (2006): 538–48; Ronnie Scharfman, "Rewriting the Césaires," *L'héritage de Caliban*, ed. Maryse Condé (Paris: Jasor, 1992) 233–46; and Marie-Agnès Sourieau, "Suzanne Césaire et *Tropiques*: de la poésie cannibale à une poétique créole," *French Review* 68.1 (1994): 69–78.

24. See Condé, "Unheard Voice" 61–66; and "Order, Disorder, Freedom, and the West Indian Writer"; T. Denean Sharpley-Whiting, *Negritude Women* (Minneapolis: U of Minnesota P, 2002).

25. Renée Riese Hubert, *Magnifying Mirrors: Women, Surrealism, and Partnership* (Lincoln: U of Nebraska P) 6.

26. Penelope Rosemont, ed., *Surrealist Women: An International Anthology* (Austin: U of Texas P, 1998).

27. Robin D. G. Kelley, *Freedom Dreams: The Black Radical Imagination* (Boston: Beacon P, 2002) 170.

28. Sharpley-Whiting, *Negritude Women* 40. For more on Nardal, see also Brent Hayes Edwards, *The Practice of Diaspora: Literature, Translation, and the Rise of Black Internationalism* (Cambridge: Harvard UP, 2003) 16–25.

29. As noted in chap. 1, Lacascade's novel *Claire-Solange, âme africaine* was published before the texts traditionally associated with Negritude's emergence. With its 1924 publication date, *Claire-Solange* preceded *La Revue du Monde Noir* (1931–32) by seven years, the journal *Légitime Défense* (1932) by eight years, Damas's poetry collection *Pigments* (1937) by thirteen years, and Aimé Césaire's *Cahier d'un retour au pays natal* (1939) by fifteen years. Suzanne Lacascade, *Claire-Solange, âme africaine* (Paris: Eugène Figuière, 1924).

30. Ann duCille, "The Occult of True Black Womanhood: Critical Demeanor and Black Feminist Studies," *Signs* 19.3 (1994): 619.

31. Arnold, "Gendering of Créolité" 36. Carole Boyce Davies, *Black Women, Writing and Identity: Migrations of the Subject* (New York: Routledge, 1994) 40.

32. Sam Haigh, *Mapping a Tradition: Francophone Women's Writing from Guadeloupe* (London: Maney Publishing, 2000) 64.

33. Haigh 68.

34. Jean-Paul Sartre, "Orphée noir," preface, *Anthologie de la nouvelle poésie nègre et malgache de langue française* xxxiii, xxxii. Translated as "Black Orpheus," trans. John MacCombie, *Massachusetts Review* 6 (1964): 40, 39.

35. Aimé Césaire, *Cahier d'un retour au pays natal (Notebook of a Return to My Native Land)*, *Aimé Césaire: The Collected Poetry*, trans. and ed. Clayton Eshleman and Annette Smith (1939; Berkeley: U of California P, 1983) 50/51. All subsequent *Cahier* references will be noted parenthetically in the text.

36. Leo Frobenius, *Kulturgeschichte Afrikas* (Frankfurt: Phaidon Verlag, 1933). Translated as *Histoire de la civilisation africaine*, trans. H. Back and D. Ermont, 3rd ed. (1936; Paris: Gallimard, 1952).

37. Pierre Desroches-Laroche, preface, "Le spiritisme dans l'intérieur de l'Afrique" ("Spiritualism in Central Africa"), by Léo Frobenius, *La Revue du Monde Noir* 5 (1932): 20.

38. Arnold, *Modernism and Negritude* 35, 50.

39. Frobenius, *Histoire de la civilisation africaine* 15. English translation is mine.

40. Georges Ngal, *Aimé Césaire: un homme à la recherche d'une patrie* (1975; Paris: Présence Africaine, 1994) 131. Translation is mine. See also Arnold, *Modernism and Negritude* 38.

41. Suzanne Césaire, "Léo Frobénius et le problème des civilisations," *Tropiques* 1 (1941): 27–36. Translated as "Leo Frobenius and the Problem of Civilizations," trans. Krysztof Fijalkowski and Michael Richardson, *Refusal of the Shadow* 82–87. Unless otherwise noted, all subsequent Césaire translations are by Fijalkowski and Richardson.

42. Janheinz Jahn, *Leo Frobenius: The Demonic Child*, trans. Reinhard Sander, Occasional Publication of the African and Afro-American Studies and Research Center (Austin: U of Texas at Austin, 1974), 5–6. To my knowledge there have been no statements supporting or disputing Jahn's claim. My thanks to Dorian Stuber and Stanka Radovic for their assistance with Jahn's translation of *Ebenmässigkeit der Bildung*.

43. J. Michael Dash, "Marvellous Realism: The Way Out of Negritude," *Caribbean Studies* 13.4 (1974): 60–61.

44. Sharpley-Whiting, *Negritude Women* 41.

45. Suzanne Césaire, "Malaise d'une civilisation," *Tropiques* 5 (1942): 43–49. Translated as "A Civilization's Discontent," *Refusal of the Shadow* 96–100.

46. Rabbitt, "Suzanne Césaire's Significance" 543.

47. Lacascade 62.

48. Etienne Léro, "Misère d'une poésie," *Légitime Défense* 1 (1932): 12. Translated as "Poverty of a Poetry," trans. Fijalkowski and Richardson, *Refusal of the Shadow* 58. Unless otherwise noted, all subsequent Léro translations are by Fijalkowski and Richardson.

49. Arnold, *Modernism and Negritude* 37.

50. Sourieau 71. This and subsequent translations from Sourieau are mine.

51. Édouard Glissant, *Le discours antillais* (1981; Paris: Gallimard, 1997) 61. Translated as *Caribbean Discourse: Selected Essays*, trans. J. Michael Dash (Charlottesville: UP of Virginia, 1989) 42/43.

52. Marita Bonner, *The Purple Flower*, in *Frye Street and Environs: The Collected Works of Marita Bonner*, ed. Joyce Flynn and Joyce Occomy Stricklin (Boston: Beacon P, 1987) 41, 46.

53. Richardson, introduction, *Refusal of the Shadow* 7.

54. André Breton, *Manifeste du surréalisme*, 1924, *Oeuvres complètes*, ed. Marguerite Bonnet (Paris: Gallimard, 1988) 1:319. Translated as *Manifesto of Surrealism*, trans. Richard Seaver and Helen R. Lane, *Manifestoes of Surrealism* (Ann Arbor: U of Michigan P, 1969) 14. For an informative discussion of the specificity with which French colonial discourse defined and legislated racial difference in the Caribbean, see Joan Dayan, *Haiti, History, and the Gods* (Berkeley: U of California P, 1995).

55. Breton makes the claim about surrealism and childhood in the *Manifeste du surréalisme* (340). Both Suzanne Césaire and Aimé Césaire depict poetry as a conduit to an unmediated relationship with nature, the former in "Alain et l'esthétique," *Tropiques* 2 (1941): 57; the latter in "Poésie et connaissance," *Tropiques* 12 (1945): 162.

56. One hears echoes of this language in Sartre's comparison (discussed earlier) of the black and white peasant. See "Orphée noir" xxxii.

57. J. Michael Dash, *The Other America: Caribbean Literature in a New World Context* (Charlottesville: UP of Virginia, 1998) 36.

58. Dash, *Other America* 38.

59. Richardson, introduction, *Refusal of the Shadow* 11.

60. Suzanne Césaire, "André Breton, poète," *Tropiques* 2 (1941): 31-37. This essay is not among those included in Richardson and Fijalkowski's *Refusal of the Shadow*. All translations are mine.

61. André Breton, "Poèmes," *Tropiques* 3 (1941): 38–41.

62. André Breton, "Pour Madame," *Tropiques* 3 (1941): 41. In the Francophone Caribbean a *chabine* is a woman who, according to Michel Leiris, has "une combinaison paradoxale de traits des races noire et blanche" ("a paradoxical combination of traits from the black and white races"). A *chabine*, for example, may have fair coloring (blonde hair, blue eyes, and pale skin) but other features (nose, lips, and hair texture) suggestive of individuals of African ancestry. The male form of *chabine* is *chabin*. See Leiris, *Contacts de civilisations en Martinique et en Guadeloupe* (Paris: Gallimard/UNESCO, 1955) 161. Translations of Breton and Leiris are mine.

63. Breton, *Second manifeste du surréalisme*, 1930, *Oeuvres complètes* 784–85. *Second Manifesto of Surrealism, Manifestoes of Surrealism* 128.

64. Suzanne Césaire, "Misère d'une poésie," *Tropiques* 4 (1942): 50. This essay is not among those included in Richardson and Fijalkowski's *Refusal of the Shadow*. Translation is mine with the exception of the final sentence, which is from the Condé article "Unheard Voice" (64).

65. Aimé Césaire opens his argument with the contention that poetic knowledge is superior to its scientific counterpart because the latter encourages summation rather than engagement. Aimé Césaire, "Poésie et connaissance" 157, 169 (trans. as "Poetry and Cognition" by A. James Arnold in Aimé Césaire, *Lyric and Dramatic Poetry, 1946–82*, trans. Clayton Eshleman and Annette Smith [Charlottesville: UP of Virginia, 1990]) xlii–lvi; and by Richardson and Fijalkowski as "Poetry and Knowledge," *Refusal of the Shadow* 134–52.

66. Condé, "Unheard Voice" 62.

67. Sourieau 73.

68. J. Michael Dash, "*Caraïbe Fantôme:* The Play of Difference in the Francophone Caribbean," *French and Francophone: The Challenge of Expanding Horizons*, ed. Farid Laroussi and Christopher L. Miller, spec. issue of *Yale French Studies* 103 (2003): 94.

69. Suzanne Césaire, "1943: Le Surréalisme et nous," *Tropiques* 8–9 (1943): 15. Translated as "1943: Surrealism and Us," *Refusal of the Shadow* 124.

70. Kesteloot 232/256.

71. Jean-Claude Michel, *Les écrivains noirs et le surréalisme* (Sherbrooke: Éditions Naaman, 1982) 107. Michel has published an abridged, English-language version of this text under the title *The Black Surrealists* (New York: Peter Lang, 2000). See also Sharpley-Whiting, *Negritude Women* 90–91.

72. Rabbitt, "Suzanne Césaire's Significance" 545.

73. Condé, "Unheard Voice" 65; Michel, *Les écrivains noirs et le surréalisme* 107. Translation is mine.

74. Suzanne Césaire, "Le grand camouflage," *Tropiques* 13–14 (1945): 267. Translated as "The Great Camouflage," *Refusal of the Shadow* 156.

75. J. Michael Dash, "*Le Je de l'autre*" 87.

76. Antonio Benítez-Rojo, *The Repeating Island: The Caribbean and the Postmodern Perspective,* trans. James Maraniss (Durham: Duke UP, 1992) 3.

77. Condé, "Unheard Voice" 66.

78. Condé, "Unheard Voice" 65.

79. Jean Bernabé, Patrick Chamoiseau, and Raphaël Confiant, *Éloge de la Créolité/In Praise of Creoleness,* bilingual ed., trans. M. B. Taleb-Khyar (Paris: Gallimard, 1993) 13/75.

80. Sourieau 77.

81. The term *béké* refers to white descendants of French colonists, especially those of aristocratic origins, who settled the Caribbean. *Békés* are generally thought to be distinguishable from *les métropolitains* (whites from metropolitan France) by their distinct accent and rather passionate attachment to the Caribbean—two characteristics Césaire chooses to describe the unnamed white group in "Le grand camouflage" (270). For more on socio-racial categories in the Francophone Caribbean, see Leiris, "Les relations entre catégories fondées sur l'origine," *Contacts de civilisations en Martinique et en Guadeloupe* 117–87.

82. Glissant 69.

83. Verse from Léon-Gontran Damas, "Blanchi," *"Pigments" suivi de "Névralgies"* (Paris: Présence Africaine, 1972) 59–60.

84. Carolina González, "An Interview with Ángela Hernández Núñez," *Callaloo* 23.3 (2000): 1000.

85. I have only discussed six of the seven essays in this chapter. The seventh is Suzanne Césaire, "Alain et l'esthétique," *Tropiques* 2 (1941): 53–61.

86. SallyAnn H. Ferguson, "Dorothy West and Helene Johnson in *Infants of the Spring,*" *Langston Hughes Review* 2.2 (1983): 22.

87. Ronnie Scharfman, "De grands poètes noirs: Breton rencontre les Césaire," *Nouveau monde, autres mondes: surréalisme et Amériques,* ed. Daniel Lefort, Pierre Rivas, and Jacqueline Chénieux-Gendron (Paris: Lachenal & Ritter, 1995) 230, 231. Scharfman's title translates as "Of Great Black Poets: Breton Meets the Césaires." All translations are mine.

88. Remembering his first encounter with *Tropiques,* Breton writes, "La mercière martiniquaise, par une de ces chances accessoires qui accusent les heures fortunées, ne devaient pas tarder à se faire connaître pour la soeur de René Ménil, avec Césaire le principal animateur de *Tropiques*" ("The Martinican haberdasher, by one of those additional acts of chance that indicate propitious moments, lost no time in introducing herself as the sister of René Ménil, the principal animator of *Tropiques* with Césaire"; "Un grand poète noir," 120/192).

89. Scharfman 234.

90. Clarisse Zimra, introduction, *Lone Sun,* by Daniel Maximin, trans. Clarisse Zimra (Charlottesville: UP of Virginia, 1989) xxv.

91. John D. Erickson, "Maximin's *L'Isolé soleil* and Caliban's Curse," *Callaloo* 15.1 (1992): 127.

92. Daniel Maximin, *L'Isolé soleil* (Paris: Seuil, 1981) 16/7. All subsequent Maximin references will be noted parenthetically in the text. The "poem" of which Marie-Gabriel speaks is Césaire's 1945 essay "Le grand camouflage."

93. Zimra, introduction, *Lone Sun* xxv.

94. H. Adlai Murdoch, *Creole Identity in the French Caribbean Novel* (Gainesville: UP of Florida, 2001) 121.

95. Murdoch, *Creole Identity* 101.

96. Scharfman, "Rewriting the Césaires" 236.

97. Although Maximin gives the article's title as "Qu'est-ce que le martiniquais?" ("What Is a Martinican?" [192/191]), the phrase comes from but does not provide the actual title for Césaire's "Malaise d'une civilisation." Maximin 192/190.

98. Murdoch, *Creole Identity* 120.

99. Murdoch, *Creole Identity* 109.

100. Suzanne Césaire, "1943: Le Surréalisme et nous" 18/126. See also Aimé Césaire, *Cahier d'un retour au pays natal* 48; and Damas, "Blanchi," *"Pigments" suivi de "Névralgies"* 60. The Senghor statement to which I refer is the famous "L'émotion est nègre comme la raison est hellène." From Léopold Sédar Senghor, *Liberté I: Négritude et humanisme* (Paris: Seuil, 1964) 24.

4. Black Modernism in Retrospect

1. Dorothy West, *The Living Is Easy* (1948; New York: Feminist P, 1982) 70. Subsequent references to the novel and all other West writings will be noted parenthetically in the text.

2. Ann duCille, *The Coupling Convention: Sex, Text, and Tradition in Black Women's Fiction* (New York: Oxford UP, 1993) 114.

3. Lorraine Elena Roses, "Interviews with Black Women Writers: Dorothy West at Oak Bluffs, Massachusetts, July, 1984," *Sage* 2.1 (1985): 47.

4. Mary Helen Washington, preface, *The Richer, the Poorer: Stories, Sketches, and Reminiscences,* by Dorothy West (New York: Doubleday, 1995) xii.

5. Dorothy West, "Dear Reader," *Challenge* 1.1 (1934): 39.

6. Editorial, *New Challenge* 2.2 (1937): 3.

7. Washington, preface, *Richer, the Poorer* xv; editorial, *New Challenge* 2.2 (1937): 3. See also Sharon L. Jones, "Reclaiming a Legacy: The Dialectic of Race, Class, and Gender in Jessie Fauset, Zora Neale Hurston, and Dorothy West," *Hecate* 24.1 (1998): 155–64. Richard Wright published his famous "Blueprint for Negro Writing" in *New Challenge* 53–65. The essay echoed the sentiments of the issue's editorial.

8. James Robert Saunders and Renae Nadine Shackleford, eds., *The Dorothy West Martha's Vineyard: Stories, Essays and Reminiscences by Dorothy West Writing in the "Vineyard Gazette"* (Jefferson, NC: McFarland & Co., 2001); and Verner D. Mitchell and Cynthia Davis, eds., *Where the Wild Grape Grows: Selected Writings, 1930–1950* (Amherst: U of Massachusetts P, 2005). *The Wedding* would go on to become a made-for-television movie starring Halle Berry. See "Oprah Winfrey Presents: *The Wedding,*" dir. Charles Burnett, perf. Halle Berry, Shirley Knight, Carl Lumbly, Michael Warren, Cynda Williams, and Lynne Whitfield; ABC, 1998.

9. David Levering Lewis, *When Harlem Was in Vogue* (1981; New York: Penguin Books, 1997) 3.

10. Deborah E. McDowell, "Conversations with Dorothy West," *The Harlem Renaissance Reexamined,* ed. Victor A. Kramer (New York: AMS P, 1987) 273.

11. For more on the origins and history of the "Black Brahmins," to which Dorothy West's family belonged, see Adelaide M. Cromwell, *The Other Brahmins: Boston's Black Upper Class, 1750–1950* (Fayetteville: U of Arkansas P, 1994); and Willard B. Gatewood, *Aristocrats of Color: The Black Elite, 1880–1920* (Bloomington: Indiana UP, 1990) 119–23.

12. Trudier Harris, *Saints, Sinners, Saviors: Strong Black Women in African American Literature* (New York: Palgrave, 2001) 119, 121.

13. Alain Locke, "The New Negro," *The New Negro,* ed. Alain Locke (1925; New York: Touchstone, 1997) 7, 6.

14. Locke, "New Negro" 10–11.

15. Locke, "New Negro" 11.

16. Elise Johnson McDougald, "The Task of Negro Womanhood," *The New Negro,* ed. Alain Locke (1925; New York: Touchstone, 1997) 369.

17. McDougald 369.

18. McDougald 382.

19. McDougald 380.

20. Cherene Sherrard-Johnson, *Portraits of the New Negro Woman: Visual and Literary Culture in the Harlem Renaissance* (New Brunswick: Rutgers UP, 2007) 10; McDougald 370.

21. Sherrard-Johnson, *Portraits of the New Negro Woman* 10. Sherrard-Johnson provides the following description of McDougald's portrait: "In Reiss's portrait of educator and social organizer Elise Johnson McDougald, which accompanies McDougald's essay 'The Task of Negro Womanhood,' her golden-brown skin contrasts with her white clothing, which blends into a white background to give the portrait a celestial quality" (25).

22. McDougald 380.

23. W. E. B. Du Bois, "The Damnation of Women," *Darkwater: Voices from within the Veil* (1920; Mineola, NY: Dover Publications, 1999) 96.

24. Du Bois, "Damnation of Women" 95. For more on the master-slave dialectic, see Hegel, "Independence and Dependence of Self-Consciousness: Lordship and Bondage," *The Phenomenology of Mind,* trans. J. B. Baillie (New York: Harper Torchbooks, 1967) 228–40.

25. Du Bois, "Damnation of Women" 107.

26. Joy James, *Transcending the Talented Tenth: Black Leaders and American Intellectuals* (New York: Routledge, 1997) 54.

27. Du Bois 107.

28. Locke, "New Negro" 12.

29. Randolph and Owen founded the *Messenger* in 1917, and, until it ceased publication in 1928, the journal was one of the major African American periodicals of the Harlem Renaissance era. Abby Arthur Johnson and Ronald Maberry Johnson, *Propaganda and Aesthetics: The Literary Politics of African-American Magazines in the Twentieth Century* (Amherst: U of Massachusetts P, 1979) 57.

30. Johnson and Johnson 57.

31. "New Negro Woman," editorial, *Messenger* (July 1923): 757.

32. "New Negro Woman."

33. For more on Kelly Miller's views on African American women in the public sphere, see Giddings, *When and Where I Enter* 120; and Anne Stavney, "'Mothers of Tomorrow': The New Negro Renaissance and the Politics of Maternal Representation," *African American Review* 32 (1998): 538.

34. Susan Gillman and Alys Eve Weinbaum, "Introduction: W. E. B. Du Bois and the Politics of Juxtaposition," *Next to the Color Line: Gender, Sexuality, and W. E. B. Du Bois* (Minneapolis: U of Minnesota P, 2007) 17–18.

35. Claudia Tate, *Domestic Allegories of Political Desire: The Black Heroine's Text at the Turn of the Century* (New York: Oxford UP, 1992) 14.

36. Elizabeth Ammons, *Conflicting Stories: American Women Writers at the Turn into the Twentieth Century* (New York: Oxford UP, 1992) 7; Tate 97.

37. For more on these exceptions, see Stavney 551.

38. Ammons 8. Both Ammons and Paula Giddings address the social and economic conditions limiting black women's access to the lifestyle dictated by the cult of true womanhood. Paula Giddings, *When and Where I Enter: The Impact of Black Women on Race and Sex in America* (1984; New York: William Morrow, 1996) 47.

39. Giddings 54. Emphasis added. See also Nella Larsen, *Quicksand* and *Passing*, ed. Deborah E. McDowell (1928, 1929; New Brunswick: Rutgers UP, 1986).

40. Lisa Rado, "Primitivism, Modernism, and Matriarchy," *Modernism, Gender, and Culture: A Cultural Studies Approach*, ed. Lisa Rado (New York: Garland, 1997) 296.

41. Suzanne Lacascade, *Claire-Solange, âme africaine* (Paris: Eugène Figuière, 1924) 67.

42. Stavney 549.

43. Stavney 548. Stavney undertakes an illuminating reading of Winold Reiss's *Brown Madonna*, the portrait featured on the frontispiece of the first edition of Locke's *New Negro* anthology. She argues that along with its idealized depiction of black motherhood, the portrait's "prefatory location . . . situates the true black woman outside the discursive body of black writing defined by the text" (Stavney 546). From this reading one might deduce that the true black woman precedes but does not participate in the modernist project(s) represented by the New Negro.

44. Du Bois, "Damnation of Women" 107; "New Negro Woman."

45. duCille 114.

46. Ammons 7.

47. Ann Heilmann, *New Woman Fiction: Women Writing First Wave Feminism* (New York: St. Martin's, 2000) 1.

48. Maria Balshaw, *Looking for Harlem: Urban Aesthetics in African-American Literature* (London: Pluto P, 2000) 46.

49. Balshaw 46.

50. Houston A. Baker Jr., *Modernism and the Harlem Renaissance* (Chicago: U of Chicago P, 1987) 4.

51. Locke writes that, "with the Negro rapidly in process of class differentiation, if it ever was warrantable to regard and treat the Negro *en masse* it is becoming with every day less possible, more unjust and more ridiculous." Locke, "New Negro" 5–6. While alone this comment seems merely to highlight the increasing diversity of the African American population, alongside moments in the essay privileging artists, intellectuals, and other "enlightened minorities," the statement suggests the class separatism that Cleo seeks.

52. Tate 14.

53. Maryse Condé, "Order, Disorder, Freedom, and the West Indian Writer," *Post/Colonial Conditions*, ed. Françoise Lionnet and Ronnie Scharfman, spec. issue of *Yale French Studies* 83 (1993): 126.

54. Pamela Peden Sanders, "The Feminism of Dorothy West's *The Living Is Easy*: A Critique of the Limitations of the Female Sphere through Performative Gender Roles," *African American Review* 36.3 (2002): 437.

55. Harris 108.

56. Stavney 543.

57. Nella Larsen, *Quicksand*, ed. Thadious M. Davis (1928; New York: Penguin, 2002), 104.

58. Sanders 439.

59. duCille 114.

60. Stavney 543.

61. Henry Louis Gates Jr., "The Trope of a New Negro and the Reconstruction of the Image of the Black," *America Reconstructed, 1840–1940*, spec. issue of *Representations* 24 (1988): 132.

62. Lawrence R. Rodgers, "Dorothy West's *The Living Is Easy* and the Ideal of Southern Folk Community," *African American Review* 26.1 (1992): 169.

63. Farah Jasmine Griffin, *"Who Set You Flowin'?" The African-American Migration Narrative* (New York: Oxford UP, 1995) 85.

64. duCille 114.

65. Rodgers 169.

66. Sanders 443.

67. Likewise, the family of Rachel Pease Benson, West's mother, "feared her good looks would get her into trouble with white men in the South" and thus sent her to live in New England. See Washington, preface xii.

68. Marita Bonner, *The Purple Flower*, in *Frye Street and Environs: The Collected Works of Marita Bonner*, ed. Joyce Flynn and Joyce Occomy Stricklin (Boston: Beacon P, 1987) 37.

69. duCille 114. See also Griffin 84.

70. Zora Neale Hurston, *Their Eyes Were Watching God* (1937; New York: Harper & Row, 1990) 182.

71. Tate 8.

72. duCille 114.

73. Tate 11.

74. Ammons 7.

75. Du Bois, "Damnation of Women" 163–64.

76. Rodgers 169.

77. Griffin 87.

78. Rodgers 169.

79. Wallace Thurman, *Infants of the Spring* (1932; New York: Modern Library, 1999) 79.

Conclusion

1. Édouard Glissant, *La Lézarde* (1958; Paris: Gallimard, 1997). Translated as *The Ripening* by Michael Dash (London: Heinemann, 1985).

2. Rey Chow, "The Old/New Question of Comparison in Literary Studies: A Post-European Perspective," *ELH* 71 (2004): 295.

3. Deborah E. McDowell, *"The Changing Same": Black Women's Literature, Criticism, and Theory* (Bloomington: Indiana UP, 1995) 20. Although McDowell is referring specifically to African American women's literature, the manner in which her statement acknowledges intraracial, intra-gender difference suggests its applicability to diasporic analysis as well. Two of the most famous writers to reject the term *feminist* are Condé and, in African American literature, Alice Walker, who coined what McDowell describes as the culturally specific yet racially unmarked term *womanist*

(McDowell 20). For the neologism's definition, see Alice Walker, *In Search of Our Mothers' Gardens: Womanist Prose* (San Diego: Harcourt, 1983) xi–xii.

4. Cheryl A. Wall, "Introduction: Taking Positions and Changing Words," *Changing Our Own Words: Essays on Criticism, Theory, and Writing by Black Women,* ed. Cheryl A. Wall (New Brunswick: Rutgers UP, 1989) 2; Barbara Smith, "Toward a Black Feminist Criticism," *All the Women Are White, All the Blacks Are Men, but Some of Us Are Brave,* ed. Gloria T. Hull, Patricia Bell Scott, and Barbara Smith (Old Westbury, NY: Feminist P, 1982) 159. Smith's essay was originally published in 1977.

5. C. Hugh Holman and William Harmon, *A Handbook to Literature,* 5th ed. (New York: Macmillan, 1986) 390.

6. Toni Morrison, *Sula* (New York: Knopf, 1973) 92.

7. Thadious M. Davis, introduction, *Passing* (1929; New York: Penguin Books, 1997) xxvi.

8. Davis xxvi–xxvii.

9. Maryse Condé, *En attendant le bonheur (Heremakhonon)* (1988; Paris: Robert Laffont, 1997). Translated as *Heremakhonon,* trans. Richard Philcox (Boulder: Three Continents P, 1996). All subsequent references to the novel will be noted parenthetically in the text.

10. Vèvè Clark, "Developing Diaspora Literacy: Allusion in Maryse Condé's *Hérémakhonon,*" *Out of the Kumbla: Caribbean Women and Literature,* ed. Carole Boyce Davies and Elaine Savory Fido (Trenton: Africa World P, 1990) 312.

11. Aimé Césaire, *Cahier d'un retour au pays natal (Notebook of a Return to My Native Land),* 1939, *Aimé Césaire: The Collected Poetry,* trans. and ed. Clayton Eshleman and Annette Smith (Berkeley: U of California P, 1983) 82/83.

12. Maryse Condé, "The Stealers of Fire: The French-Speaking Writers of the Caribbean and Their Strategies of Liberation," *Journal of Black Studies* 35.2 (2004): 163.

13. Clark 312.

14. Condé, "Stealers of Fire" 159.

15. H. Adlai Murdoch, *Creole Identity in the French Caribbean Novel* (Gainesville: UP of Florida, 2001) 3.

16. Suzanne Lacascade, *Claire-Solange, âme africaine* (Paris: Eugène Figuière, 1924) 66.

17. James Clifford, "Traveling Cultures," *Cultural Studies,* ed. Lawrence Grossberg, Cary Nelson, and Paula Treichler (New York: Routledge, 1992) 109.

18. Murdoch 2. The Guyanese Félix Éboué was "the first Antillean to serve" as governor of Guadeloupe. He held the post from 1936 to 1938. Gary Wilder, *The French Imperial Nation-State: Negritude and Colonial Humanism between the Two World Wars* (Chicago: U of Chicago P, 2005) 353 n. 58.

19. Murdoch 88.

20. Susan Z. Andrade, "The Nigger of the Narcissist: History, Sexuality and Intertextuality in Maryse Condé's *Heremakhonon,*" *Callaloo* 16.1 (1993): 220.

21. Countee Cullen, "Heritage," 1925, *The Norton Anthology of African American Literature,* ed. Henry Louis Gates Jr., Nellie Y. McKay, et al. (New York: Norton, 1997) 1311.

22. Leah Hewitt, "Rencontres explosives: les intersections culturelles de Maryse Condé," *L'Œuvre de Maryse Condé: questions et réponses à propos d'une écrivaine politiquement incorrecte* (Paris: L'Harmattan, 1996) 46.

23. Andrade 218; Murdoch 75.

24. Jessie Redmon Fauset, *There Is Confusion* (New York: Boni & Liveright, 1924).

25. Stuart Hall, "Cultural Identity and Diaspora," *Identity: Community, Culture, Difference*, ed. Jonathan Rutherford (London: Lawrence & Wishart, 1990) 224, 231.

26. Frantz Fanon, *Les damnés de la terre*, 1961 (Paris: Gallimard, 1991) 194. Translated as *The Wretched of the Earth*, trans. Constance Farrington (New York: Grove P, 1963) 153.

27. When Véronica's students ask her to discuss *Les damnées de la terre*, she admits: "Hier ils ont voulu m'entraîner dans une discussion des *Damnés* que je n'ai pas lus. *Mea culpa! Mea maxima culpa!*" ("Yesterday they wanted to drag me into a discussion of *The Wretched of the Earth* that I haven't read. Mea culpa! Mea maxima culpa!"; Condé 58/32–33).

28. See Homi K. Bhabha, "Of Mimicry and Man: The Ambivalence of Colonial Discourse," *The Location of Culture* (New York: Routledge, 1994) 85–92.

29. Maryse Condé, "Order, Disorder, Freedom and the West Indian Writer," *Post/Colonial Conditions*, ed. Françoise Lionnet and Ronnie Scharfman, spec. issue of *Yale French Studies* 83 (1993): 125–26, 133. See Jacques Roumain, *Gouverneurs de la rosée* (Paris: Bibliothèque Français, 1946). Translated as *Masters of the Dew*, trans. Langston Hughes and Mercer Cook (London: Heinemann, 1982). The novel depicts the efforts of protagonist Manuel to conscientize and revitalize his village after returning to Haiti from a stint cutting sugarcane in Cuba. According to Condé, Roumain presents Annaïse as the figurative and, upon becoming pregnant, literal vessel through which Manuel reconnects with his native land.

30. Murdoch 99–100.

31. Toni Morrison, *Tar Baby* (New York: Knopf, 1981) 45.

32. Evelyn Hawthorne, "On Gaining the Double-Vision: Tar Baby as Diasporean Novel," *Black American Literature Forum* 22.1 (1988) 102.

33. Julia V. Emberley, "A Historical Transposition: Toni Morrison's *Tar Baby* and Frantz Fanon's Post Enlightenment Phantasms," *Modern Fiction Studies* 45.2 (1999): 404.

34. Emberley 410.

35. Léopold Sédar Senghor, "Black Woman" ("Femme noire"), *The Collected Poetry*, trans. Melvin Dixon (Charlottesville: UP of Virginia, 1998) 8–9/270–71; Judylyn S. Ryan, "Contested Visions/Double-Vision in *Tar Baby*," *Modern Fiction Studies* 39 (1993) 608.

36. Ryan 612.

37. Ryan 613.

38. W. E. B. Du Bois, *The Philadelphia Negro: A Study* (1899; Philadelphia: U of Pennsylvania P, 1996) 7.

39. Jadine reads Césaire to Son during their New York sojourn (Morrison, *Tar Baby* 229).

40. Aimé Césaire, *Cahier* 44/45.

41. This observation is inspired in part by Brent Edwards reading of *décalage*. See Edwards, *The Practice of Diaspora: Literature, Translation, and the Rise of Black Internationalism* (Cambridge: Harvard UP, 2003) 14.

42. Fanon, *Les damnés de la terre* 280/232.

43. Maryse Condé, *Les derniers rois mages* (Paris: Mercure de France, 1992). Translated as *The Last of the African Kings*, trans. Richard Philcox (Lincoln: U of Nebraska P, 1997) 127/82.

44. Condé, *Les derniers rois mages* 127/82.

45. Clifford, 110.

46. Dorothy West, *The Living Is Easy* (1948; New York: Feminist P, [1988]) 141.

47. Linda Bosniak, "Citizenship Denationalized," *Indiana Journal of Global Legal Studies* 7.2 (2000): 477.

48. See Natalie Melas, "Versions of Incommensurability," *World Literature Today* 69 (1995): 275.

49. The French original reads, "Il s'agit de prendre conscience du formidable amas d'énergies diverses que avons jusqu'ici enfermées en nous-mêmes" ("It is a matter of becoming conscious of the formidable mass of different energies that until now have been trapped within us"). Suzanne Césaire, "Malaise d'une civilisation," *Tropiques* 5 (1942): 48/100.

Bibliography

Aas Rouxparis, Nicole. "Espace antillais au féminin: présence, absence." *French Review* 70 (1997): 854–64.

Addams, Jane. *Twenty Years at Hull-House.* 1910. New York: Penguin Books, 1998.

Ahearn, Edward J. "Black Woman, White Poet: Exile and Exploitation in Baudelaire's Jeanne Duval Poems." *French Review* 51.2 (1977): 212–20.

Ako, Edward O. "*L'Étudiant noir* and the Myth of the Genesis of the Négritude Movement." *Research in African Literatures* 15 (1984): 341–53.

Alexander, Elizabeth. "'We Must Be about Our Father's Business': Anna Julia Cooper and the In-Corporation of the Nineteenth-Century African-American Woman Intellectual." *Signs* 20.2 (1995): 336–56.

Allen, Carol. *Black Women Intellectuals: Strategies of Nation, Family, and Neighborhood in the Works of Pauline Hopkins, Jessie Fauset, and Marita Bonner.* New York: Garland Publishing, 1998.

Ammons, Elizabeth. *Conflicting Stories: American Women Writers at the Turn into the Twentieth Century.* New York: Oxford UP, 1992.

Andrade, Susan Z. "The Nigger of the Narcissist: History, Sexuality, and Intertextuality in Maryse Condé's *Heremakhonon.*" *Callaloo* 16.1 (1993): 213–26.

Antoine, Régis. *La littérature franco-antillaise: Haïti, Guadeloupe, Martinique.* Paris: Karthala, 1992.

Anzaldúa, Gloria. *Borderlands/La Frontera: The New Mestiza.* San Francisco: Aunt Lute Books, 1987.

Arnold, A. James. "The Gendering of Créolité: The Erotics of Colonialism." *Penser la créolité.* Ed. Maryse Condé and Madeleine Cottenet-Hage. Paris: Karthala, 1995. 21–40.

———. *Modernism and Negritude: The Poetry and Poetics of Aimé Césaire.* Cambridge: Harvard UP, 1981.

Baker, Houston A., Jr. *Modernism and the Harlem Renaissance.* Chicago: U of Chicago P, 1987.

Balshaw, Maria. *Looking for Harlem: Urban Aesthetics in African-American Literature.* London: Pluto P, 2000.

———. "New Negroes, New Women: The Gender Politics of the Harlem Renaissance." *Women: A Cultural Review* 10.2 (1999): 127–38.

Baudelaire, Charles. *The Flowers of Evil.* Trans. James McGowan. New York: Oxford UP, 1993.

———. *Les fleurs de mal.* 1857. Ed. John E. Jackson. Paris: Librairie Générale Française, 1999.

Bauland, Peter. "Expressionism in Modern American Drama." *Amerikanisches Drama und Theater in 20. Jahrundert.* Ed. Alfred Weber and Siegfried Neuweiler. Göttingen: Vandenhoeck & Ruprecht, 1975. 15–35.

Benítez-Rojo, Antonio. *The Repeating Island: The Caribbean and the Postmodern Perspective.* Trans. James Maraniss. Durham, NC: Duke UP, 1992.

Berg, Allison, and Merideth Taylor. "Enacting Difference: Marita Bonner's *Purple Flower* and the Ambiguities of Race." *African American Review* 32 (1998): 469–80.

Berliner, Brett A. *Ambivalent Desire: The Exotic Black Other in Jazz-Age France.* Amherst: U of Massachusetts P, 2002.

Bernabé, Jean, Patrick Chamoiseau, and Raphaël Confiant. *Éloge de la créolité/In Praise of Creoleness.* Bilingual ed. Trans. M. B. Taleb-Khyar. Paris: Gallimard, 1993.

Bernheimer, Charles, ed., *Comparative Literature in the Age of Multiculturalism.* Baltimore: Johns Hopkins UP, 1995.

Bhabha, Homi K. *The Location of Culture.* New York: Routledge, 1994.

Blanckeart, Claude. "Of Monstrous Métis? Hybridity, Fear of Miscegenation, and Patriotism from Buffon to Paul Broca." *The Color of Liberty: Histories of Race in France.* Ed. Sue Peabody and Tyler Stovall. Durham, NC: Duke UP, 2003. 42–70.

Bolovan, Margaret M. "André Breton." *Dictionary of Literary Biography. Literature Resource Center.* Thomson Gale. University of Texas Libraries. Austin, 10 July 2007, http://galenet.galegroup.com.ezproxy.lib.utexas.edu.

Bonner, Marita. *Frye Street and Environs: The Collected Works of Marita Bonner.* Ed. Joyce Flynn and Joyce Occomy Stricklin. Boston: Beacon P, 1987.

Bosniak, Linda. "Citizenship Denationalized." *Indiana Journal of Global Legal Studies* 7.2 (2000): 447–509.

Breton, André. *Manifeste du surréalisme.* 1924. *Œuvres complètes.* Ed. Marguerite Bonnet. Vol. 1. Paris: Gallimard, 1988.

———. *Manifestoes of Surrealism.* Trans. Richard Seaver and Helen R. Lane. Ann Arbor: U of Michigan P, 1969.

———. "Poèmes." *Tropiques* 3 (1941): 38–41.

———. "Un grand poète noir." *Tropiques* 11 (1944): 119–26.

Burton, Richard D. E. "Between the Particular and the Universal: Dilemmas of the Martinican Intellectual." *Intellectuals in the Twentieth-Century Caribbean.* Ed. Alistair Hennessy. London: Macmillan, 1992. 186–210.

Busia, Abena P. A. "But Caliban and Ariel Are Still Both Male: On African Colonial Discourse and the Unvoiced Female." *Crisscrossing Boundaries in African Literatures, 1986.* Ed. Kenneth Harrow, Jonathan Ngaté, and Clarisse Zimra. Washington, DC: Three Continents P and the African Literature Association, 1991. 129–40.

Capécia, Mayotte. *"I Am a Martinican Woman" and "The White Negress": Two Novelettes.* Trans. Beatrice Stith Clark. Pueblo, CO: Passeggiata P, 1997.

——. *Je suis martiniquaise.* Paris: Éditions Corrêa, 1948.

——. *La négresse blanche.* Paris: Éditions Corrêa, 1950.

Cappetti, Carla. *Writing Chicago: Modernism, Ethnography, and the Novel.* New York: Columbia UP, 1993.

Carby, Hazel V. "Policing the Black Woman's Body in an Urban Context." *Critical Inquiry* 18 (1992): 738–55.

——. *Race Men: The W. E. B. Du Bois Lectures.* Cambridge: Harvard UP, 1998.

——. *Reconstructing Womanhood: The Emergence of the Afro-American Woman Novelist.* New York: Oxford UP, 1987.

Césaire, Aimé. *Cahier d'un retour au pays natal.* 1939. *Aimé Césaire: The Collected Poetry.* Trans. and ed. Clayton Eshleman and Annette Smith. Berkeley: U of California P, 1983.

——. "Poésie et connaissance." *Tropiques* 12 (1945): 157–70.

——. "Poetry and Knowledge." *Refusal of the Shadow: Surrealism and the Caribbean.* Ed. Michael Richardson. Trans. Krzysztof Fijalkowski and Michael Richardson. New York: Verso, 1996. 134–46.

Césaire, Ina. Personal interview. 27 March 2001.

Césaire, Suzanne. "Alain et l'esthétique." *Tropiques* 2 (1941): 53–61.

——. "André Breton, poète." *Tropiques* 3 (1941): 31–37.

——. "Le grand camouflage." *Tropiques* 13–14 (1945): 267–73.

——. "Léo Frobenius et le problème des civilisations." *Tropiques* 1 (1941): 27–36.

——. "Malaise d'une civilisation." *Tropiques* 5 (1942): 43–49.

——. "1943: Le Surréalisme et nous." *Tropiques* 8–9 (1943): 14–18.

Chick, Nancy. "Marita Bonner's Revolutionary Purple Flowers: Challenging the Symbol of White Womanhood." *Langston Hughes Review* 13.1 (1994): 21–32.

Chow, Rey. "The Old/New Question of Comparison in Literary Studies: A Post-European Perspective." *ELH* 71 (2004): 289–311.

Clark, Vèvè. "Developing Diaspora Literacy: Allusion in Maryse Condé's *Hérémakhonon.*" *Out of the Kumbla: Caribbean Women and Literature.* Ed. Carole Boyce Davies and Elaine Savory Fido. Trenton, NJ: Africa World P, 1990. 303–19.

Clifford, James. "Traveling Cultures." *Cultural Studies.* Ed. Lawrence Grossberg, Cary Nelson, and Paula Treichler. New York: Routledge, 1992. 96–116.

Cohn, Robert Greer. "Intimate Globality: Baudelaire's *La Chevelure.*" *French Studies* 42 (1988): 292–301.

Colvile, Georgiana. *Scandaleusement d'elles: trente-quatre femmes surréalistes.* Paris: Jean-Michel Place, 1999.

Condé, Maryse. *En attendant le bonheur (Heremakhonon).* 1988. Paris: Robert Laffont, 1997.

——. *Heremakhonon.* Trans. Richard Philcox. Boulder: Three Continents, 1996.

——. "La littérature féminine de la Guadeloupe: recherche d'identité." *Présence Africaine* 99–100 (1976): 155–66.

——. *La parole des femmes: essai sur des romancières des Antilles de langue française.* 1979. Paris: L'Harmattan, 1993.

——. *The Last of the African Kings.* Trans. Richard Philcox. Lincoln: U of Nebraska P, 1997.

——. *Les derniers rois mages.* Paris: Mercure de France, 1992.

——. "Négritude césairienne, Négritude senghorienne." *Revue de Littérature Comparée* 3.4 (1974): 409–19.

——. "Order, Disorder, Freedom, and the West Indian Writer." *Post/Colonial Conditions.* Ed. Françoise Lionnet and Ronnie Scharfman. Spec. issue of *Yale French Studies* 83 (1993): 121–35.

——. "The Stealers of Fire: The French-Speaking Writers of the Caribbean and Their Strategies of Liberation." *Journal of Black Studies* 35.2 (2004): 154–64.

——. "Unheard Voice: Suzanne Césaire and the Construct of a Caribbean Identity." *Winds of Change: The Transforming Voices of Caribbean Women Writers and Scholars.* Ed. Adele S. Newson and Linda Strong-Leek. New York: Peter Lang, 1998. 61–66.

Conklin, Alice. "Who Speaks for Africa? The René Maran–Blaise Diagne Trial in 1920s Paris." *The Color of Liberty: Histories of Race in France.* Ed. Sue Peabody and Tyler Stovall. Durham, NC: Duke UP, 2003. 302–37.

Cooper, Anna Julia. *A Voice from the South: The Voice of Anna Julia Cooper.* Ed. Charles Lemert and Esme Bhan. New York: Rowman & Littlefield, 1998.

Corzani, Jack. *La Négritude.* Fort-de-France: Désormeaux, 1978. Vol. 3 of *La littérature des Antilles-Guyane françaises.* 6 vols. 1978.

——. *Splendeur et misère: l'exotisme littéraire aux Antilles.* Point-à-Pitre: GURIC, Centre d'Enseignement Supérieur Littéraire, 1969.

Cromwell, Adelaide M. *The Other Brahmins: Boston's Black Upper Class, 1750–1950.* Fayetteville: U of Arkansas P, 1994.

Cullen, Countee. "Heritage." 1925. *The Norton Anthology of African American Literature.* Ed. Henry Louis Gates Jr., Nellie Y. McKay, et al. New York: W. W. Norton, 1997. 1311.

Damas, Léon-Gontran. *Pigments.* 1937. Paris: Présence Africaine, 1962.

——. *"Pigments" suivi de "Névralgies."* Paris: Présence Africaine, 1972.

Dash, J. Michael. "*Caraïbe Fantôme*: The Play of Difference in the Francophone Caribbean." *French and Francophone: The Challenge of Expanding Horizons.* Ed. Farid Laroussi and Christopher L. Miller. Spec. issue of *Yale French Studies* 103 (2003): 93–105.

——. "*Le Je de l'autre*: Surrealist Ethnographers and the Francophone Caribbean." *L'Esprit Créateur* 47.1 (2007): 84–95.

———. "Marvellous Realism: The Way Out of Negritude." *Caribbean Studies* 13.4 (1974): 57–70.

———. *The Other America: Caribbean Literature in a New World Context.* Charlottesville: UP of Virginia, 1998.

Davies, Carole Boyce. *Black Women, Writing and Identity: Migrations of the Subject.* New York: Routledge, 1994.

Davis, Thadious M. Introduction. *Passing.* By Nella Larsen. 1929. New York: Penguin Books, 1997. vii–xxxii.

———. *Nella Larsen, Novelist of the Harlem Renaissance: A Woman's Life Unveiled.* Baton Rouge: Louisiana State UP, 1994.

Dayan, Joan. *Haiti, History, and the Gods.* Berkeley: U of California P, 1995.

Desroches-Laroche, Pierre. Preface. "Le spiritisme dans l'intérieur de l'Afrique." ("Spiritualism in Central Africa.") By Léo Frobenius. *La Revue du Monde Noir* 5 (1932): 20.

Dewitte, Philippe. *Les mouvements nègres en France, 1919–1939.* Paris: L'Harmattan, 1985.

Dillon, Kim Jenice. "Marita Bonner." *The Concise Oxford Companion to African American Literature.* Ed. William L. Andrews, Frances Smith Foster, and Trudier Harris. New York: Oxford UP, 2001. 40–41.

Douthwaite, Julia V. *Exotic Women: Literary Heroines and Cultural Strategies in Ancien Régime France.* Philadelphia: U of Pennsylvania P, 1992.

Du Bois, W. E. B. "The Damnation of Women." *Darkwater: Voices from within the Veil.* 1920. Mineola, NY: Dover Publications, 1999.

———. *The Philadelphia Negro: A Study.* 1899. Philadelphia: U of Pennsylvania P, 1996.

———. *The Souls of Black Folk.* 1903. *The Norton Anthology of African American Literature.* Ed. Henry Louis Gates Jr. and Nellie Y. McKay. New York: Norton, 1996. 613–740.

———. "The Talented Tenth." *The Negro Problem: A Series of Articles by Representative American Negroes of To-day.* Ed. Booker T. Washington. New York: James Pott & Co., 1903. 31–75.

duCille, Ann. *The Coupling Convention: Sex, Text, and Tradition in Black Women's Fiction.* New York: Oxford UP, 1993.

———. "The Occult of True Black Womanhood: Critical Demeanor and Black Feminist Studies." *Signs* 19.3 (1994): 591–629.

Editorial. *New Challenge* 2.2 (1937): 3–4.

Edwards, Brent Hayes. "Black Globality: The International Shape of Black Intellectual Culture." Diss. Columbia U, 1998.

———. *The Practice of Diaspora: Literature, Translation, and the Rise of Black Internationalism.* Cambridge: Harvard UP, 2003.

Emberley, Julia V. "A Historical Transposition: Toni Morrison's *Tar Baby* and Frantz Fanon's Post-Enlightenment Phantasms." *Modern Fiction Studies* 45.2 (1999): 403–31.

English, Daylanne K. "Selecting the Harlem Renaissance." *Critical Inquiry* 25.4 (1999): 807–21.

Erickson, John D. "Maximin's *L'Isolé soleil* and Caliban's Curse." *Callaloo* 15.1 (1992): 119–30.

Ezra, Elizabeth. *The Colonial Unconscious: Race and Culture in Interwar France.* Ithaca, NY: Cornell UP, 2000.

Fabre, Michel. *From Harlem to Paris: Black American Writers in France, 1840–1980.* Urbana: U of Illinois P, 1991.

———. "The Reception of *Cane* in France." *Jean Toomer and the Harlem Renaissance.* Ed. Geneviève Fabre and Michel Feith. New Brunswick: Rutgers UP, 2001. 202–14.

Fanon, Frantz. *Black Skin, White Masks.* Trans. Charles Lam Markmann. New York: Grove P, 1967.

———. *Les damnés de la terre.* 1961. Paris: Gallimard, 1991.

———. *Peau noire, masques blancs.* Paris: Seuil, 1952.

———. *The Wretched of the Earth.* Trans. Constance Farrington. New York: Grove P, 1963.

Fauset, Jessie Redmon. *There Is Confusion.* New York: Boni & Liveright, 1924.

Ferguson, SallyAnn. "Dorothy West and Helene Johnson in *Infants of the Spring*." *Langston Hughes Review* 2.2 (1983): 22–24.

Foucault, Michel. *Discipline and Punish.* Trans. Alan Sheridan. New York: Vintage Books, 1979.

Frazier, E. Franklin. *Black Bourgeoisie.* 1957. New York: Free Press Paperbacks, 1997.

Friedman, Susan Stanford. "Definitional Excursions: The Meanings of *Modern/Modernity/Modernism*." *Modernism/Modernity* 8.3 (2001): 493–513.

Frobenius, Leo. *Histoire de la civilisation africaine.* 1936. Trans. H. Back and D. Ermont. 3rd ed. Paris: Gallimard, 1952.

———. *Kulturgeschichte Afrikas.* Frankfurt: Phaidon Verlag, 1933.

Gaines, Kevin K. *Uplifting the Race: Black Leadership, Politics, and Culture in the Twentieth Century.* Chapel Hill: U of North Carolina P, 1996.

Gates, Henry Louis, Jr. "Harlem on Our Minds." *Critical Inquiry* 24 (1997): 1–12.

———. "The Trope of the New Negro and the Reconstruction of the Image of the Black." *America Reconstructed, 1840–1940.* Spec. issue of *Representations* 24 (1988): 129–55.

Gatewood, Willard B. *Aristocrats of Color: The Black Elite, 1880–1920.* Bloomington: Indiana UP, 1990.

Giddings, Paula. *When and Where I Enter: The Impact of Black Women on Race and Sex in America.* 1984. New York: William Morrow, 1996.

Gikandi, Simon. "Picasso, Africa, and the Schemata of Difference." *Modernism/Modernity* 10.3 (2003): 455–80.

———. *Writing in Limbo: Modernism and Caribbean Literature.* Ithaca, NY: Cornell UP, 1992.

Gillman, Susan, and Alys Eve Weinbaum. "Introduction: W. E. B. Du Bois and the Politics of Juxtaposition." *Next to the Color Line: Gender, Sexuality, and W. E. B. Du Bois.* Minneapolis: U of Minnesota P, 2007.

Gilroy, Paul. *The Black Atlantic: Modernity and Double Consciousness.* Cambridge: Harvard UP, 1993.

Glissant, Édouard. *Caribbean Discourse: Selected Essays.* Trans. J. Michael Dash. Charlottesville: UP of Virginia, 1989.

———. *La Lézarde.* 1958. Paris: Gallimard, 1997.

———. *Le discours antillais.* 1981. Paris: Gallimard, 1997.

———. *The Ripening.* Trans. Michael Dash. London: Heinemann, 1985.

González, Carolina. "An Interview with Ángela Hernández Núñez." *Callaloo* 23.3 (2000): 999–1010.

Griffin, Farah Jasmine. *"Who Set You Flowin'?" The African-American Migration Narrative.* New York: Oxford UP, 1995.

Haigh, Sam. *Mapping a Tradition: Francophone Women's Writing from Guadeloupe.* London: Maney Publishing for the Modern Humanities Research Association, 2000.

Hall, Stuart. "Cultural Identity and Diaspora." *Identity: Community, Culture, Difference.* Ed. Jonathan Rutherford. London: Lawrence & Wishart, 1990. 222–31.

Harper, Frances Ellen Watkins. *Iola Leroy, or Shadows Uplifted.* 1893. Boston: Beacon P, 1987.

Harris, Trudier. *Saints, Sinners, Saviors: Strong Black Women in African American Literature.* New York: Palgrave, 2001.

Harvey, Sir Paul, and J. E. Heseltine, eds. *The Oxford Companion to French Literature.* 1959. Oxford: Oxford UP, 1993.

Hawthorne, Evelyn. "On Gaining the Double-Vision: *Tar Baby* as Diasporean Novel." *Black American Literature Forum* 22.1 (1988): 97–107.

Hegel, Georg Wilhelm Friedrich. *The Phenomenology of Mind.* Trans. J. B. Baillie. New York: Harper Torchbooks, 1967.

Heilmann, Ann. *New Woman Fiction: Women Writing First Wave Feminism.* New York: St. Martin's, 2000.

Hewitt, Leah. "Rencontres explosives: les intersections culturelles de Maryse Condé." *L'Œuvre de Maryse Condé: questions et réponses à propos d'une écrivaine politiquement incorrecte.* Paris: L'Harmattan, 1996. 205–16.

Higonnet, Margaret R., ed. *Borderwork: Feminist Engagements with Comparative Literature.* Ithaca, NY: Cornell UP, 1994.

Hill, Errol. "The Revolutionary Tradition in Black Drama." *Theatre Journal* 38.4 (1986): 408–26.

Holman, C. Hugh, and William Harmon. "Expressionism." *A Handbook to Literature.* 5th ed. New York: Macmillan, 1986. 194–95.

hooks, bell. "The Oppositional Gaze: Black Female Spectators." 1992. *Feminist Film Theory: A Reader.* Ed. Sue Thornham. New York: New York UP, 1999. 307–20.

Hubert, Renée Riese. *Magnifying Mirrors: Women, Surrealism, and Partnership.* Lincoln: U of Nebraska P, 1994.

Huggins, Nathan Irvin. *Harlem Renaissance.* New York: Oxford UP, 1971.

Hughes, Langston. *The Big Sea.* 1940. New York: Hill & Wang, 1963.

———. "The Negro Artist and the Racial Mountain." 1926. *The Norton Anthology of African American Literature.* Ed. Henry Louis Gates Jr., Nellie Y. McKay, et al. New York: Norton, 1997. 1267–71.

Hurston, Zora Neale. "How It Feels to Be Colored Me." 1928. *I Love Myself When I Am Laughing . . . and Then Again When I Am Looking Mean and Impressive: A Zora Neale Hurston Reader.* Ed. Alice Walker. Old Westbury, NY: Feminist P, 1979. 152–55.

———. *Their Eyes Were Watching God.* 1937. New York: Harper & Row, 1990.

Jahn, Janheinz. *Leo Frobenius: The Demonic Child.* Trans. Reinhard Sander. Occasional Publication of the African and Afro-American Studies and Research Center. Austin: University of Texas at Austin, 1974.

James, C. L. R. *The Black Jacobins: Toussaint L'Ouverture and the San Domingo Revolution.* 1938. New York: Random House, 1963.

James, Joy. *Transcending the Talented Tenth: Black Leaders and American Intellectuals.* New York: Routledge, 1997.

Jameson, Fredric. "Modernism and Imperialism." *Nationalism, Colonialism, and Literature.* By Terry Eagleton, Fredric Jameson, and Edward W. Said. Minneapolis: U of Minnesota P, 1990. 43–66.

Jardel, Jean-Pierre. "Représentations des 'Gens de Couleur' et du métissage aux Antilles." *L'Autre et nous: scènes et types.* Ed. Nicolas Bancel et al. Paris: ACHAC/SYROS, 1995. 115–20.

Johnson, Abby Arthur, and Ronald Maberry Johnson. *Propaganda and Aesthetics: The Literary Politics of African-American Magazines in the Twentieth Century.* Amherst: U of Massachusetts P, 1979.

Jones, Sharon L. "Reclaiming a Legacy: The Dialectic of Race, Class, and Gender in Jessie Fauset, Zora Neale Hurston, and Dorothy West." *Hecate* 24.1 (1998): 155–64.

Kelley, Robin D. G. *Freedom Dreams: The Black Radical Imagination.* Boston: Beacon P, 2002.

———. *Race Rebels: Culture, Politics, and the Black Working Class.* New York: Free P, 1994.

Kesteloot, Lilyan. *Black Writers in French: A Literary History of Negritude.* Trans. Ellen Conroy Kennedy. Philadelphia: Temple UP, 1974.

———. *Les écrivains noirs de langue française: naissance d'une littérature.* Brussels: Université Libre de Bruxelles, 1965.

Krasner, David. "Whose Role Is It Anyway? Charles Gilpin and the Harlem Renaissance." *African American Review* 29.3 (1995): 483–96.

Kutzinski, Vera M. *Sugar's Secrets: Race and the Erotics of Cuban Nationalism.* Charlottesville: UP of Virginia, 1993.

Lacascade, Renée, and André Pérye. *L'île qui meurt.* 3rd ed. Paris: Calmann-Lévy, 1930.

Lacascade, Suzanne. *Claire-Solange, âme africaine.* Paris: Eugène Figuière, 1924.

Lanser, Susan Sniader. "Compared to What? Global Feminism, Comparison, and the Master's Tools." *Borderwork: Feminist Engagements with Comparative Literature.* Ed. Margaret R. Higgonet. Ithaca, NY: Cornell UP, 1994. 280–300.

Lara, Oruno. *Question de couleurs (Blanches et noirs): roman de mœurs.* Paris: Nouvelle Librairie Universelle, 1923.

Larsen, Nella. *Quicksand* and *Passing.* Ed. Deborah E. McDowell. Rutgers: Rutgers UP, 1986.

Leiris, Michel. *Contacts de civilisations en Martinique et en Guadeloupe.* Paris: UNESCO/ Gallimard, 1955.

"Le mois littéraire." *Le Nouvelliste* (Point-à-Pitre, Guadeloupe) 6 Dec. 1924: 2 and 10 Jan. 1925: 1–2.

"Le mot 'nègre.'" Editorial, *La voix des nègres* (Paris), Jan. 1927: 1.

Léro, Étienne. "Misère d'une poésie." *Légitime Défense* 1.1 (1932): 10–12.

———. "Poverty of a Poetry." *Refusal of the Shadow: Surrealism and the Caribbean.* Ed. Michael Richardson. Trans. Krzystof Fijalkowski and Michael Richardson. New York: Verso, 1996. 55–58.

Levin, Harry. "What Was Modernism?" *Eighteen Essays in World Literature.* Ed. Stanley Burnshaw. New York: New York UP, 1962. 307–29.

Lewis, David Levering. *When Harlem Was in Vogue.* 1981. New York: Penguin Books, 1997.

Lewis, Shireen K. *Race, Culture, and Identity: Francophone West African and Caribbean Literature and Theory from Négritude to Créolité.* Lanham, MD: Lexington Books, 2006.

Lincoln, C. Eric. *The Black Muslims in America.* Boston: Beacon P, 1973.

Lionnet, Françoise. "Reframing Baudelaire: Literary History, Biography, Postcolonial Theory, and Vernacular Languages." *diacritics* 28.3 (1998): 63–85.

Löbbermann, Dorothea. "Harlem as Memory Place: Reconstructing the Harlem Renaissance in Space." *Temples for Tomorrow: Looking Back at the Harlem Renaissance.* Ed. Geneviève Fabre and Michel Feith. Bloomington: Indiana UP, 2001. 210–21.

Locke, Alain. "Negro Youth Speaks." *The New Negro.* Ed. Alain Locke. 1925. New York: Touchstone, 1997. 47–53.

———. "The New Negro." *The New Negro.* Ed. Alain Locke. 1925. New York: Touchstone, 1997. 3–16.

Lucky, Crystal J. "Black Women Writers of the Harlem Renaissance." *Challenging Boundaries: Gender and Periodization.* Ed. Joyce W. Warren and Margaret Dickie. Athens: U of Georgia P, 2000. 91–106.

Makward, Christiane P. *Mayotte Capécia, ou l'aliénation selon Fanon.* Paris: Éditions Karthala, 1999.

Maran, René. *Batouala.* Trans. Barbara Beck and Alexandre Nboukou. London: Heinemann, 1973.

———. *Batouala: véritable roman nègre.* 1921. Paris: Albin Michel, 1938.

Maximin, Daniel. *L'Isolé soleil.* Paris: Seuil, 1981.

———. *Lone Sun.* Trans. Clarisse Zimra. Charlottesville: UP of Virginia, 1989.

McClary, Susan. *Georges Bizet: Carmen.* Cambridge Opera Handbooks. New York: Cambridge UP, 1992.

McDougald, Elise Johnson. "The Task of Negro Womanhood." *The New Negro.* Ed. Alain Locke. 1925. New York: Touchstone, 1997. 369–82.

McDowell, Deborah A. *"The Changing Same": Black Women's Literature, Criticism, and Theory.* Bloomington: Indiana UP, 1995.

———. "Conversations with Dorothy West." *The Harlem Renaissance Re-examined.* Ed. Victor A. Kramer. New York: AMS, 1987. 265–82.

———. "Introduction: Regulating Midwives." *Plum Bun: A Novel without a Moral.* By Jessie Redmon Fauset. 1929. Boston: Beacon P, 1990. ix–xxxiii.

McHenry, Elizabeth. *Forgotten Readers: Recovering the Lost History of African American Literary Societies.* Durham, NC: Duke UP, 2002.

McKay, Claude. *Banjo: A Novel without a Plot.* New York: Harcourt, 1928.

McKay, Nellie Y. "Black Theater and Drama in the 1920s: Years of Growing Pains." *Massachusetts Review* 28 (1987): 615–26.

———. *Jean Toomer, Artist: A Study of His Literary Life and Work, 1894–1936.* Chapel Hill: U of North Carolina P, 1984.

Melas, Natalie. *All the Difference in the World: Postcoloniality and the Ends of Comparison.* Stanford: Stanford UP, 2007.

———. "Versions of Incommensurability." *World Literature Today* 69 (1995): 275–80.

Mendelsohn, Michèle. "Reconsidering Race, Language and Identity in *The Emperor Jones.*" *Eugene O'Neill Review* 23.1–2 (1999): 19–30.

Ménil, René. "De l'exotisme colonial." *Tracées: identité, négritude, esthétique aux Antilles.* Paris: Robert Laffont, 1981. 18–25.

Michel, Jean-Claude. *The Black Surrealists.* New York: Peter Lang, 2000.

———. *Les écrivains noirs et le surréalisme.* Sherbrooke: Éditions Naaman, 1982.

Mitchell, Verner D., and Cynthia Davis, eds. *Where the Wild Grape Grows: Selected Writings, 1930–1950.* Amherst: U of Massachusetts P, 2005.

Moore, Jacqueline M. *Leading the Race: The Transformation of the Black Elite in the Nation's Capital, 1880–1920.* Charlottesville: UP of Virginia, 1999.

Moreau de Saint-Méry, Médéric Louis Elie. *A Civilization That Perished: The Last Years of White Colonial Rule in Haiti.* Trans. and ed. Ivor D. Spencer. Lanham, MD: UP of America, 1985.

———. *Description topographique, physique, civile, politique et historique de la partie française de l'isle Saint-Domingue.* 2 vols. Philadelphia, 1797–98. *Eighteenth-Century Col-*

lections Online, 18 June 2007, http://galenet.galegroup.com.ezproxy.lib.utexas.edu/servlet/ECCO.

Morrison, Toni. *Sula.* New York: Knopf, 1973.

———. *Tar Baby.* New York: Knopf, 1981.

Mosse, George L. *Toward the Final Solution: A History of European Racism.* New York: Howard Fertig, 1978.

Mulvey, Laura. "Visual Pleasure and Narrative Cinema." *Narrative, Apparatus, Ideology.* Ed. Philip Rosen. New York: Columbia UP, 1986. 198–209.

Murdoch, H. Adlai. *Creole Identity in the French Caribbean Novel.* Gainesville: UP of Florida, 2001.

Musser, Judith. "African American Women and Education: Marita Bonner's Response to the 'Talented Tenth.'" *Studies in Short Fiction* 34 (1997): 73–85.

———. "'The Blood Will Flow Back to You': The Reactionary Proletarian Fiction of Marita Bonner." *Canadian Review of American Studies/Revue Canadienne d'Études Américaines* 32.1 (2002): 53–79.

Nardal, Paulette. "Éveil de la conscience de race/Awakening of Race Consciousness." *La Revue du Monde Noir* 6 (1932): 25–34.

"The New Negro Woman." Editorial. *The New Negro Woman's Number.* Spec. issue of *Messenger* 5 (1923): 757.

Ngal, Georges. *Aimé Césaire: un homme à la recherche d'une patrie.* Paris: Présence Africaine, 1994.

North, Michael. *The Dialect of Modernism: Race, Language, and 20th Century Literature.* New York: Oxford UP, 1994.

Nunes, Zita C. "Phantasmatic Brazil: Nella Larsen's *Passing,* American Literary Imagination, and Racial Utopianism." *Mixing Race, Mixing Culture: Inter-American Literary Dialogues.* Ed. Monika Kaup and Debra J. Rosenthal. Austin: U of Texas P, 2002. 50–61.

Orlando, Valérie. *Of Suffocated Hearts and Tortured Souls: Seeking Subjecthood through Madness in Francophone Women's Writing of Africa and the Caribbean.* Lanham, MD: Lexington Books, 2003.

Perkins, Kathy A. Introduction. *Black Female Playwrights: An Anthology of Plays before 1950.* Bloomington: Indiana UP, 1989. 1–17.

Poole, Gabriele. "'Blarsted Niggers!' *The Emperor Jones* and Modernism's Encounter with Africa." *Eugene O'Neill Review* 18.1–2 (1994): 21–37.

Pound, Ezra. *Make It New.* London: Faber & Faber, 1934.

Rabbitt, Kara. "Suzanne Césaire." *île en île.* 23 June 2007, www.lehman.cuny.edu/ile.en.ile/paroles/cesaire_suzanne.html.

———. "Suzanne Césaire's Significance for the Forging of a New Caribbean Literature." *French Review* 79.3 (2006): 538–48.

Rado, Lisa. "Primitivism, Modernism, and Matriarchy." *Modernism, Gender, and Culture: A Cultural Studies Approach.* Ed. Lisa Rado. New York: Garland, 1997. 283–300.

Régismanset, Charles. "Exotisme." *La dépêche coloniale et maritime* (Paris) 7–8 Dec. 1924: 2.

Rice-Maximin, Micheline. *Karukéra: présence littéraire de la Guadeloupe.* New York: Peter Lang, 1998.

Richardson, Michael, ed. *Refusal of the Shadow.* Trans. Krzystof Fijalkowski and Michael Richardson. New York: Verso, 1996.

Rodgers, Lawrence R. "Dorothy West's *The Living Is Easy* and the Ideal of Southern Folk Community." *African American Review* 26.1 (1992): 161–72.

Rooks, Noliwe. *Hair Raising: Beauty, Culture, and African American Women.* New Brunswick: Rutgers UP, 1996.

Rosemont, Penelope, ed. *Surrealist Women: An International Anthology.* Austin: U of Texas P, 1998.

Roses, Lorraine Elena. "Interviews with Black Women Writers: Dorothy West at Oak Bluffs, Massachusetts, July, 1984." *Sage* 2.1 (1985): 47–49.

Roses, Lorraine Elena, and Ruth Elizabeth Randolph. "Marita Bonner: In Search of Other Mothers' Gardens." *Black American Literature Forum* 21.1–2 (1987): 165–83.

Roumain, Jacques. *Gouverneurs de la rosée.* 1944. Paris: Bibliothèque Française, 1946.

———. *Masters of the Dew.* Trans. Langston Hughes and Mercer Cook. London: Heinemann, 1982.

Ryan, Judylyn S. "Contested Visions/Double-Vision in *Tar Baby.*" *Modern Fiction Studies* 39.3–4 (1993): 597–621.

Said, Edward W. *Orientalism.* New York: Random House, 1978.

Sanders, Pamela Peden. "The Feminism of Dorothy West's *The Living Is Easy*: A Critique of the Limitations of the Female Sphere through Performative Gender Roles." *African American Review* 36.3 (2002): 435–46.

Sartre, Jean-Paul. "Black Orpheus." Trans. John MacCombie. *Massachusetts Review* 5 (1964): 13–52.

———. "Orphée noir." Preface. *Anthologie de la nouvelle poésie nègre et malgache de langue française.* Ed. Léopold Sédar Senghor. 1948. Paris: Quadrige/PUF, 1992. ix–xliv.

Saunders, James Robert, and Renae Nadine Shackleford, eds. *The Dorothy West Martha's Vineyard: Stories, Essays and Reminiscences by Dorothy West Writing in the "Vineyard Gazette."* Jefferson, NC: McFarland & Co., 2001.

Saussy, Haun. "Exquisite Cadavers Stitched from Fresh Nightmares: Of Memes, Hives, and Selfish Genes." *Comparative Literature in the Age of Globalization.* Ed. Haun Saussy. Baltimore: Johns Hopkins UP, 2006. 3–42.

Scharfman, Ronnie. "De grands poètes noirs: Breton rencontre les Césaire." *Nouveau monde, autres mondes: surréalisme et Amériques.* Ed. Daniel Lefort, Pierre Rivas, and Jacqueline Chénieux-Gendron. Paris: Lachenal & Ritter, 1995. 230–39.

———. "Rewriting the Césaires." *L'Héritage de Caliban.* Ed. Maryse Condé. Paris: Jasor, 1992. 233–46.

Schwarz-Bart, André. *La mulâtresse Solitude*. Paris: Seuil, 1972.

Senghor, Léopold Sédar, ed. *Anthologie de la nouvelle poésie nègre et malgache de langue française*. 1948. Paris: Quadrige/PUF, 1992.

———. *The Collected Poetry*. Trans. Melvin Dixon. Charlottesville: UP of Virginia, 1998.

Shakespeare, William. *The Tempest*. Ed. Robert Langbaum. New York: Penguin, 1987.

Sharpley-Whiting, T. Denean. *Black Venus: Sexualized Savages, Primal Fears, and Primitive Narratives in French*. Durham, NC: Duke UP, 1999.

———. "Erasures and the Practice of Diaspora Feminism." *Small Axe* 17 (2005): 129–33.

———. *Negritude Women*. Minneapolis: U of Minnesota P, 2002.

Sherrard-Johnson, Cherene. *Portraits of the New Negro Woman: Visual and Literary Culture in the Harlem Renaissance*. New Brunswick: Rutgers UP, 2007.

Smith, Barbara. "Toward a Black Feminist Criticism." *All the Women Are White, All the Blacks Are Men, but Some of Us Are Brave: Black Women's Studies*. Ed. Gloria T. Hull, Patricia Bell Scott, and Barbara Smith. Old Westbury, NY: Feminist P, 1982. 157–75.

Sollors, Werner. *Neither Black nor White yet Both: Thematic Explorations of Interracial Literature*. New York: Oxford UP, 1997.

Sourieau, Marie-Agnès. "La Revue du Monde Noir." *Encyclopedia of Latin American Literature*. Ed. Verity Smith. Chicago: Fitzroy Dearborn, 1997. 453.

———. "Suzanne Césaire et *Tropiques*: de la poésie cannibale à une poétique créole." *French Review* 68.1 (1994): 69–78.

Spillers, Hortense J. "Mama's Baby, Papa's Maybe: An American Grammar Book." *diacritics* 17.2 (1987): 65–81.

Spivak, Gayatri. *Death of a Discipline*. New York: Columbia UP, 2003.

Stavney, Anne. "'Mothers of Tomorrow': The New Negro Renaissance and the Politics of Maternal Representation." *African American Review* 32.4 (1998): 533–61.

Steen, Shannon. "Melancholy Bodies: Racial Subjectivity and Whiteness in O'Neill's *The Emperor Jones*." *Theatre Journal* 52 (2000): 339–59.

Stein, Gertrude. "Melanctha." *Three Lives*. 1909. Ed. Linda Wagner-Martin. Boston: Bedford/St. Martin's, 2000. 87–187.

Stovall, Tyler. *Paris Noir: African Americans in the City of Light*. Boston: Houghton Mifflin, 1996.

Summers, Martin. *Manliness and Its Discontents: The Black Middle Class and the Transformation of Masculinity, 1900–1930*. Chapel Hill: U of North Carolina P, 2004.

Tate, Claudia. *Domestic Allegories of Political Desire: The Black Heroine's Text at the Turn of the Century*. New York: Oxford UP, 1992.

Thaly, Daniel. *Chants de l'Atlantique suivis de Sous le Ciel des Antilles*. Paris: Garnier Éditeur, 1928.

———. *Le jardin des tropiques: Poèmes, 1897–1907*. Paris: Éditions du Beffroi, 1911.

Thurman, Wallace. *Infants of the Spring*. 1932. New York: Modern Library, 1999.

Toomer, Jean. *Cane*. 1923. New York: Liveright, 1993.

Toumson, Roger. *La transgression des couleurs: littérature et langage des Antilles, XVIIIe, XIXe, XXe siècles.* 2 vols. Paris: Éditions Caribéennes, 1989.

Toumson, Roger, and Simonne Henry-Valmore. *Aimé Césaire: le nègre inconsolé.* Fort-de-France: Vent des Îles, 1993.

Trouillot, Michel-Rolph. *Silencing the Past: Power and the Production of History.* Boston: Beacon P, 1995.

Turner, Darwin T., ed. *The Wayward and the Seeking: A Collection of Writings by Jean Toomer.* Washington, DC: Howard UP, 1980.

Vignaud, Jean. "La vie littéraire." *Le Petit Parisien* 10 Nov. 1924: 6.

Wald, Priscilla. "Geographics: Writing the Shtetl into the Ghetto." *Revista Canaria de Estudios Ingleses* 39 (1999): 209–27.

Walker, Alice. *In Search of Our Mothers' Gardens: Womanist Prose.* San Diego: Harcourt, 1983.

Wall, Cheryl A. "Introduction: Taking Positions and Changing Words." *Changing Our Own Words: Essays on Criticism, Theory, and Writing by Black Women.* Ed. Cheryl A. Wall. New Brunswick: Rutgers UP, 1989. 1–15.

——. *Women of the Harlem Renaissance.* Bloomington: Indiana UP, 1995.

Warner, Keith Q. *Critical Perspectives on Léon-Gontran Damas.* Washington, DC: Three Continents P, 1988.

Warren, Joyce W. "Introduction: The Challenge of Women's Periods." *Challenging Boundaries: Gender and Periodization.* Ed. Joyce W. Warren and Margaret Dickie. Athens: U of Georgia P, 2000. ix–xxiv.

Washington, Booker T. *Up from Slavery: An Autobiography.* 1901. New York: Modern Library, 1999.

Washington, Mary Helen. Preface. *The Richer, the Poorer: Stories, Sketches, and Reminiscences.* By Dorothy West. New York: Doubleday, 1995.

West, Dorothy. "Dear Reader." *Challenge* 1.1 (1934): 39.

——. *The Living Is Easy.* 1948. New York: Feminist P, 1982.

——. *The Richer, the Poorer: Stories, Sketches, and Reminiscences.* New York: Doubleday, 1995.

——. *The Wedding.* New York: Doubleday, 1995.

Whipps, Judy D. "Jane Addams's Social Thought as a Model for Pragmatist-Feminist Communitarianism." *Hypatia* 19.2 (2004): 118–33.

Wilder, Gary. "Framing Greater France between the Wars," *Journal of Historical Sociology* 14 (2001): 198–225.

——. *The French Imperial Nation-State: Negritude and Colonial Humanism between the Two World Wars.* Chicago: U of Chicago P, 2005.

——. "Panafricanism and the Republican Political Sphere." *The Color of Liberty: Histories of Race in France.* Ed. Sue Peabody and Tyler Stovall. Durham, NC: Duke UP, 2003. 237–58.

Wilson, Sondra K., ed. *The Crisis Reader.* New York: Modern Library, 1999.

Woolf, Virginia. *A Room of One's Own.* 1929. New York: Harcourt, 1957.

Wynter, Sylvia. "Afterword: Beyond Miranda's Meanings: Un/silencing the 'Demonic Ground' of Caliban's 'Woman.'" *Out of the Kumbla: Caribbean Women and Literature.* Ed. Carole Boyce Davies and Elaine Savory Fido. Trenton, NJ: Africa World P, 1990. 355–72.

Zimra, Clarisse. "Négritude in the Feminine Mode: The Case of Martinique and Guadeloupe." *Journal of Ethnic Studies* 12.1 (1984): 53–77.

Index